Johnny Green is the author (with Garry Barker) of *A Riot of Our Own: Night and Day with The Clash*, which was published to much acclaim in 1997 and remains in print. Described variously as 'f***ing great' (Joe Strummer's builders) and 'a touching, angry, uproarious tale' (Greil Marcus) it is a definitive account of life with The Clash.

PUSH YOURSELF JUST A LITTLE BIT MORE

BACKSTAGE AT THE TOUR DE FRANCE

Johnny Green

An Orion paperback

First published in Great Britain in 2005
by Orion
This paperback edition published in 2006
by Orion Books Ltd,
Orion House, 5 Upper St Martin's Lane,
London WC2H 9EA

1 3 5 7 9 10 8 6 4 2

A CIP catalogue record for this book is available
from the British Library.

ISBN-13 978-0-7528-7770-9
ISBN-10 0-7528-7770-4

Printed and bound in Great Britain by
Mackays of Chatham plc, Chatham, Kent

The Orion Publishing Group's policy is to use papers that
are natural, renewable and recyclable products and
made from wood grown in sustainable forests. The logging
and manufacturing processes are expected to conform to
the environmental regulations of the country of origin.

www.orionbooks.co.uk

I just wanna thank ......

The late, great Joe Strummer – for kick startin' my idea
Frank the Forger – for documentation
Ian Preece – for diggin' the vision and holdin' his nerve
Michael Ball – for sound advice
M'boy, Earl – a chip off the old block
Aubrey 'n' Kate – for the beach hut
My true love, Nesta – for matchin' me every step of the way
Pat Gilbert – for technical nous
Denise Twomey – for sure, fast fingers
Polly 'n' Ruby – for keepin' me sweet
Bill Reading – for the Big Picture
Sophie Richmond – for makin' sense of the chaos
Robin Banks – for savin' my life

For
Barry Ashby
Centre-half
Gillingham FC

Inspiration

I was raised on the Kentish banks of the Thames Estuary. Across the river was Canvey Island, the Essex oil terminal winkin' in the sun. It was the home of Dr Feelgood, a band that turned me round in my youth. We both fed off the energy and shit that flowed down the river from London. They played John the Baptist to the coming punk. It was manic rhythm'n'blues. Wilko Johnson, the guitarist, was like an electrocuted chicken. All crisp'n'sharp chords'n' shapes. The singer, Lee Brilleaux, looked mean and world-weary, like he'd been around the block quite a few times. He became a boozin' pal of mine in '78. Dingwalls in Camden Town. I lived around the corner in Rehearsal Rehearsals, The Clash HQ. Now and then, I would give him a lift for a spot of breakfast at the end of a session. I ran a school of drunken driving. One year on, we had gone different ways when I heard 'Take a Tip'. The first verse goes:

> Take a little tip from Mr Johnny Green –
> Keep your rear view mirror clean.
> An eye on the road, one behind –
> Increase your speed if you're so inclined.
> You've got to move faster –
> You've got to get along –
> You've got to go faster –
> Push your foot down to the floor.
> PUSH YOURSELF JUST A LITTLE BIT MORE

Lee died young at the age of 41. He sang like he'd lived it. That punch-line hits it on the nail. The attitude needed for Le Tour de France. For riding it, winning it, working it, reporting it or running with it just for kicks.

Chapeaux, Mr Lee Brilleaux.

Chapter 1

It was the day before. Not being a pro, I had a lot of nerves. How to do it right. I shouldn't have bothered. There's a structure, a system, a French administrative bureaucracy that has been developed over a hundred years. It's as sound and strong as the Eiffel Tower. It's called ASO. Amaury Sports Organisation is a big outfit. It deals in all sorts like golf and the Paris–Dakar rally, where Mark Thatcher did the impossible. He put the fear of God into his mum by getting lost in the Sahara. The Koh-I-Noor in ASO's jewellery box is Le Tour de France. A car-ride along the banks of the mighty Meuse took me to HQ. I was staying on an island, Outremeuse, in the old town of Liège. Simenon-ville: everything was named after Georges, roads, bookshops of course, my hotel. It was deliciously rough. The streets were of an Arab/Congo flavour. Old Georges was famous for his Maigret detective books, whopper bestsellers. Even more so for the boast that he'd fucked 10,000 women in his twentieth-century lifetime. I'd always been impressed that an ugly Belgian could pull that many birds until I realised most of them were hookers. That's cheating.

The nerve-centre of the Tour was downstream on another island. A huge exhibition centre, decidedly not ropey. I swung the motor into the dripping landscaped car-park, every turn guarded by hostile cops.

As I walked up to the entrance, an enchanted world opened up before me. A line of tropical plants led to a giant route map of this Tour painted on the lobby floor, unfolding under my feet. Look, Nîmes, a shuffler to Alpe d'Huez, a long stride to Chartres. Hanging on the walls

3

under the glass atrium, to match the destination names, were beautiful photographs of these locations. A few were familiar but most were exotic, calling to me. I felt impatient, all of a sudden, to get going. I wanted to reach them all. I felt glad that I didn't have to decide on a destination. I had no need to enter the travel agent's shop and choose. It was all before me on the floor. Just follow the arrows. Hire a car, book a room, keep yourself healthy and sane. All will be revealed. That shivering tingle of childhood on the night before Christmas. The presents wrapped under the tree, shinin' and beckonin'.

Bustle was the order of the day and smart casual was the look. Boxes and packages were being carted by characters in olive and khaki. A style that said: 'Anything you can throw at me will be dealt with cool efficiency.' We'd see about that. The one thing that stood in the way was the pass. Everyone wore one. I needed mine. The place was vast. I've never been in an aircraft hangar but that's what people trot out. It was hard to say how many 747s could be wedged in here. I've never checked out one of those up close. The potted plants led to a series of rooms and alcoves, coiffeured yet thrown-together office space. A meander brought me past every part of the outfit. Publicity, sponsors, police security, accommodation. Everyone was busy, eyes down to the computer screens.

I was only after one thing. I followed the arrows. Arrows are a big thing on Le Tour de France. When you've got that many people in strange unknown places, that many nationalities needing to be in the right place, you have to resort to gentle herding. Move 'em along. Arrows are terrific. When you need to split the main herd into groups, coloured arrows are wonderful. I was green. I followed my arrows to a clearing marked 'Press/Media'.

A few real journos milled in front of the trestle tables,

stacked with logo'd handouts. Behind, correctly and neatly attired in ASO uniform, a youngster gave me a questioning look. I was wearing my dark suit. I was jumpy. There was a lot riding on these next few minutes. A lotta planning, the hire of the motor for a month, hell. The Brief had even booked us a stack of unknown rooms. Most of all, I had set my heart'n'mind on a month's adventures. Now I had set off, I could not be stopped. The youth took my name. I used my most charming French manner on him. The Brief said that I pinned him with my twitching eye. He returned with a large brown envelope with my name on. I could see the orange windscreen sticker poking out the top. 'Oh yes, mine now. I want it.' I reached out to take the package.

'Your press card, M'sieur. For identification.'

It was back at the hotel. In my tunnel-visioned mania I had just come here with nothing. I had arrived bearing fuck all, like a Haj pilgrim at Mecca. My holy grail was within licking distance and some spotty kid was playing desk-clerk with me. I am not clear about what happened next. In my recollection, I smiled politely at the youth, shrugged in a French kinda way and said something like, 'I'm sure that if you check with M. Matthieu Desplats, your superior, you will find that all my accreditation has been filed appropriately and every criterion has been achieved. I fully understand that you are just doing your job.'

The Brief said that my face turned puce as I stiffened. He said I bared my teeth and growled in a low voice. I do recall wanting to rip the boy's head off with my hands. I wanted that package very badly. I have been an addict. I have done those things to get the gear. Whatever. The envelope came across the desk. It seemed to float towards me. Matthieu, the Press Officer, was standing there.

'Bonjour, Johnny. Ça va?'

We shook hands and a light returned to my eye. The whole room glowed. The world was a better place. I had scored.

It was bucketing it down outside, so I legged it like Gene Kelly to a café over the road. The Devil was standing next to a policewoman at the front gates. He was a colourful fixture on Le Tour. Red tights, horns, beard and trident. Every day, he'd position himself on the roadside to roar on the riders. Didi Senff was a German. He'd had the gig some ten years. Once a weirdo maverick, he was now sponsored by a clutch fluid company.

'He's sold his soul,' I said.

'He's the Devil,' said Earl.

Over evil little coffees, I rummaged through my bags of goodies. I pulled out the pass. A green laminate with a soft-focus shot of me. Kinda Robert Redford. I dangled it on the black and yellow strap. This would unlock the back-stage gates. It was the key to my heart. My precious.

Let's deal with this straight away: 'Lance Armstrong won it, didn't he?' – 'Yes he did.' If this is you, jack it in right now. There's a couple of hundred cyclists in Le Tour de France, and each one has got something going for him. The Prologue is an excellent means of staking out the runners and riders. It's a bit like the paddock at the Grand National. Each man rides solo at one-minute intervals around a 6 kilometre circuit in the town. His car, name on the front, spare bike on the roof, is right behind. Plus there's a running order in *L'Équipe*, the daily font of all sporting knowledge. The Prologue is a leisurely start to proceedings 'cos it's spread out over a whole day. The route looped over the riverbank. I loped over the bridges early on, getting different viewpoints. I followed a ramshackle brass band, wearing battered leather caps, red neckerchiefs and battered leathery faces. They were pissed. They should've been playing Reverend Al Green's 'Take Me to the River'. This song had been an inspiration to me through the dark months of uncertain planning. Instead, it was drunken oompah. I didn't care. I was glad to be there.

I wended my way upstream towards the start, pausing to watch a rider, head down in solitary work. The Prologue is an individual time-trial. A race against the clock. It makes for a good Day One but it's a phoney war. The Tour is built on team-work. It takes a pyramid to put the star-rider on top.

As I came alongside the ramp, down which each rider starts, I hit an impasse. The crowd had jammed the pavement from barriered kerb to shop-window. People had climbed onto the windowsills for a good look-out. It was solid. The intimacy was intense, but it was not for me. Three years ago, the Brief and I had travelled to Antwerp to watch a stage finish of Le Tour. We were forced to park miles away, on the city limits, even so early in the morning. A crowded slow shuffle along a claustrophobic tunnel under the river had dumped me close to the finish line. I spent the next six hours edging inch by inch through the huge crowd to lean on the roadside barrier. I wanted an uninterrupted view of the cyclists. I never quite got it. The excitement of that finish was somethin' else. I was hooked. During that long squashed wait, I had plenty of time to look across at the other side of the road. There were enclosures for VIPs, press, friends and families of the teams, guests of ASO and God-knows-who. Liggers. They had comfort, space and room – and a clear sight of the race. I envied them. I wanted to be a ligger. I vowed to make it to the other side of the tracks. Here I was.

Behind the ramp, under two large yellow scimitar-shaped horns with the sign 'Depart – Liège', was a small fenced compound. I waved my pass at the security bloke and eased inside. It was not an elitist sanctuary but I could breathe and move. A few cyclists were finishing their warm-up, minutes before the first metres of their three-week trip. They glided around each other – slowly, silently. All around the outside fence fans, five-deep, stared wide-eyed. In their lurid lycra and aerodynamic helmets, the riders resembled exotic tropical fish in an aquarium.

We were down to the last couple of dozen. The team leaders, the big fish. I could tell by their numbers. Each one finished with a 1, Lance Armstrong was 1. Jan Ullrich, his chief rival, was 11. Each was greeted by a roar. Each signed in, was given the once-over by the judges, up the ramp and off … It was at this moment in 1989 in Luxembourg, that the reigning champion, Pedro Delgado, had shot off into the crowd to sign autographs. He had won Le Tour the previous year despite failing a dope test. He got away with the scam on a technicality because the drug in question, probenecid – a masking agent for anabolic steroids – was only due to have its ban ratified by the cycling authorities at the end of that Tour, despite already being prohibited by the International Olympic Committee. His public didn't give a toss. He was hugely cheered and immensely popular. He re-emerged almost three minutes late for his official start. He never recovered the time and lost the Tour. Now Armstrong, the reigning champion, was last one off. A bunch of Belgians booed him. He didn't seem bothered. I stood alongside and tried to figure it all out.

Chapter 2

Black Magic is a car. A left-hand-drive hire car. We walked off the SeaFrance ferry at Calais into the hire car office. Our motor was ready. The lady in the navy nylon uniform led the way into the car-park. Earl and I followed the Brief, lugging our bags. Ready for the off. Ready to hit the road, Jack.

'Voici.'

A pale grey Citroën Xsara stood before us. The lady's face shone at our anticipated delight at her shiny new car.

'It's the colour of a winter's sky. Like J.G. Ballard says, "Bold not bland". I don't wanna be seen in that. It's a hatch back.'

I looked at the Brief.

'This is not acceptable,' he said.

He'd done the booking with his computer. Bright or dark colour, four-door, CD player, air-conditioning and, especially, a separate boot. Thieves love Le Tour de France. I've been nobbled twice. Teams of thieves follow Le Tour. Just like journos and fans. Another town, another mark. All those unattended vehicles. One time, outside Verdun, the whole road was done. Scores of cars, every one of 'em, stripped'n'sorted. Not a pane of glass broken. 'Professional,' said the cops. Thieves prefer hatchbacks. It's quicker, easier. I looked around the car-park. Nearly all of 'em were hatchbacks of an insipid colour.

'I demand a replacement,' said the Brief.

His calm authority rattled the lady. She nipped back to her office and returned with new keys. Looking flushed, she presented us with a big black car with a boot.

9

'No extra charge,' she said.

The chrome on the back said 'Volkswagen Magique Noir'. Black Magic. This was good ju-ju hittin' us. As soon as our feet had hit French soil. This classy upgrade was bonzer. We had serious miles in front of us.

The Brief beamed. I had known that he'd be a good team-mate for this trip. He was a lawyer. He specialised in defending the criminally insane. I figured he could come in handy. He was calm and methodical. I might well need that. He was tall and slim with a trace of a dark beard and battered sandals. He looked confusingly distinguished, like a man of authority off duty. He was partial to a drop of sport. He held a season ticket for Fulham. I'd first got to know him as the sober captain of a cricket team of dodgy drunks. I had been the off-spinner.

The third man on the team was my son Earl. He was fresh outta art college. At 23, he quite rightly spent more time in front of a mirror with his comb than with his toothbrush. He often quizzed me about my days as road manager of The Clash. Here was a chance to show off my road-craft. To see if there was life left in the old dog. But I knew that it ain't easy, treatin' your kid as an equal.

I am the passenger from hell. Earl was along as co-driver. The Brief was currently banned. I love driving. I don't give up the wheel gracefully, but I knew that these daily distances of a few hundred kilometres would do me in. Wreck the jaunt. I had to keep my cool in the back seat and swallow hard. The Brief was navigator, ridin' shotgun.

I started shouting as soon as Earl pulled away from the hotel. Every car seemed suspect, every turn dangerous as we crossed Liège. 'Fuck off, old man,' said my driver. As he parked up, I jumped out. There was someone I wanted to see. Mario Cipollini.

Cipollini is a sprinter. He is fast. He is flash. He wins in style. He breaks the rules and doesn't give a flyin' fuck. He is beautiful. The French call him 'Le Beau Mario'. He is getting old. I wanted to see Mario Cipollini, eyeball to eyeball.

I had been stalking Cipo since I got into Liège the night before the Prologue. A big presentation was held at Palais Prices Evequal, a solemn solid town hall building with gold on top. It said, 'We are your burghers. We are responsible. You can depend on us. We have put you on the map. The whole world is watching. And we can be impressive. Look at the gold. But in moderation.'

I liked the towers of red'n'yellow balloons across the façade. The square was full of craning punters. I jostled my way into the crowd for a good view of the stage. I stopped alongside the mixing desk. Old habits die hard. Freddy French was finishing up his sound-check. He was gigging here later. He's big in Belgium. Listening to his mild version of 'Born to be Wild', and clockin' his mullet, wrinkles and leather kecks, I thought I'd give it a miss.

Each of the twenty-one teams wheeled up a ramp onto the stage, one at a time. Freddy's band's amplifiers and drum kit were at the back. The lights from the truss overhead and the genies on the wings shone on the shiny new bikes. The official voicebox, Dan Mangeas, belted outta the PA system. Every rider got praise and a name-check. Most of 'em looked sheepish'n'gawky in their new strips. I watched six or seven teams take a bow. Big names got a cheer, but the Belgians didn't seem that bothered. I was checkin' out old favourites and sucking in that old vibe. I moved across to a stone archway, through which the teams were arriving. There he was. Cipollini. A mane of golden hair tossed back onto his shoulders. A suntan that said more than early July. I was stopped in my tracks, four back from the barrier. I felt hypnotised. He led his Domina Vacanza team up onto the lip of the stage. All nine Italians were introduced. Super Mario got the biggest cheer of the night. It turned into a roar as they threw their team caps across the monitors. People scrambled to grab 'em. Cipo laughed and danced a little circular jig. He looked delighted to be there. I came to my senses. I remembered I had plastic in my pocket. A magical key. I could escape this crush, unlock the barrier and walk where the air was free. I flashed the pass. The team buses were round the back. As Cipo walked to the bus door with his entourage, he stopped to talk to an elderly couple with a child. I watched him fix them with his attention. They seemed mesmerised. The bus pulled away. I was well made up.

By the next day, the Prologue, I had learnt my lesson. The green press pass was round my neck. I stood shoulder to shoulder with the international press corps. Actually, just those few dozen who'd bothered to leave their pampered sanctuary. Next to the starting ramp with the timekeepers and officials, riders warmed up in a very public fenced area for a few minutes before their off. Favoured photographers were granted access. 'Look.' Earl pulled my arm. The Brief was sliding around in there, cameras dangling like Dennis Hopper in *Apocalypse Now*. His unobtrusiveness was an asset. A shout went up from the public. I turned. Cameramen ran and clustered around one rider. Mario Cipollini. He was lovin' it, the attention. He granted his adoring fans a show of his teeth, far better than Barry Gibb. The officials had grim faces. Cipo was wearing an astonishing outfit. Time-trialists wear aerodynamic suits'n'helmets. Every nanosecond helps. Fabric and stitching designed to conduct air flow. The newest technology tested in wind tunnels for maximum efficiency. If your team could afford it. If not, wear this cheap lot. 'Kit cheats' for gaining unfair advantage? The look was *Star Trek*, but in the correct team colours. Not Cipo. He wore a one-piece skin-hugger in two-tone blue with black electrical circuits printed, fingertips to neck to ankles. His look was that of a droid from the future with his skin stripped off. He stood out, bizarre and unique. The officials, suits with the clip-boards, were frowning, pointing. Rules is rules, especially French bureaucratic rules'n'regulations. Latex one-piece suits were on the banned list. It's gotta go. Plus there's a fine comin'. Cipo seemed unfazed. He knew that he looked unashamedly wonderful. He didn't give a fuck about the cost. I was with him all the way. Two roadies appeared with nail scissors. They crouched down beside his bike and snipped away above the knees'n'elbows. Mario's discarded costume lay on the road, replaced by his golden flesh. Camera flashes, jaws droppin', a big hubbub. The Italian went up the start ramp in his new 'distressed' look to an ovation. I joined in. I'd figured from all I'd seen'n'read that he'd be hot stuff. The effect of his presence was truly fantastic. Waves of energy rippled off him. Everyone bar the jobsworths was touched and showed it. We shouted'n'smiled. The passive audience burst into animated life. It was uncanny. I needed more of it. In this dour sporting arena, I wanted a hit of his vibrancy. I hadn't seen Cipo on his bike yet. Pelting at full tilt. I wanted to see him win a stage. To witness this god in all his glory. I desired a touch of his flesh. To feel his ju-ju.

Mario was no stranger to fines. They were always in Swiss francs, making it seem dodgier. They were always in piddly amounts. Tokenism. It was the price he paid for being a rebel. The stunts were worth the dough. I'd chip in for Cipo. He has always loved dressing up. I guess cycling gear ain't bad for show-offs. Figure-hugging lurid lycra. Big bollock bulges. Mario has moved the grand entrance beyond Elton John or Kiss territory. There was a point, always, to his wayward kit. There have been many. In 1997 he wore green, yellow and American-flag shorts to match his jersey. Fine. In '98, in Dublin, he wore the green with 'Peace' on it. Spot on, but fine. He's done topless, accompanied by a topless model. Hell, he's had a picture of Pamela Anderson on his handlebars. I'm far more grabbed by this than sprocket ratios. He's worn the maillot jaune for real. Between 1993 and '99, he won a stage every year. In '99, he did four wins on the trot. To celebrate, he dressed up in a toga with a stripper as Cleopatra alongside. The team wore silver jerseys with the legend, 'Veni, Vidi, Vici'. Big fines. Cipo's a poseur, but he delivers. Not like footballers in crap teams in the lower divisions who wear customised gold boots. Ronaldo? Yeah.

Best of all has been his imperial wave as he crossed the line as winner. He always, like a true champion, had a nanosecond in hand to acknowledge his people. We loved him for it. ASO didn't. Cipo didn't fit in neatly. He didn't know his station. The burghers had no time for such extrovert ructions. Handy for them was the fact that Mario never once made it up a serious gradient. As soon as Le Tour de France arrived at the foot of the Alps or the Pyrenees, Cipo got off his bike. Bad back, bad knee, bad any body part. This did not go down well with the organisers. Cipo was not felt to be playing the endurance game. Too right. He was there to explode like a Roman candle. His push was all or nothing. Never dutiful mediocrity. I relate to exhibitionist extremists. Like Iggy Pop. When he took class A drugs, he was out of it more than anybody else. When he was clean, he was purer than anyone. Cipo, in his prime, could beat anyone in a sprint. He didn't do mountains.

This went down very badly with Jean-Marie Leblanc, Le Tour director. Leblanc is known (by me) as the Pork Butcher. He looks like one. His face is mottled and marbled, balding on top with impressive jowls underneath. He rolls up his shirt-sleeves to reveal forearms like York hams. Jean-Marie had been a pro cyclist himself, ridin' two Tours at the back end of the '60s. He knew the score. His need for conformity was rattled by Cipo's don't-give-a-fuck attitude. For four years running, Mario sat watching the letterbox, waiting for his Tour invitation. He won the World Championship in 2002. Still, he was banished. I was well pissed off. So were a lot of thrill-seekers. He should've been resplendent in his rainbow jersey in 2003. I'd had it in mind to do something about it. I wanted to let Leblanc know how I felt about Cipo's exclusion. I made plans to hurl red paint at the Butcher. I stalked him for a coupla days, wearin' a Cipollini T-shirt I made. I was gonna shout, 'We wuz robbed, you mean-spirited petty-minded cunt.' A number of things stayed my hand. Paranoia'n'survival, for a starters. Those gendarmes can be mean. I've been beaten up by British coppers, broken jaw'n'ribs. I feared worse in France with someone of Leblanc's status. Cipo himself put on a very dignified front. Like Jimmy Greaves being left out of the England World Cup team in '66 by Alf Ramsey. He did say that he'd been 'treated no better than meat on a butcher's slab'. Thing was, as I watched the Butcher's modus operandi close up, I was shocked to find that I liked him. This podgy bigwig was quite a man of the people himself. He could glad-hand'n'press the flesh. He put himself about. I saw him have long talks with punters while strollin' solo. No minders. He was approachable. And I knew that he loved to play the saxophone, like Bill Clinton and Lisa Simpson. He probably had visions of himself blowin' away on stage at Madison Square Gardens alongside Bruce Springsteen. He couldn't be all bad … He also knew that Mario Cipollini was a big draw. His last chance to be a contender.

I was still flushed with the buzz back at the Hotel

Simenon. I discovered there that Marlon Brando was dead. For me, it was some deal. For Earl, it was a tragedy. He loved the movies. He'd spent the past three years studyin' film-making at university. He was steeped in film lore. He knew the history and the legends. He could quote frame and performance. Marlon was a giant. Brando, to him, was an actor with whoppin' parts, parts he carefully chose and made his own. Then, pissed off with the fame but not the money, he hid away on his own tropical island in the South Pacific. I looked at the pictures of the house on the atoll. Beautiful and remote. The sheer volume of people who get to be a celebrity, like every Joe Public dreams, then run'n'hide away. Agnetha from ABBA, the blonde bird voted Best Bottom in the World. Some soubriquet. Took the money and ran to her little Swedish island. A recluse who slowly, over years, opened back up to the harsh world. A German man befriended her. She showed him kindness. He moved onto her island, in a hut. Alas, he was a stalker. She moved away from him. He blew his brains out. She returned to being a recluse. Is this the real Greta Garbo story? The fame gets to Tour riders too. Some handle it so beautifully, like Mario Cipollini, that they must have been born for it.

Most riders are team players. They never get to hit the spotlight. Then there are the losers. Beautiful losers and abject failures. Le Tour has created its own title, Lanterne Rouge, for the last man in the race. Crowds applaud. He usually milks it. He knows that the infamy will bring appearance money at races around the country after Le Tour is over. I watched one of 'em, Jay Sweet, a few years ago, holding his arms aloft like a champion with a great shit-eating grin. 'Chapeaux', went the roar. The word means 'hats'. As in 'Hats off for him', meaning 'Bravo'. Those old photos where every bloke is wearing a hat. Then they throw 'em up in the air as a celebration. Am I the only one who wondered if every bloke got his own hat back afterwards? Come to that, I also wondered in those TV shots of Palestinians celebrating by firing automatic guns into the air, what happens to the bullets? Do they eventually come down on some poor sod's head doing bad hair damage?

Over a greasy kebab'n'chips with mayonnaise, we remembered a home-town boy. Liège produced the most magnificent loser in the history of Le Tour de France. Georges Goffin was a king. He was born here on April Fool's Day. At the age of 26, he decided to ride Le Tour. He did so under the name of Georges Nemo. No one, including his wife, knew why. He jacked it in on the first day. Not to be beaten, he had another go two years later. He didn't last the first day out. At the ripe old age of 39, in 1922, he gave it one last shot. 'Third time pays for all,' says Bilbo Baggins. Georges Nemo dropped out on the first day. Chapeaux!

Cycling ain't the only game with such heroes. In pre-corporate times, John Thorneycroft Hartley made it through to the semi-finals of the All-England Men's Singles at Wimbledon in 1879. The problem was that he was a vicar. His parish was in Yorkshire. Having won the quarter-final on a Saturday, he raced off up north to give his sermons on the Sunday. Having done his Matins'n'Evensong, he arrived by horse and carriage at Thirsk station at the crack of dawn. The 250-mile train journey got him into King's Cross at two in the afternoon. He had half an hour to dash across London for his tennis match. He was starving'n'knackered. C.F. Parr beat him 6–0, 6–0, 6–0. Chapeaux!

Earl was sorting out music for the motor. I asked for Motorhead. Lemmy understands this stuff well

You know I'm born to lose,

And gamblin's made for fools,
But that's the way I like it baby,
I don't wanna live for ever …
The ace of spades.

Lemmy also wrote a great road song called 'White-Line Fever'. It's a great blur of a lyric between drivin' down the highway and snortin' class A stimulants. A fine way to spend a young life. For true rockin' road music, the soundtrack had to be Chuck Berry, 'Promised Land'. As soon as Chuck sings, you can just picture the vastness of America. The thousands of miles that need to be eaten up by the tyres. Funny to remember that when Le Tour first started in 1903, the USA had only 10 miles of surfaced road in the entire country. Chuck Berry can just list place-names and it's rockin'. It don't seem to work in France, no matter how you try. 'Route 66'? Flagstaff, Arizona; don't forget Winona. Yeah, but forget Châteauroux or Rouen. Le Tour once tried to sponsor its own music. Kraftwerk were commissioned. Ralf Hutter loved cycling. With his partner, Florian Schneider, Ralf loved machines for making music. Disengaged computers'n'droid voices begat techno. The romantic French ASO hated the cold Germanic tribute to Le Tour de France. The gig was off. In 1983, the record gradually assumed cult status and got sorta re-adopted. I never heard it blarin' outta speakers at Le Départ or L'Arrivée though.

I heard loads of Sheryl Crow, though. Her voice would accompany us as we drifted away from the podium after the presentation ceremony each day. Official muzak. I'm sure her music was played for artistic merit only. It is very easy for some to be cynical about product placement in these corporate times. Le Tour would naturally acknowledge Sheryl's presence as Lance's bird. She did pop up in person from time to time.

Down at the race, I sidetracked the civic eateries. The burghers of Liège were stuffing their faces with charcuterie et fromage in their fenced-in enclosure, Le Village, distinctive with white tent roofs, pointy like the Mound Stand at Lords or a Ku Klux Klan hood. It was a guarded enclosure right behind the start line where regulars and daytrippers met to eat, drink and trade information. There was a lot of nervous tension zingin' around. First day outta twenty on the road, for real. More miles in front than a sane mind could comprehend. Smart people looked at it 'one day at a time'. I didn't. I saw it as a whirr of flashin' activity for three weeks, one huge block of time, with slight pauses for rest'n'victuals. For me, one point of the exercise was to 'derail'n'derange the senses'.

The riders, almost 200 of 'em, were nervously sorting themselves out. Like batsmen stepping to the crease, straps pulled, clothing tugged, every metal joint double tightened. I joined in the fray, movin' amongst them in their enclosure. I was just soaking up the ambience, head swivellin'. Boof! I was next to Mario Cipollini. The moment had come. He and I were an island in a space all around us. I pulled my Dictaphone outta my pocket. He was perched comfortably on his cross-bar. He slowly turned towards me. Le Beau Mario seemed huge, perfectly in proportion. I looked down at his muscular thighs, bronzed and smooth. I wanted to stretch out my hand and stroke his bare flesh down to his knee with my palm. I knew that action would give me a lifetime's good ju-ju. I looked up and into his eyes. He locked me into his warm gaze. I had no sense of time. I asked him, 'Can we speak in English?' 'No.' 'En Français?' 'Non.' Mario smiled the widest radiant smile. It radiated through me, like waves of orgasm. 'Italiano,' he said. 'No,' I laughed. He laughed. I shrugged. We laughed louder'n'louder. Still our eyes held each other. 'Ah well, fuck it,' I said, still laughing. He eased his look forward and moved off slowly, the laughter still loud. I was transfixed, watching him move away in slow motion. Then I floated behind him towards the gate of the enclosure, grinning ecstatically, insanely.

The spell was broken by Earl, grinning on the other side of the wire. He was holding his camcorder with one hand. His thumb in the air. He had captured the moment on film. But it wasn't necessary. It was imprinted on my psyche. Some hit. Some buzz. People who have met Elvis Presley have said that the moment of contact with him was remarkable. It seemed that you were the centre of Elvis's universe. He beamed all of his attention on you. Made you feel as if you were the most special person in his world for an eternal instant.

It was a big 'fuck off' to those who say 'Never meet your heroes.' I've met one or two in my time. They've been interesting and rewarding. Never anything like this.

As a youth, I collected footballers' autographs. I would hang around the big hotels in London, waiting for teams to leave for a match. A small group of pimply teens would loiter on the steps. One time, Manchester United were staying at the Russell Hotel in Russell Square. It was an old-fashioned gaff, with a stroppy doorman in a ludicrous 'circus' uniform with gold-braided top hat'n'tails. I loved that team. As they filed out, I latched on to Denis Law. He was my favourite player. 'Sign this, please, Denis.' He did. 'Going to a match son?' he asked. 'I'm going to see you at Chelsea, Denis,' I replied. 'Do you want a lift?' He pointed at the waiting team coach. Did I. I followed him onto the half-full coach nervously. 'Sit here,' said Denis, flickin' his eyes at the next seat. I looked up to the front. The rest of United were boarding. Bobby Charlton was coming down the aisle. 'What's the fucking kid doing on here?' he barked. 'He's with me,' said Denis. Charlton scowled and moved past me. I sat in a trance on the coach journey across London, staring out of the windows and back to the legends come to life. Nothing was said. As the coach pulled up inside Stamford Bridge, Denis Law nipped up to the front seat where Jackie Crompton, the trainer, sat. As I drew level, Denis handed me a ticket to the main stand. 'Enjoy yourself.' 'Thanks.'

I'm not big on having heroes so I guess it's turned out alright. Workin' in rock'n'roll, I got to bump into all kinds of big-name celebrities. Big deal. It's only the strange and wonderful that stick in the memory. I was waiting for the lift at the Grosvenor Park Hotel in London. As the doors opened, I went to move inside. There stood Roy Orbison. He was dressed all in black. So was I. His face was as white as a sheet. Like a man who never saw daylight. He wore big shades. So did I. A huge minder stood motionless next to him. I stepped forward, put out my hand and said, 'Roy, I love your music.' He didn't move a muscle. He looked embalmed. 'Roy is mighty pleased to have made your acquaintance,' said the American minder. I was spooked and delighted. We travelled down to the lobby in silence. What can you say to a man whose life unrolled like one of his tragic numbers. He divorced his wife Claudette in November '64. They re-married in August '65. Ten months later, Claudette, pretty, pretty, pretty Claudette, bought it inna motorbike crash. Roy never took the shades off again. In September '68, while Roy was out on the road, his house caught fire. His two sons, Roy Jr and Tony, were killed. I'm impressed that Roy kept gigging until his fatal heart attack in '88. It puts into perspective Tyler Hamilton's reason for quittin' Le Tour down south. He said he was upset at the death of his dog, Tugboat.

Cycling fans get to rub shoulders with their heroes easy at Le Tour. It's a tradition. It's the People's Race. It comes to them. Nothing changes. A punter can hang out at the start or finish and pat 'em on the back. Team coaches ain't sealed off. The riders have to make their own way on'n'off them through the crowd. I love this accessibility about the event. It belongs to a bygone era of assumed intimacy. Fans can wander where they will and feel that they are active participants. Modern paranoia has brought security to the fore in other sports. The rise of celebrity culture has resulted in those stars becoming unapproachable and unobtainable to the common people who put 'em there in the first place. And they wonder why they're outta touch! In the Roman Empire, a slave was employed to run alongside the Emperor, saying to him: 'Remember you are human. Remember you will die. Remember you are no different to any other citizen.' There was no need for this bloke on Le Tour de France.

As they lined up elegantly behind Mr Mayor, I scuttled to a traffic island with bollards a hundred metres in front of them. A civil ceremony of protocol followed. A member of each team, the wearer of each prize jersey, dignitaries and the Pork Butcher, were in line behind a silk ribbon. A young rider, chosen at random, read out the traditional speech on behalf of le peloton. It spoke of honour and sportsmanship. Shades of medieval chivalry. The young rider was Thomas Voeckler. I only realised that just happened to be him way after, lookin' back at the pics. A good choice by Le Tour. His day would come soon. Up went the balloons, clouds of red'n'yellow. Up went the roar. The ribbon was cut. The flag was waved out of the sunroof by the Butcher to signal the Grand Départ. I had hoped he'd stand up there 'n' blow his saxophone. The Butcher was in a red Skoda. All the biggie-wiggies were. A good colour. They were numbered. Leblanc's was No. 1. It was driven by roadie supreme, Belgian Bob. Robert Lelangue was cool. He drove his boss under impossibly chaotic conditions. A bald bloke with specs. Cycles buzzing round the car, crowds spillin' off the pavement, hordes of journos runnin' in front of his bonnet. All the way round the circuit, he was two car-lengths behind the leader. Precision drivin'. Pick ups'n'drops for the Pork Butcher were always right place, right time. As an ageing road manager, it was always a delight for me to stand back and watch Bob in action. I made small talk with him. There was nothing much to say. His performance and my admiration said it all.

Belgian Bob had an oppo in red Skoda number 7. This roadie was also entrancing. He didn't have Bob's cool but he did take care of business. His thing was being morbidly obese. Christ, he was fat. He was fuckin' huge around the waist. Special ASO uniforms must've been run up for him in outsize suppliers. His drivin' seat must've been modified in a garage so that he could fit behind the wheel. It is a wonderful testimony to Le Tour that oddball weirdos are not only tolerated but actively encouraged.

Le peloton rode straight at me.

> Onward, onward,
> Rode the six hundred …
> Theirs not to question why
> Theirs but to do or die …

Crouched on the little traffic island, the cyclists went to the left, to the right of me. I was swallowed up in a sea of colour. Wave upon wave of blue, red, green, gold, white, seamlessly obliterating everything. To have washed up on the best beach in the world. I gave thanks to Cipo. I looked out for him in the pack. It was impossible to make out individuals. There were others by me, clinging to the bollards. All had huge cameras clicking'n'whirrin' away. The top photographers. This was the prime location for the crème-de-la-crème. Victorian ladies'n'gentlemen would sit, with a picnic, on a hill overlooking a battlefield in the Crimean War. The Charge of the Light Brigade as an amusing sporting event, eye-glass to hand. This was much closer.

What great ju-ju! I touched the blue stone in my pocket. It's carried always in that tiny pocket on the right hip of my jeans. Haven't you ever wondered why Herr Levi sewed that on? When I'm getting dressed, the ju-ju stone is the first detail I check. It's ultramarine blue, shiny (but then I rub it between finger'n'thumb in dodgy moments), about an inch long, half as much wide'n'deep, tapered. A splintered vein of off-white crystal shines like Colombian cocaine. If it ain't where it should be, I panic. Like the ravens leaving the Tower of London, I would fall. If it's awol, everything shuts down 'til it's found. I went days hunting under beds, lifting chair cushions, turning out the rubbish bin. I was saying nothin' in quiet desperation. Lady Luck had left me. My daughter, Polly, had brought it back from some trip lost in time. Right then, I knew it was special. Don't ask! Your rationality doesn't apply. I felt its force straight away. One time, it was away for days on end. I was bereft. I just about ground to a halt.

'Have you seen my ju-ju stone?' I eventually asked Nesta, my wife.

'No. Only my own.'

She'd been given a purple stone, similar, yet to her it was a souvenir of no importance. The sort of trinket a kid spends her money on in a heritage shop. For some unknown reason (you gettin' the picture?), I said, 'Can I have a look?' Nesta dug it out. It was my blue stone. I went mental. Waves of paranoia swept over me.

'That's mine. How could you do this to me? You're like Delilah, cuttin' off Samson's hair to sap his strength.'

I snatched it back. I seem to have passed some test.

Since then, if it slips out of a suit pocket, I know. If it falls down the side of the settee while I'm watchin' the telly, the stone emanates its presence to me. You can see why I strongly relate to Bilbo, Frodo and Gollum.

I'm not secretive about my ju-ju stone. I don't wear it around my neck – no hippie flaunting, it's true. But when stuff's goin' down, the hairy times, out it comes.

I was not alone. Right from the off, at the Prologue, I was surprised to see Jan Ullrich cross himself discreetly on the start ramp. It wasn't quite what I'd expected from a hedonistic boy raised in Communist East Germany. The mark of the papacy was strong throughout le peloton, whether shown by the movement of fingertips, or hung on a chain around the neck. I saw one bloke, Gonzalez, suckin' a large crucifix as he crossed the finish line triumphantly in Nîmes. I could get it if an entire cycling team of devout Italians decamped to Lourdes when the race was in the Pyrenees. It made perfect sense to me to nip over to St Bernadette's grotto for a swift Catholic blessing. God knows, some teams on the slide needed a miracle. Like chemicals, if faith can nick you a couple of metres on your rival, it's worth the shot.

Objects, movement, people and places make up an invisible web of psycho-support. The riders don't question. Nor do I. For me, it ain't worship. I can do without the formal and the orthodox. But the rituals run deep in music like sport. Elvis wore a token of every major world religion.

'No point in takin' chances,' he said.

Gut feelin' is a serious component of rock'n'roll. To do it because it feels right. The power that emanates from the dead is not universal. It's a personal mix, chosen by the individual to stimulate and sustain. There was a whole bunch of characters awaiting me along the way. Paris was The End and Jim Morrison was buried there. Some places are charged either because of a special event, or just because of their name. I went to them to plug into the ju-ju, or rather they called to me. I merely responded.

Ju-ju is as vital a source of energy to this trip as filling up the tank of Black Magic with diesel. It sparks the flame of enthusiasm. It blows it on up into a bonfire of passion. Ju-ju sweeps me along intuitively, protecting and guiding. It may be medieval gobbledegook. It might be cheap animism. It most certainly undermines the worn-out fabric of reason and rationality. There may be no logic to it but it sure does work. And it's fun.

The movement of the teams was infectious. When the back-up cars had followed the cycles, I legged it across to the car-park. I was carrying a yellow'n'black rucksack that said 'Liège – Le Tour de France'. It was a freebie for the press, filled with pens, news releases, a watch, anything for a favourable write-up. In a side pocket was a stoneware flagon of local gin. A thought-out gift for journalists. My gin-drinkin' days are done. A lifetime's intimacy with alcohol is over. The booze very nearly did me in. But it would be a sin to waste the liquor. As I crossed the leafy park back to the car, I was on the look-out for someone. I knew I would recognise him immediately. I was certain he would be here amongst the trees on the periphery of the mob. A boozer, a serious drinker, a man with an unquenchable curiosity for the intensity of life. I'd never be so shallow as to call him an alcoholic. I spotted him straight away. I suffered no doubt. That stone bottle of gin was weighing heavy in my hand. I was becoming more aware of it with each step. It was pressing on my brain. I didn't want to think of the consequences. I had to double take the guy as he came towards me. Smart, yet worn khakis. He'd shaved. Made an effort to meet the world on some kinda terms. He was up and about on a Sunday morning. I could tell that there was a lack of purpose in him, an injury that was not evident to the naked eye. He glanced around in self-protection, not wonder. I slowed and our eyes locked. His were blood-shot. I scanned his face, his blotched clean skin. His hands shook. He was not wary. He reacted to my openness with confusion. As if it had been a long time since anyone had offered him kindness. I explained, in French, the bottle, Le Tour, the gig. He took awhile to get on top of it. A gift. Of booze. Good booze. It registered. I felt the need to tell. It's the nearest I get to 'My name is Johnny; I'm an alcoholic.' We parted. I managed six steps through the wooded park by the lake. I let a couple of photographers walk past me. Until I couldn't hold it in. I didn't want to hold it in. Tears flowed, I sobbed, I choked. I cried because he was me. The man I gave the stone bottle of gin to was myself. I hope he enjoyed it. God bless Le Tour de fucking France.

Chapter 3

I wanted to lighten my spirits. It's hard to do in Belgium. The race onlookers had a 'Well, we're here, ain't we? Show us!' look on their pudding faces. I knew that look well. I may have been a little biased against the country and its population. There was still the matter of an outstanding warrant for my arrest. A driving cock-up of some years ago. A getaway after a gig. In Louvain, I had been by the side monitors, as usual, while The Clash belted it out to a lumpy crowd of Belgian students. The gig was in a circus tent in a field of mud. The stage sank into the mud with the band's passionate runnin'n'jumpin'. It listed like a sinking ship. The steeper the angle, the more manic were Strummer, Jones, Simenon at the mikes. Topper's drum kit was falling over. Great chaotic gig. The audience applauded politely. Drivin' the hire van outta town, I was demonstrating the stand-up jockey position. The front bumpers demolished a coupla 'Keep Right' bollards in the middle of the road. The laughter stopped when the Belgian police nicked me. I had been drinking the excellent national brew. I never responded to the bail conditions. Every year, an update on the fine from the court would land on my mat along with the Christmas cards. Every year, I ignored it. I never intended to return to Belgium.

Charleroi, Namur. The same kinda muted reaction along the route. Four days in Belgium was a drag. It rained. The cold winds blew. The cyclists crashed. Bandages'n'plasters started appearing on heads, arms'n'legs. A Spanish rider, Angel Vicioso of the Liberty team, copped it bad. He looked a mess. I instantly warmed to him – his jaw was wrapped in gauze. He became Sid Vicious. To inject a little familiarity and lookin' for idiosyncratic distractions, Earl and I played with silly names. Andrea Noe was 'Doctor'. A trail of 'Pleasant dreams, Mr Bond' jokes followed. Maryan Hary sadly got trimmed 'cos of time early on. The Belgian, Marc Wauters, became Choppy Waters. This is schoolboy stuff. Benny Salmon. Jakob Piil, the breakaway specialist. Vladimir Karpets rode so well that he stopped being a snigger. Jan Kirsipuu was an old hand. He won the first day's bunch sprint against the odds. It won him no respite from his given name, 'the Potato Boy'. He just looked like a spud. We had bags-full of nicknames. It passed the car journeys. It personalised the bunch, gave me someone to point at and say, 'Ooh, look.' If one of 'em had a good day or an unexpected burst of form, it would raise a cheer. If there was one unfancied non-star we loved more than anyone, it was Ronny Scholtz. Ronny was German. He rode in the sky blue of the Gerolsteiner team. They were sponsored by a mineral-water company. Hence, the 'German Water Boys'. I never saw Ronny drink any. Their bus had fizzy bubbles on the side. Ronny was a team man, a domestique, helping his leader, Georg Totschnig, make eventual seventh, and leading out his sprinter, Danny Hondo, to fuck-all wins. No matter. We loved Ronny Scholtz. Every day, he got our loudest shout. Repetitive jokes gain power the more you say'n'share 'em. These anonymous team members in the pack became personalised and came to life.

Very ominously, so did Gian Matteo Fagnini. A bad crash at speed on a wet, slippery road broke his collarbone. Fagnini was a senior pro on the Domina Vacanze team. He was the lead-out man for Mario Cipollini. He had been, down all the years. This gig means going full tilt at the front inside the last kilometre, with yer man right behind your back wheel. Slipstreaming. Keepin' the way open. Fighting off rivals. Towin' your team's top sprinter. At the key moment, Fagnini would peel off to the side. This should leave Cipo with a clear run to the line at breakneck speed. Arms aloft, massive smile, another win. Another precious stage victory to add to his total of twelve. That was the theory. Trouble was, every other team was tryin' to pull the same stunt. The jostlin'n'jinkin' heads down, elbows out, stretch right across the road, was the sight. And now Cipollini, the striker, had no team-mate to cross the ball. No assists. It didn't look good for Mario. Or me, wanting to be there when it happened. If it happened.

The old men of speed were giving way to the younger generation of up'n'coming sprinters. Of course. Ain't it always? Passin' the baton. Cipo, Erik Zabel, even Alessandro Petacchi, the heir apparent, were being clipped by Tom Boonen, Thor Hushovd and the Aussies. Thing was, for me, these new kids were too busy tryin' too hard to win. In their earnest endeavours to be first across the line, they were neglecting to develop their panache. Or maybe they had none. I love the swagger of a man at the top of his game. Sure, the final result is paramount. But the intricacies and tricky touches are what bring a smile to my lips. I fully understand that money drives modern sport. Sponsors provide the dough. They wish to be identified as winners. But results fade quickly with time. Style and panache lift things above the performance of the common man. Winners make me clap my hands. Flash brings a gleam to my eye and a 'Yeah!' to my throat. Little Richard didn't need lipstick, mascara and a towerin' pompadour hair-do to sing 'Tutti Frutti' but it made his performance memorable. Jerry Lee Lewis could've just plonked the keys to 'Great Balls of Fire'. As well, he kicked away his stool, let his greasy curled quiff fall all over his face and jumped on top of the piano. It was unforgettable. This new generation of cyclists needed to strut their stuff as well as deliver the goods.

It was still the best show in town. From the press area, behind the line, or alongside the line, right on the barrier, leanin' out, cranin' the old neck, hearin' the aural Mexican wave of the crowd's roar. Seein' coloured specks become people in a flash. So fast, so close. I stared so hard to figure out the winner, often only by the thickness of the rubber inna tyre. We weren't a gamblin' family. As a boy, my old man told me that at the races there were geezers who predicted photo finishes. We are talkin' pre-television. When the horses were too close to call for the judges, a photograph would be requested. In the time gap between the tight finish and the judges' announcement these geezers would bet on the result. It was all down to the incredible sharpness of his eye against some rheumy-eyed old bookie. I was gettin' better with these bikes.

The crazy yelling of punters was more of a collective guttural sigh in Belgium. The sight of the publicity caravan failed to bring a twinkle to their eyes. When free key-rings'n'sachets of 'Grand Mère' instant coffee were thrown, even the kids hardly bothered to catch 'em in the air or bend down to pick 'em up. Horns were honked. The correct response of the crowd was a cheer'n'a wave. Not here. It was a blank stare.

I couldn't figure it. It was gettin' to me. In Charleroi, before the start, the torpor was overpowering. I walked away from the assembly. In the empty grey back streets, I was surprised to see quite a few riders slowly killing time, solo or in pairs. Pissed off. They didn't look up for it. I was brooding on the legacy of this town.

If there was a plaque on the wall for Arthur Rimbaud, I must've missed it. It was to Charleroi he walked as a youth. He was on the lam from his home-town to the south, Charleville. He was on the run from his family, his school, from conventional thought, word'n'behaviour. I'd been to his old house last year, when Le Tour breezed through that town. I was accompanied by the Mentor. He was my old professor. The place was now a museum with little in it other than his suitcase and his poetry. He had shocked the local burghers badly. Now he brought in tourism. Hushed-up'n'smoothed-out. Heritage is money. His escape to Charleroi did not provide enough relief or stimulation for him. Arthur ended up in Paris, under the respectable tutelage of the poet, Verlaine. Rimbaud's drugged'n'drunken debauchery, his foul-mouthed outspoken honesty, entranced Verlaine, then wrecked his life and sent him mad. Rimbaud jacked in poetry at the end of his teens. He never wrote another verse. He fucked off to Ethiopia to sell guns. Endlessly itchy feet. He died at 37 and inspired a rock'n'roll generation: Jim Morrison, Patti Smith, Keith Richards, Pete Doherty and on and on.

Charleroi nowadays had no such vivacity. The press centre was in an agricultural warehouse. It leaked in the pouring rain. The journos clung to a free beer stall. Out in the streets, I was joined by Berlin Tom. Tom was tall and thoughtful, with a pony-tail and big plastic specs. He always seemed to be workin' up a left-field angle for his column in a German newspaper.

'What's new, Johnny?' he asked.

'Not a lot. Change and decay in all around I see,' I said.

I doubted he was familiar with the number.

I continued. 'O, Thou who changest not, abide with me.'

Tom looked blank. When in Rome … He'd obviously never been to a Cup Final.

'I was thinkin' 'bout Marc Dutroux,' I said.

Dutroux was a local here. He was the monster who'd abducted little girls. He'd used them for his one-way sexual needs. Then they died. He was a Belgian Fred West. Fred had stuck 'em upright under the patio. Marc had carved out, constructed and equipped a series of 'play-rooms' and dungeons in his basement. One of the girls, Sabine Dardenne, survived to tell the world. She is remarkably cool about what Dutroux put her through. It's as if the whole nightmare has taught her William Burroughs' maxim 'The Face of Evil is almost always the Face of Total Need.' The neighbours said of Marc, as those of Fred had done, 'He was a quiet man who kept himself to himself.'

I'm fuckin' sure he did! He'd hardly get legless down the boozer and risk blurtin' it all out.

It's always the shy, silent ones: Dennis Nielsen, Peter William Sutcliffe, Jeffrey Dahmer. Dutroux would have quietly joined the A-list of sadistic killers but for the rumours. The whole saga had been a complicated mess. Lots of questions, like: how come it had escaped police notice for so long? How come Dutroux had escaped from police custody? The rumours spoke of connections. Child sex rings involving top cops, burghers, even government ministers. There had been huge demonstrations in protest by shocked townspeople in these very streets. A very dark ju-ju hung over the town. I could feel it.

Berlin Tom said, 'The route today went right past Marc Dutroux's house. ASO had demanded that the building be demolished before Le Tour arrived. The council had agreed. But it wasn't done.'

The street was fillin' up. Le peloton was stackin' up like a crash on the M25. None of 'em looked in a hurry to get goin'. I leaned on a lamp-post, using the handy list I kept in my pocket to put names to numbers. Just to break the ennui. Sebastien Joly looked grim near the front. Nicolas Portal suddenly joined him. The big boys, Armstrong,

Ullrich, Hamilton were tucked anonymously in the middle. Karpets had a doppelgänger – same style, same long barnet – a French bloke, name of Brochard. Team leader of AG2R Prévoyance. But he didn't quite carry the mean look off. No mean drive. We called him Faux Karpets. I was enjoying Salvatore Commesso. He had the face of the devil, beard'n'eyes'n'razor teeth. He stood out from the pack of anonymity. In the less important races of the cycling season, Commesso did pretty good. He'd made his mark as a solid pro. He wore the flame-red of Team Saeco. That was Cipo's old team, in the days when they were as fuckin' cool as a catanaccio defence at Inter Milan. Mario himself was posing for photos off to the side. Everyone wanted a slice of his action. He seemed delighted to share it around. He chatted enthusiastically with a crippled youth in a wheelchair.

A big man in dungarees'n'boots shouted, 'Eh, Mario,' from the punter side of the barrier.

Cipo turned and lit up the bloke's life with his smile. The man started climbin' over the wire. Serious mistake. The Belgian cops had snarlin' great dogs on leads. Lots of 'em. He never managed to get both feet on the ground.

I almost kissed the Brief when he announced, 'I couldn't find a hotel in this town. I'm afraid that it's a bit of a drive. We are over the border in France.' Earl drove round the Maubeuge ring road three times before we clocked the Hotel de Paris. I was screamin' abuse from the rear. Maybe Belgium had sapped my tolerance. Maybe I was an appalling passenger. For sure, gettin' lost is a major road crime. Especially, if you stay lost'n'do fuck all. A well-honed trick is to ask three different people on the pavement, on the basis that one will be drunk/ drugged/mad as a hatter; one will be a visitor to the place; one will know exactly where you should go. In the poncy dining room, we were studying maps and press releases, waiting for the zander et frites. The maître d' led a crocodile of eight or nine scruffy men between the tables. They were loud. They had Zone Technicale passes on. They went beyond a door. I knew the score. It happened regularly to roadies with bands. The hotel wants the dosh but not the raucous behaviour. Stick 'em in the back room. The waiter came'n'went with large trays of drinks. Every time the door swung, the noise of the crew flooded across the genteel restaurant. At least they were outta sight.

Elvis Presley is the King. Denis Law was the King. Albert is King of the Belgians. He didn't look regal when I bumped into him on the stairs in Namur. He was fat'n'bald. He wore a brown sports jacket and brown shoes. Brown shoes, as Frank Zappa pointed out, don't make it. I dunno if the history of cycling has anyone called the King. Surely Eddie Merckx would have to be a serious contender. I'd seen Eddie around Le Village, time to time. Quite often, shovelling fresh cream gâteaux into his gob by the plateful. The first time I realised that the Cakeman was Eddie, I nipped over and shook his hand. Then I walked back to Earl and pulled that old '50s stunt. I held out my right hand and said to him, 'Shake the hand that shook the hand.' Meaningless fun. Like the Everly Brothers singin' 'I ain't gonna wash for a week, oh-no-no,' because some bird's kissed Don or Phil on the cheek. It's justa different cookie age.

The Cakeman was looking trimmer as he stood at the bottom of the steps with Albert, his king. Hair brushed, whistle on. He looked nervous, which was strange 'cos Eddie didn't seem the nervous type. He was relentless and ruthless. He had the nickname of 'The Cannibal' because he ate up his opponents. He could not bear to have rivals in front of his bike at any time. He took 'em all. No easy days for Eddie. He had won five Tours in six years between 1969 and '74. At the same time, he won the Giro d'Italia, the other big cycle race, five times. He was sponsored by Italian coffee and sausage makers, but loved here in Belgium, his home country. He was the first to cash in on the knick-knacks of fame: Eddie Merckx key-rings, tea-towels, T-shirts. He was a household name in my youth. He was that bit older than me. Just like mates would say to you, if you had a camera, 'Who the fuck d'ya think you are? David Bailey?' so, if you overtook a mate on yer bike, they'd say, 'Who d'ya think you are? Eddie fuckin' Merckx?'

The Rolling Stones must've learnt a trick or two from Eddie. By the late '70s, their merchandising on tour was earning 'em more than their ticket sales. Eddie knocks around Le Tour still. He has serious clout. His son, Axel, is a rider himself nowadays, with Team Lotto-Domo. The boy does all right. He was to come twenty-first in this race, but it must be tough – always the comparison with the old man. Julian Lennon, Rolan Bolan, Ziggy Marley. It's never gonna cut it. Maybe my boy would finish this road trip and sell insurance.

Earl'n'I were pushed out the way by the royal security. The entourage entered the building: the Pork Butcher and Eddie alongside King Albert, who was nodding'n'blinking at the statistics he was obviously being told. The Butcher himself was being fed facts'n'figures by his PA, Agnes Gougeat. I loved to watch Agnes. Same old ASO outfit, olive'n'khaki skirt. Glasses. Short dark hair. She combined on-the-spot attention with a distant thoughtfulness. She was always a step or two ahead of her boss, the Butcher, pointing things out to him, leading him across to introductions. She whispered background details. I could see his eyes light up with 'Right! I got that!' when she stepped back from him. There were times, back-stage yet so public, when the

Butcher stood still, like a little boy lost at the zoo but knowing mummy and daddy will come back to find him. He would tilt his thick neck backwards, lift his head up and stare around in wonder. Agnes would rescue him. Gently bustlin' him along with her folders and mobile in hand. He was a great front man. He had the common touch. He needed Agnes to make the act work. She was the star to me.

Namur had welcomed its king by wearing silly hats. There were two lines of old men waddling in formation. It didn't look military, mad not joyous. They wore puce robes with white hats. Cone heads, turbans, like the ends of a rack of lamb to keep one's fingers clean. The hats matched the slippers. White'n'fluffy. I couldn't figure if they were goin' home to sleep or just got up. They looked as dozy as the King.

The next start was at Waterloo. I'd had enough.

'Let's skip it,' I said to the Brief.

He was scoffin' croissants. I was guzzling caffeine. Earl was still in bed. He liked to time his exit to the last moment. I could guess what was comin'. The big match of 1815. Napoleon versus Wellington. Stalemate. A last-minute winner from Field-Marshal Blücher. I've seen the big earth mound with the lion on top marking the battlefield a few times; the motorway to Brussels goes right past it. Hey, wouldn't it be a great idea for obsessives to dress up as dragoons'n'hussars with flintlocks'n'sabres? Stitch perfect replica Cuirassier uniforms? A mini re-enactment in honour of the visit of Le Tour de France? A twenty-one-cannon salute? A few black stallions with imperial plumage? No thanks. It's not big. It's not clever. We don't want it, thank you very much. Any more than I wanna squirm through crap Zorba-the-Greek bazouki dancing done by the local plumber'n'his mates in a taverna in Crete. Or some clumsy cod-flamenco dancing done as 'colour'n'heritage' by the local hairdresser for a bit of pin money to taped backing music in Tossa del Mer. None of this stuff has heart or passion. Like tribute bands, it's cheap pastiche.

'A bit sour, you grumpy old man,' said Earl. 'They're only havin' fun. F-U-N.'

We drove over cobblestones called pavés. The route outta Belgium was by the back roads'n'farm tracks. Shades of Willy Voet, the Team Festina roadie, who got pulled'n'nicked near here with a van load of drugs. He was tryin' to slip across this border in '98. The bust was obviously a set-up. It brought doping to the front page. It ain't left the headlines since. The cobbles were flat'n'rounded at the edge, like loaves of bread. The trackway ran between fields of wheat and potatoes, ditches on each side. Punters were camped out already, hours before the race was due. Tourists on bikes were tryin' it out. Bouncin', bobblin' – it looked tricky 'n'uncomfortable. Thin racing wheels'n'tyres wouldn't like it. Some big other races, notably Paris–Roubaix, used these cobble tracks. Covered in thick mud that seeped from the fields, they were chosen deliberately for their tough going. 'The Hell o' the North' is a one-day race that is famed for its rugged conditions in bad weather. These two sections in this Tour were a nod o' the head to the past, tradition, heritage, tokenism. The Pork Butcher had cut his teeth around here, in Lille. He'd been a student at the university here. Leblanc had begun his career as a sports journalist here with *La Voix du Nord*, before moving to Paris as cycling correspondent of *L'Équipe*. Maybe it was his bit of nostalgia. In which case, all those poor cunts who hurt themselves when they crashed here later on that day would be tolerant of an old man's fancy. Some big guns went down: Mario Cipollini, Paolo Bettini in his King of the Mountains polka-dots, Lance

Armstrong himself, though gently. Silly 'cos it's as flat as Norfolk.

The Brief got excited for a moment. Not that he wished it. If Armstrong was knocked back by a crash, the whole Tour might open out into a competitive race. The Brief had been despondent since Liège, when Lance had seemed head and shoulders better than everyone, including Jan Ullrich, his nearest rival.

'That's it. It's all over. He's got it in the bag.' The Brief was used to weighing up the odds in the court. 'Only a crash will level it.'

As if to prove the point, another crash took out two other contenders. Iban Mayo fell into a ditch. He ripped his shorts, grazed his thigh, bruised his spirit and lost his drive. Which was a tragedy for all those Basque fans waiting in the Pyrenees for Mayo to arrive and clean up. He was done for. Maybe next time it would be Lance. Another early crash victim who never fully recovered was Christophe Moreau. He'd been around. He'd been a Tour de France rider for getting on ten years and achieved considerable success, finishing in fourth place in the millennium Tour. The Festina Doping Carnival of 1998 had sucked Moreau in. He twisted'n'squirmed but finally admitted to being a drug fiend. He'd got a six-month ban. Still, he carried a lot of French national hope. But he was getting on in years. He tried to fool his public by growing a strange vertical strip of hair between his lower lip and chin. It looked pubic. Is that what they call a 'Brazilian'? Earl named him 'Cheesey' Moreau. His bird was decidedly tasty. She was one of the Crédit Lyonnais beauties who presented le maillot jaune on the podium each day.

I stood on the cobbles and cheered. I lifted my feet and danced. My knees sprung high, above my saggin' waist. I didn't care. I pointed my toes. Faster, higher. I kept my arms to my side. Rigidly, as if gaffa-taped. The jig got wilder.

'Who's this?' I shouted at Earl, watchin' outta the car window.

'A madman? Dunno.'

'Michael Flatley, *Riverdance*, Lord of the fuckin' Dance,' I said.

I was dancin' with joy because I realised that this cobbled road was 20 miles inside France.

Chapter 4

It was a long walk from the press centre to the finish line. A coupla miles. The map was crap.

'Let's follow this,' said the Brief, pointing at rue Gambetta.

He was spot on. The street took us past the massive headquarters of Cofidis. I'm not sure what Cofidis does, apart from sponsoring a major cycle team. Something to do with telephones, money, credit. It seems to do well. Apart from its choice of star riders. British hopes had rested solely on David Millar, Cofidis team leader. He had been rated. He was cool. But he'd got busted for EPO weeks before the off. He'd been lifted out of a café with his girl by the coppers. He'd shown 'em some works with traces, kept in an ornamental box on his mantelpiece. Purely as a reminder, you understand, of the one time he had stupidly jacked the gear up. It was, you must believe, a ju-ju reminder to clean living. I could dig it. The coppers, everyone else, couldn't. Monsieur Migraine, his boss, didn't buy it. The Butcher wasn't convinced either. He was out. So was Migraine. The parking lot beyond the railings was empty. Gone to the race, maybe. Or into hiding. Cofidis couldn't even manage a winner in their home-town of Lille. Interestingly, wherever I went during Le Tour and the French realised I was English, they laughed about Millar. It don't matter that he's a Scotsman who grew up in Hong Kong and lives in Biarritz. He's a fuckin' Brit. His bust was no big deal to me. So he took a pick-me-up – shrug – don't we all? One baker in Besançon mimed crankin' up in his elbow.

'Why not?' he said.

We live in a drug culture. Always have.

Cipo didn't manage a win that day either. I was in place, ready. He wasn't. He was off the pace. Again. The razzamatazz was splendid. The rush, the buzz of the sprint was as good as ever. It's just that I'm a fan. I don't possess a fair-minded sporting rationale. I wanted to bask in the after-glow of Mario's success. I wanted more. I wanted to stroke his ju-ju thigh. Next time. If you're a fan, you're an optimist.

Bed was Albert. The bells woke me. I flung open the French windows. It was a glorious morning. The bells were ringing from the church across the way. I almost stepped onto the small veranda above the town centre to greet the morning. Then I remembered I was naked. The last time, I was on tour in '77, in some bird's flat in Montmartre. The white dome of Sacre Coeur was right above me. A street market below. I stepped forward, full of joie de vivre and a hangover. The cries from the market traders made me realise I was behavin' as if I was in a Carry On film.

The basilica of Albert summed up the First World War. The spire was hit by a shell during the Battle of the Somme in 1916. The top leaned over at a crazy angle. It held firm right through the rest of the war. Soldiers marched carefully in Albert, avoiding going underneath the steeple. It could be any moment. It could be you. Shortly after the elevens of 1918, when the Armistice was signed, the spire fell to the ground. Ju-ju. Now it is restored. Gold leaf shining.

Black Magic had found the hotel in Albert on auto-pilot. The Brief had his maps out. Earl had his headphones on and his eyes open. Unnecessary. The hotel was in rue Gambetta. It was full of Brits. These were not Tour fans but war buffs. The town was geared for the heritage industry. It flogged death. Shop windows with trench warfare coffee-table books, Passchendaele tea towels, menus in Franglais. An old bi-plane strung up from the ceiling of the railway station. I watched an old boy in a flat cap hobble up to a cash point. He took his time examining the machine. He looked like a virgin at it. In went the plastic. His shakin' fingers did the business. He stood, staring. Nothing. He waited. Nothing. He peered closely. Started bashing the keys. Muttering. His shoulders sagged as he walked away. He peered over his shoulder at the bank. Cursin', confused as to how he'd got ripped. This is the modern world.

I needed some dough myself. I'd hang on. Earl was rubbin' his eyes. The Brief joined me at the motor. He was carrying several supermarket bags.

'I've stocked up. Could be a long day.'

It was Team Time-Trial day. A one-off extravaganza where all nine team members ride a short course of 40 miles in aerodynamic formation. First five home register on the clock for the lot. The twenty-one teams are staggered over almost two hours. Cambrai was the far side of the Somme. War graves sat on the rounded hills. Immaculate white rockery walled gardens. The Tommy Café was closed. Pity. I'd fancied the full English and a nice cuppa tea. Two dummies in British squaddie uniform and tin hats guarded the doorway with a howitzer like a pet dog at their feet. We hung a leftist down to the Thiepval Memorial. I could see it from miles away: the largest British war memorial on the planet. A huge series of stacked stone arches, like an open-plan cathedral, surrounded by lawns that could grace Wembley. On the vertical slabs were the names of every Tommy killed in the First World War whose smashed-up body was never found, never given a decent burial: 73,000 of them. The list of names scrolled up into the sky. Like the beginning of *Star Wars*. Regiment by regiment. There were all the usuals. Guards'n'Fusiliers. The Artists' Rifles. The Northern Cyclists Battalion. The Huntingdon Cycling Battalion. Three Brits were checking for relatives. One of 'em, Alec, told me that the very first bloke killed in the entire war was a squaddie on a bike. His officer sent him over the hill on a reconnaissance. Shot. He never returned.

I turned to Earl. 'It does make me wonder if I would have joined up like this lot.' Served king'n'country. I would hope that I wouldn't be conned by national hysteria. Tricked into it by government media. Fly the flag. Lay down my life. Twenty thousand killed on the first day of the Somme. A million dead between July and November.

'It certainly puts things into perspective,' I said.

'Too much fuckin' perspective,' said Earl.

'Yeah, all that weepin''n'a'wailin' about the New York City Trade Towers. Sad, but only a coupla thousand. With this lot, it was deliberate, calculated and extended.'

Nationalism is an ugly sight.

I huddled under canvas in Le Village in Cambrai to keep out of the drizzle. It was a squash. Lots of journos were there, catchin' up on world news from the newspaper racks. One American was takin' up far more than his fair share. He probably reckoned he was a ringer for Michael Moore. Yeah, and I'm Robert Redford. He was extremely fat. No, no, massively fuckin' obese. He waddled. His sweatshirt rippled like a waterbed when he moved. Tiers of chins hung below his loud mouth. His glasses were vast David Hockney rejects. I was certain he had permanently bad hair. I couldn't prove it. He wore a Nike baseball cap way too small. I was standing next to him. It was as tight as a rush-hour tube. I was reading the day before's *Guardian*. It had a glorious photograph of some fan riding full gallop, bareback on a white stallion, in a field alongside le peloton. On the pavé cobble stones. He held a giant stars'n'stripes billowing out behind him. I held the picture up to the American.

'Look at this.'

It was a friendly overture.

'Oh that's crap. It's stupid. Whadya expect in an English paper?'

The Yank turned away, dismissing me. I boiled. I was real close to sinkin' my fist deep into the rolls of fat round his vast gut. I had mind to pick up the nearest tubular chair and smash it on top of his fat head. I wanted to pull out my lock-knife and slit his bulging cheeks ear to ear. I was a model of restraint. It was a long way to Paris. I would plot revenge. The fucker would rue the day he crossed me.

The Grand Square was an impressive piece of burgher architecture. I was not usually an admirer of dull and solid. But the Hotel de Ville had golden bells adorned with turbaned nigger boys. The art of colonialism. Just as the Congo had made Belgium, under Leopold III, the fourth wealthiest nation a century ago, at the birth of Le Tour de France. It had all been thanks to the production of rubber: tyres for bicycles and, later, cars. The Congo had ended in horrendous bloodshed and slaughter, as colonialism often does. It was an appropriate setting for Kurtz in Conrad's *Heart of Darkness*.

A shop bore the sign 'Mick + Joe', next door to an optician's with a huge neon pair of green glasses. Just like I wore in punk days. I was even named Johnny Greenglasses. A moment's nostalgia for my old muckers, The Clash. The teams were parking up in their tour buses. I was chewin' a free bowl of pork'n'beans when the heavens opened. I wiped my spex to see Domina Vacanza right before me. Through the windscreen, I clocked a pair of shinin' teeth. Cipo was in the front seat, laughing away with a tasty blonde bird. We may have only been separated by a pane of glass, but Mario was inhabiting a different universe from me. I had a plastic waterproof on with the hood up. He wore shorts. A Swiss journo told me that Cipollini owned 400 suits, kept in a special room. Bravo!

A girl on a stage in the rain was dancin' on tiptoes to Bowie's 'Let's Dance'. She wore a sash with 'Miss Cambrai' on it, like a beauty queen. Fuck it, she was a beauty queen. Miss Tank. No one gave a toss. All eyes were on the starting line. The nine were abreast, held by the saddle by nine pretty girls in tight wet T-shirts. The Manfred Mann/Ready Steady Go count down: 5–4–3–2–1. The girls let go. The bikes were slippin''n'a'slidin' all over the wet flagstones.

The name of the game is formation. Many variations. Indian file. Double chain. The Brief was fond of the wedge-shaped flying duck. This was no place to check 'em out. Too ceremonial. The TV would've been good if sterile. But then I might as well have stayed at home. The Brief stuck a finger on the map. 'There!' We had our own race against the clock to get there. Chicaning through empty villages, careering down tiny lanes. Our vantage point was a sugar-beet factory 10 miles from the finish. It was lashin' it down. A squat man in a tan linen suit sat sodden on a fishing stool, an umbrella forlornly above his sodden hair. The only elevation on the flat fields was a great pile of manure next to the route. A family of five had climbed onto the top of the stinkin' heap. They reclined in deck chairs on their grandstand of shit. Our badges of the elite meant nothing here. All men were equal. Apart from the cop with the gun. Every side road onto the course was police protected to stop doolallies pootlin' out in front of the two-wheel hell-fer-leathers. It was so great. The speed of each team passing. A blast of spray that I welcomed. No steppin' back gingerly from the kerb, bus-goin'-through-puddle routine on the high street. I felt the air move. A five-minute gap. Blue hazy motorbike lights, horns. Kids shoutin', 'They're comin'.' I counted the number in each team. Some were short. The stragglers came by in a while to huge encouragement. I doubt they noticed. It was down to the individual to keep up. Stickin' together meant more effective shape and greater shared effort. By our position, three-quarters of the way round, no team was waiting or helping mates who had dropped off the back. That was their problem. So long as there were five together across the last line, naturally with the big hitter, Lance, Jan, Georg. If you fucked up on the road, no mate had the time, energy or inclination to sacrifice themselves for you. Harsh road-craft that applied here as it did to U2 roadies in Des Moines, Iowa, and to sailors of HMS *Belfast* overboard in the Straits of Malacca. The Mentor had learnt his lesson last year, the hard way. He had fucked up big time at Alpe d'Huez. Derailed my previous dry run at Le Tour. He wouldn't get a second crack at it. The individual gives it all to his team and his leader.

'Lance Armstrong won it, didn't he?'

'Well, yeah, but there is his team, US Postal.'

'How does it work?' asked Earl.

'Armstrong has the crème-de-la-crème. Each member of his team is a specialist, but he is never allowed to compete for personal glory. That is not the case in the other teams. Riders are given their moment on climbs, sprints or breakaways,' said the Brief.

'Don't Landis, Hincapie, and the rest of US Postal get pissed off?' asked Earl.

'They are professionals. They are in the best team. They are well paid. Le Tour winner traditionally turns over all his prize money to his team-mates. Then there is the kudos. It is a terrific springboard to a leader's position with another team. Look at Tyler Hamilton and Roberto Heras,' continued the Brief.

In the 1947 Tour, Apo Lazarides, Stan to his mates, was a French domestique for Rene Vietto's team. Vietto had an aching foot. He told the doctor, on a rest day, to cut off a toe.

'I'll be lighter in the mountains,' he said cheerfully.

He turned to Stan and told him to do the same. To have a toe amputated like his team leader.

Lazarides queried, 'Why? I don't need to.'

'Because I say so,' said Vietto.

Stan had the operation. He walked with a wobble till the day he died. Vietto's toe is preserved in formaldehyde in a bar in Marseille.

US Postal cleaned up in Cambrai.

That night, the restaurant in Albert was full and hushed. Most of the covers were terribly English. Eyes down in earnest discussion on whether to have the fish or the duck, the white or the red. It was George Herbert's hymn, 'You in your small corner; And I in mine.' The chef got it. He came out of the kitchen and sauntered over to our table, wipin' his mitts on his apron.

He beamed. 'You're with Le Tour.'

Books'n'maps for the morrow were piled by the salt'n'pepper. My pass sat on top. He saw.

'Yeah.'

He wanted an account of the day's play. Being French, he never said, 'US Postal won, didn't they?'

'They did so comfortably and impressively,' said the Brief, 'but it must be acknowledged that the official rules have been changed this year. The margin between teams on today's Time-Trial has been limited so that no single team, and for that read US Postal, may get too far ahead.'

'I get it,' I said. 'The organisers have doctored the race to stop Armstrong becoming untouchable so early on.'

'He's unstoppable,' said Earl, shaking his head in admiration.

The chef's eyes gleamed as the three of us each gave our four-penn'orth, full of animation and detail about all twenty-one teams, the triumphs and the fuck-ups. He was after the big picture. Totality. He wanted to touch Le Tour. Although it had come close, so close to him, he'd been choppin' carrots instead. But he could shake the hand that shook the hand. I gave him the press sheets of that day's results. He was well made up as he went back to work. Our grub was delicious'n'bounteous. I wanted to roar'n'holler. I wanted to dance on the table-tops in hobnail boots. I wanted to tell the room about the day that had just been. That everyone was an active part of Le Tour de France. Not separate from it. Not passive. Not distant. Not at all like Formula One. To watch motor racing costs an arm'n'a leg. In a custom-built stadium of little or no charm. A constructed theme park for speed. Punters are kept well clear of the action. Health'n'safety, of course, but you can't get intimate behind walls of wire. It might've taken the deadly crush of Hillsboro' but football woke up to that some time ago. Thank God! If the fencing had still been up at Selhurst Park, we would never have enjoyed the passionate intensity of Eric Cantona's honourable karate kick on that Palace thug. Formula One has become disengaged. Drivers are hidden away in their cars behind helmets. Punters can't get to pat Jenson Button on the back. They can only see a machine. Computers and scientific innovation help the rich teams like Ferrari. Technology cheats. In cycling, the rider is the driver and the engine. There's only so much can be done with pedal, chain, cog, wheel. So Ferrari wins'n'wins. Michael Schumacher may well be a genius. Like Lance Armstrong. But Schumacher relies on technology far more than is healthy for a clean fight.

I'd been browsin' the papers. Some bloke in *The Independent* said of the British Grand Prix, 'The illusion that it [Formula One] is doing any more than stage the most expensive processions since the old Red Square parades of ballistic rocketry, is as shredded as an old tyre.' Then again, Bernie Ecclestone's rise to power makes him hugely attractive. From second-hand cars to Top Ten Richest Men in Britain, he's pushed himself more than most. I love the tale that he was out in Italy at the Grand Prix in the early '80s. A beautiful woman was modelling T-shirts for Armani. She was Slavica, a Croatian. He looked up and bought her a can of Coke. He proposed. She's his wife. Some instinct.

With the morning papers, a spot of breakfast. It was lunch for the others. Local products were used and highlighted. In Amiens, smoked fish, eel, carp'n'trout. The hot dish of the day was steamin' in giant woks. Queues formed. Motorbike photographers barged straight to the front. I guess six hours balancin' pillion in'n'out the cars and peloton on hairpin bends taking nanosecond pictures don't make you inclined to queue patiently. The Picardy fricassée went down well. I had three bowls. The Sacred Bleedin' Heart Cookery School of Amiens had rustled up this new dish of mushrooms, onions, garlic, crème fraiche and ham. The riders stuck to hi-energy bars. Christ knows what's in 'em There were boxes of 'em stacked up'n'dished out next to the signing-in stage. For research rather than culinary delight, I went over to grasp a handful. The food roadie wasn't havin' it. He shooed me away, protectively leanin' over his goodies. I couldn't talk him round.

'Fuck you. I didn't really want one anyway,' I muttered childishly.

The Brief, a man of less confrontational aspect, got the same treatment. I suddenly twigged. 'That's where the dope is,' I said. 'The hi-energy bars are secretly crammed full of the very latest performance-enhancing chemicals. No need for pills or needles. What could be more innocuous!'

The Brief visited a display of local macaroons. Quite a pile of Monsieur Trogneaux's exceedingly good coconut cakes found their way into his squirrel bag. One of Le Village's functions was as a Mediterranean café. Some of the riders used it like that on a daily basis. Two of Cipo's team liked to wheel up, dismount'n'park their bikes on the railings. They were acting laddish. They put their cleated feet up on spare chairs. Helmets on the table. Sipping thimbles of espresso, nibblin' macaroons. Their shirts were unzipped.

The Brief commented. 'Very spotty, these boys.'

It was true. Purple boils, small red skin explosions across their chests, yellow heads askin' for a squeeze, black heads.

'Just acne,' I said. 'Stress. Maybe it's a change in the water. My old mum swore by that.'

'Maybe it's the hi-energy bars,' said the Brief. 'I'm familiar with the effects of medication in mental hospitals. This has all the hallmarks of steroid usage.'

They flirted with the travellin' waitresses. I liked their relaxed style. Maybe it was a long-term pull. Maybe the boys were settin' up a quick shag for the night. Three weeks' worth of testosterone is a volatile bag to carry around. The hostesses liked the flirtin' of the domestiques, once their own gig was done. I was up close to a Brioche Baker Boy rider. I looked at his face. Like cops today, I thought, so young. Still with bum-fluff. I checked his number. It was Maryan Hary. One of the tanned Italians looked up at the sky and wrinkled his nose. More rain. Again.

I wanted to up the ante with Mario. A part of me felt it was beautiful as it was. The purity of non-verbal vibration. The other side said, 'Pick into his brain while you've got the chance.' The sprinting days would be over by Quimper, in a few days. I went up to Pascale, sippin' coffee nearby. She was the official Tour translator. I had seen her at a coupla press conferences.

'Can you help me, Pascale? I wanna talk to Mario Cipollini. I can't speak Italian. Will you be go-between?'

I knew she spoke half-a-dozen languages. She was pale of skin, with the fairest Françoise Hardy-length hair. She wore the palest coloured clothes. Her appearance allowed her to slip into any situation and merge. I knew that her fragile doll-like demeanour was an illusion. She had toured the world with theatre companies. She knew the road well.

'Of course. Fix it up with Mario and let me know,' said Pascale.

I nipped over to the Domina Vacanza bus. An Italian woman in black, smoking a cigarette on the steps, said, 'Sure.' She gave me her mobile number. For one person only, I was gonna be a real journalist. But I didn't wanna know about his braking capacity.

The punters' pageant that was the Publicity Caravan set off from the old stone Circus building. Wildly decorated floats advertised the wares of Le Tour's sponsors in an enthusiastic carnival. It covered every mile of the course precisely one hour ahead of the race. It wound a big loop through the town. The crowd went loopy. Ten-deep and in good voice. Earl and I had to go shopping for film. He needed some state-of-the-art new mini-digital bollocks. We cut across the dog-leg to the town centre. A spotty youth in a camera shop looked blank.

'Try the department store,' he said.

'Where's that?' I asked.

'In Place Gambetta.'

'Of course.'

The store had the rare film. Ju-ju. It also had an interesting window display. A grey Peugeot that had crashed through the glass. Security men and broken glass everywhere. It was a serious accident and yet, with the bizarre carnival that is Le Tour de France in town, it had the appearance of a major art installation.

The caravan was trundling along right outside. Cochoneau Pork Products did a very nice red-checked cap. I don't do caps. Earl caught one. The giant cheesebox of La Vache qui Rie was next. Ten foot high, circular, the driver's windscreen was a mesh. A covered door on the side. There were no windows. It was impossible to identify the driver.

'If you were a multi-millionaire but with little imagination or flair and you wanted an adventure to brighten up your dull life, like, say, take in Le Tour de France end to end, but you were really, really famous and you had a problem with fame and being recognised, what would you do?'

'Hide in that cheese-box,' said Earl. 'Who did you have in mind?'

'It's obvious,' I said. 'Phil Collins. He's in there.'

Phil was a rock star whose idea of a great day out was to be driven in his deluxe speed-boat around Lake Geneva near his Swiss tax-exile home. Dull man, dull music. Tosser. Every day after Amiens we waved'n'shouted at Phil when he passed. He was so nifty with the media that no one managed to get a photo of him in the whole Tour.

Earl handled Black Magic round the Paris Périphérique. The Brief did the signs. I tried not to go hoarse. I buried myself in Hank Williams. Ol' Hank was the greatest of country singers by a mile. He wrote about his own tragic life with no punches pulled. He sang his lonesome songs like he meant them. All passion, intensity'n'raw feeling. In the years '47 to '52, he took off like a rocket from nothin' to bestselling country'n'western artist in the USA. His records, 'Cold, Cold Heart', 'Hey Good Lookin'', 'Lovesick Blues', 'Jambalaya', so many, went mega. He got to the top by giggin'. Hank Williams was out on the road most days'n'nights. From town to town by car'n'bus with no motorways to ease the miles. Hard work. A long slog. All year round. Hank's drive'n'determination delivered the goods. Made him the best. Created some of the greatest music ever to come outta America. Hank had a bad back that had him in chronic pain a lotta the time. Hank had women problems that caused him pain. He sure liked to drink'n'drug it. He had a doctor in most of the towns he visited on tour. If in doubt, he'd take along his own, Toby Marshall. Toby claimed to be a doctor and shot Hank up with morphine. He also handed out Hank's chloral hydrate, a strong hypnotic sedative. Hank was electric live on stage. Folk don't ever say, 'Hank Williams – Drug Cheat.'

In the pourin' rain with wipers swishin', the road from Paris led right out west to the tip of Brittany. Quimper. Hank was singin' 'Lost Highway'. It suited perfectly. He died of an overdose in the back of his limo with his white cowboy boots on. It was New Year's Day 1953. Hank Williams was twenty-nine. He was being driven by an eighteen-year-old student to yet another gig. Although he lived on the wild side of life, Ol' Hank loved Jesus. One of the Lord's great buildings was due in front of us.

Le Tour de France was comin' to Chartres. The twin towers of the cathedral would provide a magnificent backdrop for the sprint finish. One to wow every television viewer. Maybe it did. It didn't work out that way in real life. I went to Berlin in 1980, gigging. I never got to see the Berlin Wall 'cos I never left the bar. In Chartres, I never got to see the cathedral that many say is the finest in Christendom. I was stuck on an airfield on the edge of town.

This was always happening with bands. I'd come back from America. Friends would say, 'I'll bet you saw some sights.' I'd reply, 'Yeah.' What I meant was. 'No. Airport–hotel–gig–airport.'

Hard graft and you've gotta ring-fence rest'n'victuals for self-preservation. Le Tour's a bit that way. The infrastructure is so sprawlin' and unwieldy that it frequently has to be sited on an industrial estate or closed-off ring roads. Airports are popular. The runways are handy, with lotsa space on the side for the Zone Technicale.

It was a mad dash for the doorway of the press buildings from the car. The rain was that stuff out of a roadie's hosepipe on a film set. The beginning of *Don't Look Now*. Raindrops that bounce back up. The ASO staff in the foyer applauded our drenched appearance. A tourist office woman handed me a free T-shirt with a picture of Chartres cathedral on it.

'So that's what it looks like. I can tell my friends.'

The shirt fell to bits in the first wash. The rain dripped off my hair, down my neck as I chomped a free sandwich. I was watching the race on multi-television. A five-man breakaway from the main bunch. The excitement was, could they, would they, stay fast enough to keep a big enough gap from the relentless power of le peloton? It was like a fish swimming for its life away from a shark. Or, to turn it on its tail, like a fisherman tryin' to reel in a marlin on a hook. Hemingway kinda thrill. In no man's land, TV's the only way to see it. Until the last kilometre, when the race goes under the red inflatable over the road, the Flamme Rouge. Only one place to be. I legged it across the soakin' grass, zig-zaggin' through the electricians' trucks, hoppin' over their wrist-thick cables. I was gettin' my timing good. I had time to clean my spex in the rain and there they were. Stuey O'Grady, Jakob Piil and Thomas Voeckler, who instantly became maillot jaune. He was already French national champion in a tricolour jersey. Now he became a French hero.

I couldn't see the cathedral from the motel either. Redemption would have to wait. At least I had crossed the Line. Only just, but it was significant. I felt relieved. Lightened a little. France is two countries. North and South. The border that divides them is the Line. It is as straight as a ruler on a map. It runs exactly through the tip of the spire of Chartres cathedral on the left and the white line down the centre of Main Street in Disneyland on the right. Join up these two points right across France. That is the Line. Paris don't count. It is a capital city. Capitals always have their own ambience. (For the sake of this argument, New York City is the capital of the USA. Don't expect logic.) Also, Brittany is an exception and will be dealt with in Quimper. North of the Line is grim, tight, mean, shut-off. South of the Line is heaven. Those photos of a single file of Tour de France riders in the middle of a glorious field of sunflowers. Every year, in the colour mags'n'coffee-table books. They ain't taken outside Calais. English tourists sitting at a roadside table in a little café, to watch Le Tour sippin' chilled rose. Béziers not Boulogne.

We headed south, in the slipstream of a convoy. Findus Lasagne was part of the Caravan. They'd been in the same concrete motel, designed in the style of a Swedish open prison. A huge, garish picture of a steamin' pile of lasagne on the sides of the vans. At that time of the morning, it made me wanna fuckin' puke. The pic looked that way too. Did they throw mini-samples of the gook to the crowds? Did it blind some poor sod by accident? Would anyone take it home'n'eat it? I know everyone loves a freebie but that was pushin' it.

The boulangerie window opposite the car-park was a picture. It was culinary art. I was drawn across the road like a magnet. Proved my point about the Line. Pies, meat, cheese, spinach. Small flans that fitted into the palm of your hand. Twists'n'plaits of flaky pastry. All arranged, like an art exhibition, around models and pictures of Le Tour. So much more than function. Someone had been busy since dawn. Madame, behind the counter, beamed at me as I made my choices. I complimented her on her beautiful shop. I bought a bunch. I wouldn't have minded her as well. Her eyes shone; she'd been at the mascara. Her mouth turned elegantly down at the edges, as if she'd seen a bit too much of humanity. Although it was after nine o'clock in the morning, her crimson lipstick was well in place. For a second, I thought of offering her a lift to Quimper.

I was noshin' the Pithiviers pie, the local Old Orléans speciality, full of liver'n'kidney. Offal makes a great kick-start to a day.

'Excuse me. Are you English?'

'Mmm ...'

'Will the teams' vehicles park near here?'

He came from Sheffield.

'Yeah.'

I'd seen the signs wired up on the plane trees.

'If you stay right here, you can meet the cyclists.'

It was a wide avenue with low barriers.

'Really?'

His shyness was evaporating. I stood up on the portable triangular pissoir.

'Are you following the whole Tour?'

'Yeah.'

I turned to look at him politely without pissin' down my trousers.

'Do you talk to the riders every day then?'

'No. I watch 'em and what's goin' on around 'em. If you ask riders how they are and what their prospects are, they'll always tell you that they're feelin' fit'n'strong and that they're confident of doin' well. If I ask 'em what happened, they can't tell me any better than I know already. Or else it's like a goal scorer. "The ball came over from the left, I was in the right place. I stuck out my foot and in it went." '

Like musos, they're so wrapped up makin' it, in the eye of the hurricane, they're not often the best people to ask.

'Thanks, mate.'

It was rare to see a Brit.

A band greeted me. They were dressed as huntsmen in blue velvet, hats'n'boots. Brass instruments were popular. Or maybe they were huntsmen dressed as musicians; it was hard to say. They swanned around a lot, tryin' to look great, now'n'then makin' a lot of noise. They fitted in well into the setting. Bonneval was pretty. A crenellated stone wall around a moated town en fleur. The sponsors and their suppin' guests had been squeezed like a piece of plasticine into a small park between the two. The shape of Le Village was so bendy'n'flexible, it went most places. It was the sheer volume of motors, motorbikes, vans'n'trucks that restricted where Le Tour can'n'can't go. Car sharin' must be a future option. That's the sensible take. Truth is that three weeks' mega-travel in a vehicle with the same person can require interpersonal skills of a very high level and regular therapy sessions. Or just turn into a monster and blow it all out. I favour the latter.

The riders were mixin' in Le Village before the daily signing. Blokes from different teams were joshin'n'chattin. Like any old game, it would be a small world. And this lot spent three weeks in a bubble, cyclin' along. There was bound to be friendship across competitive teams. A natter over a coffee before kick-off.

A bit of yik-yak whilst wheelin' around slowly warmin' the muscles, signin' autographs, posin' for photos with punters. Not US Postal. They kept themselves to themselves, especially and especially Lance Armstrong. Maybe that's what it takes to be a killer. Perfect focus. No distractions. US Postal in their dark blue would appear like a rash at the last minute. They'd sign in and stack up at the startin' gate. Straight to business. They ran a tight ship. It didn't go down well with the French. Sure the American tourists didn't care. They queued up by the team bus chantin' loudly. They didn't wanna see other riders. US Postal didn't wanna put themselves about. A perfect marriage.

The trick cyclist was doin' his thang. A young man on a customised BMX. He had a lotta pads on his angles. Elbows, knees, wrists, head. I supposed he was expecting to fall off a lot. He had a go at me for leaving a pile of greasy dried wild boar sausage on one of his portable ramps. He did wheelies, front wheel, rear wheel. He got some idiot in his ring. Laid 'em down'n'hopped this way'n'that over their body'n'head. Same thing every day. He was very good. I never once saw the paramedics in action. He'd be there without his ramps, at the finish line, doin' the same stunt with an entranced, patient but restless crowd. I didn't know if he had a twin brother or the fast driver on the crew. Maybe he hitched a ride in a chopper.

The Brief dropped the bombshell.

'Cipo's gone.'

'Whadya mean "gone"?'

'Pulled out of Le Tour. Injuries. Petacchi's gone with him. Same reason.'

I felt a long moment's disbelief before I went numb. Can't be. Can't be. Fuck it. It wasn't just that the two best, flashest sprinters weren't around any more. Tough as that was. It meant that the dream was unfulfilled. I had gotten one hell of a buzz from Cipollini's charisma. I wanted to be there when he won. To see'n'feel Le Beau Mario at his very best. Where he belonged. First across the line in a crazy sprint. In full flight. I'd seen all the photos. I'd got one framed above my desk in my room. I wanted to bask in his radiance, at his side when he does what he does. I felt fuckin' cheated. Cheated by the rain'n'slippery roads of Belgium'n'France (north of the Line.) The crashes had done for my man. The misery of northern Europe had done for the Lion King – so far from home, his natural habitat of the sun-kissed Mediterranean. The French laughed. Said he'd be back on the beach already. I didn't blame him. I felt like fuckin' off. No interview now. No chance of strokin' his beautiful magical thigh. We may not see his like again. At least Ronny Scholtz was still goin' strong. Road-craft kicked in. The show must go on. Quimper, here I come. Chapeaux, Cipo.

The biggie-wiggies' cars were parked through an arch. The floral displays right across the town were glorious. Flower-beds, verges, window-boxes were explodin' with fresh colour. The car-park was in a mental hospital. This beautiful loony-bin had been an abbey since the ninth century. Saint Florentin had flourished in wealth and power. The French Revolution of 1789 did for that. Sold by the state, the abbey became a spinning mill and a tapestry manufacturer. It converted to lunacy in 1862. There was only a population of 4,500 in Bonneval. Must've been a lotta full moon risin' in the fields round about. The asylum was a big gaff. The width of a medieval wall took me into a secret garden. A quiet world of elegant building in parkland, tailor-made for frazzled brains. It looked very attractive. The Brief admired it, whipped off a few shots with his camera and shot off. Bit too much like work, I supposed.

I was still thinkin' 'bout Hank Williams. His endless road-work took a terrible toll on his body'n'mind. Yet that's what produced such magnificent words'n'music. He took drugs. They enhanced his battered performance. They lifted his spirits. They gave him access in his innermost being. In short, Ol' Hank might've stayed a sharecropper without the gear. The world would be a poorer place without him. For sure, he never got close to his pension. Hell, quality not quantity is the measurin' stick. Like any self-respectin' drug fiend, he took a doctor on his crew. He wouldn't be the last. It was always said that Keith Richards travelled everywhere on tour in the '70s with his own personal doctor'n'prescription pad. Rule number one: protect your source. Prohibition never stopped nothin'. If folk want to, they will do. A big problem is self-medication. Gettin' the dose wrong is the disaster. Tales of pro cyclists on EPO. EPO has the effect of thickening the blood. It is whispered that the soigneurs, the trainers, have to wake up riders in the middle of the night in case their blood thickens'n'sets like toothpaste. They make their boys jog on the spot or ride exercise bikes to move the blood round. I dunno. Wild rumours, urban myths, the truth? Who cares? This should be doctors' stuff. Hank's doc, Toby Marshall, was a dodgy choice. Toby had already done a year in St Quentin for armed robbery when he met Ol' Hank. He bought his degree and the medical 'qualifications' of Chicago University of Applied Sciences and Arts from a travelling salesman at a filling station for $25. No place but the Land of the Free.

'A man's gotta do whatta man's gotta do.'

Toby helped Hank do it. He might've been dodgy but he gave it his best unskilled shot. He just meant well. Which was always Jacques Anquetil's point. He was a five-times Tour-winning Frenchman. This cool ruler always maintained that riders need stuff, gear, like every other human being, apart from Amish communities and some followers of John Knox's Presbyterian Church. And me, nowadays. Ol' Jacques said that if doctors were allowed to dish it to all who wanted it, carefully, scientifically, how much happier, fitter, wiser, safer, equal all le peloton would be. This wisdom didn't go down too well at Head Office. Thirty years on, Eric Cantona talked about Jacques Anquetil.

'An artist in my eyes, is someone who can lighten a dark room.'

Eric saw no difference between Jacques riding a mountain stage, a goal from Maradonna and the poems of Arthur Rimbaud.

'Here are the high-wire artists of the soul, people who can do the impossible, who are on another plane. They are flawless only in the expression of their excellence.'

Thing is, the Greats, like Hank, Jacques, George Best, produce work that the rest are not capable of. Yet they are judged by conventional standards.

Commentating is based on the assumption that more information produces greater understanding. Facts 'n'figures, statistics, competitive comparisons. A means of coverin' up the embarrassment of silence. And to give employment to ageing ex-pros. Numerical listing on a grand scale has reached its nadir with the Olympic Games. Baffling chronicles of split-times, head-wind speeds, training and race comparisons. Season's best, season's worst. Endless apologies for athletic injuries, medical details. Too much fuckin' detail. I just wanna see the race.

The bell was ringin'. Time was called for the riders to take their positions. A number of the riders had their women around. I spoke to Choppy Wauters, playin' with his two little kids. I wondered how it worked. He said his missus'n'kids followed him around in a camper van. It was lovely to be with 'em, morning'n'evening. I didn't get to ask him if she parked on his team hotel car-park. Whether he managed to nip out to the van to give her one. No one was sayin' much about the role of shaggin' and the effect on athletic stamina. George Best swore on the benefits of pre-match shaggin'. Mostly the thinking is yogic. Loss of semen equals loss of strength. Samson'n'Delilah. I wasn't too sure where Sheryl Crow fitted into Lance's thinking'n'training. Christophe Brandt was kissin' his bird bye-bye – a sweet-faced Belgian boy with freckles. His woman looked decidedly rock'n'roll. Dressed in black dungarees with dyed hair. Small, but Christophe was on his bike so she didn't have to stand on tiptoe for a snog. She looked rather bold in these demure surroundings. I've seen many a fine band fall apart by takin' their birds on the road. It ain't misogynist. Merely, the band stops pullin' to the middle. Stops interactin' like a band. Each individual pulls outward, separately. That consideration'n'intuition fractures.

Christophe Brandt was the first name I heard when I walked into the press centre at Angers. The frantic drive around Le Mans had taken far less than twenty-four hours. Berlin Tom, my left-field journo confidante came up.

'Have you heard about Christophe Brandt?'

'Does he hold the world in the palm of his hand?' I replied.

'He holds fuck-all,' said Tom, the Teuton.

Poor Christophe had failed a dope-test. Got the chop from Le Tour. De rigueur. The quotes for the press were flying.

Claudy Criquielion, the Lotto Domo manager, said, 'I had to send him home. Our sponsor is a national institution.'

The Pork Butcher said, 'It's in the interest of the whole world, everyone.'

Bah! Not mine! Did they think Brandt was gonna deal to the rest of le peloton?

The astonishing fact was that his drug of choice was methadone. I was gob-smacked. Methadone ain't what is normally considered 'performance enhancin'. It's a synthetic opiate. I.G. Farben, the German pharmaceutical company and makers of 'Zyklon B', developed methadone as a heroin substitute. It's a serious pain-killer. The Nazis took it on board big-time in the Second World War when their morphine supply line was severed. Nowadays, the green gungy liquid is used as a smack replacement right across the civilised world. It don't give the buzz but it stops withdrawals. It is six times more addictive than heroin. It's a crap drug. I never liked it one bit but it sure killed pain. Ridin' Le Tour must cause pain. Brandt must've been in pain. Maybe he'd had a habit.

He said, 'Search me! I dunno how that gear got into my bloodstream. Must've been contaminated vitamin pills.'

Well, yeah, that was like the Italian rider of a coupla years ago. Cocaine was his bust. Blood-test affirmative. Oh, perhaps it was those bon-bons his wife brought back for her mother from a recent holiday in Colombia. Must've been contaminated with local cocaine. He'd sucked on one of her sweeties. That must've been it. He got off scot-free. I wondered where that sweet shop was. In all my years of tastin' class As, I've never heard of sherbet lemons filled with high-grade Bogota Flake.

I was sharing rumours over fresh cream gâteaux with Berlin Tom. He was cool because, unusually for a journalist, he understood that Le Tour de France opened up a way of lookin' at France, at the world. Not reducin' it to a race. ASO gave a Guide Touristique in its press pack. It was dedicated to grandee, Elie Wermelinger, who died in 1993. Wermelinger was a historian, gourmet, traveller and observer. He understood the deep link between the race, the country it races through and the history of that countryside. It was Elie who brought into play innovations like the volcano, Puy-de-Dôme and Alpe d'Huez. He dressed up in shorts'n'felt hat. He'd run a casino in Biarritz, been an army officer, cavorted with film-star lovers, crossed the Sahara. Elie Wermelinger pushed himself. By doing so, he flavoured Le Tour with his character. It was a way of makin' the French aware of the richness of their own land. This tourist guide listed every town'n'region passed through, stage by stage, right across the cultural board. I found that bloke's width of vision an inspiration. I've taken all this from the guide.

The trestle tables of the press centre groaned under the weight of guide books piled up next to laptops. Along with the Touristique, every journo got a guide Historique. This encyclopaedia of facts'n'figures detailed riders, teams, times, stages, winners. It ran potted biographies stretching back the full century. It had every hill with the exact elevation. It had the lot at its fingertips. There was a Guide Hebergement. Which team was in what hotel on which night. With phone numbers.

The Big Book was our Bible. The Livre de Route carried day-by-day information. A concise appreciation of start'n'finish towns just in case a journo couldn't be arsed to flick through and précis the Touristique. A quote from Antoine Blondin, the literary doyen, hand-picked to slip into a quality newspaper column. Town plans, race map, off-course map to speed up A to B. High-point account on that stage from an earlier race to nick for quoting. Arrivals in all villages along the way, timed at three varying speeds. It had all the varying times, like the Caravan, the opening and closing of the Village. Particular problems. A cross-section of ups'n'downs. I was told in it where I could buy priority petrol in case punters jammed up the filling station. The pack was very full of detail. ASO had done a brilliant job. All in French; no concessions to insular Americans except a chunk of the Touristique. So brilliant that none of the 1,200 journalists needed to set foot outside of this hall. A lotta them didn't bother. It was all done for 'em. All they had to do was open their eyes to the banks of TV screens, watch the race and press the keys on their laptops. No need to phone in copy to their editors in some distant foreign city. Winning lists were dished out round the tables minutes after the results. So were chilled bottles of Aquarel-sponsored water.

I'd been given a free bottle of Cointreau as I'd walked in. It went down well with the hacks. My Guide Touristique told me that Adolphe Cointreau was a specialist in elixirs here in Angers. In the nineteenth century, he produced Guignolet d'Anjou, then moved on to his famous self-named 'delicious orange digestive liquor'. The company, now Remy-Cointreau, had an annual production run of 30 million bottles a year, of which 75 per cent is exported. My bottle was wasted on me. And so it went. A journo could roam from town to town with all the colour and knowledge he needed for his article in his freebie yellow backpack from Liège. I read the articles by this lot on a daily basis. I could've sworn they were really there.

Robert Millar rode in eleven Tours. He was from Glasgow. He didn't piss about. He said of an earlier generation of reporters following Le Tour in the eighties:

'Those guys see the race on TV, then ask you what's happened. You see them sleeping during the day because they've been drunk the night before. If I think they're useless, I tell them so.'

Journos are just part of the game. On the inside, co-dependent, umbilically linked. They have to flag up drama'n'excitement at every stage. Even when there ain't a lotta action. Just like football commentators on the box, every attack has to be voiced in tones that suggest an imminent goal. Edge-of-the-seat stuff. Which ain't the case. And in this case, Lance Armstrong versus the rest of the world, it was no real contest. As the Brief had noted from the off. So every twitch, every nodule of bullshit, is flagged up to epic levels. ASO look after this lot. The press are treated well. They expect it. If the finger buffet ain't up to scratch, voices are raised, deputations are gathered. The roads are cleared. Hotels are arranged and booked. The flow of news and information is relentless and thorough. Le Tour de France has to reach the world. These men'n'women work hard to get there. But they rarely rock the boat. Sponsors bank-roll the Great Spectacle. No one wants the product to be anything less than shiny. Rough, ready, dodgy have no place here. Ain't that just like the record companies.

Matthieu ran a tight ship. He was ASO's man in the press room. From his desk by the front door, he monitored the comings'n'goings. His young, friendly staff counted 'em in and counted 'em home. He gauged the mood of the hall. If there was a problem, he was the point of access, the font of all knowledge. He was cool. Brittany was his home. He loved to sail. I was imagining him tacking round the harbour, givin' his Saucy Sue a ride round the bay. Whoops! Matthieu was a big-time sailor. Tall ships, three masters, ocean-goers, round-the-worlders. Those custom-built racin' yachts with a team of military efficiency. He was a diplomat. He wasn't big on cycling. In his coupla years with Le Tour, he'd got into it. Now he appreciated what was goin' on. But, like a lot of the journos, he was removed from the livin' buzz. His area exuded calm vibes. Nothing was too much trouble. There was no trouble. One time, the screens went down blank. The cries of dismay rose to screams'n'panic. Journos leggin' it up'n'down the rows, wavin' their arms in despair — like a bunch of junkies when the gear's run out. Matthieu kept his cool, organised his technicians, put on a replay and fronted out the mania that was in his face. Impressive.

There were all nationalities. The big French outfits, like *L'Équipe*, ruled the roost. One of their writers was outasight. He looked like David Blunkett dressed for a safari. He carried under his arm a little wire-haired dog with a fringe over its eyes. Spit the Dog, from *Tiswas*. On cold wet days, David tucked his doggie under his sleeveless down jacket. They looked so self-contained together. It was certainly a good twist on the usual sight in France of a poor castrated drop-shouldered man who had been nagged into the humiliation of taking his wife's dog, a glorified hairy rat, for a walk. David also carried an old-fashioned ribbon typewriter. He would bash out his copy on the noisy keys. Not for him the ominous electric click of the laptop.

The nationalities tended to group together. Americans, naturally. Us'n'them, though they were probably unaware they were doin' it. The French were excellent at eye-ballin' as a means of protectin' their territory. Chairs, table space. I was pluggin' in one time. I wanted to check the Gillingham FC website. Close season signin's (ha!). Details of 'friendly' wins (ha!). This French bloke figured I was gettin' too close to him. I was havin' problems with continental plug sockets. He moved his head like a turtle's to within 6 inches of mine. He opened his sleepy hooded eyes, blasted me with his stale boozy breath, and attempted to give me the evil eye. I held the look for a bit. It was laughable. Having been raised in an area of gypsies, I knew the true power of an old pikey woman's evil eye. This bloke was an innocent.

They came from all over the planet. My favourites were

the Colombians. There were three of 'em. Very fired up. Full of passion. They didn't bother with the cloistered academic world of the press centre. They were out'n'about, down on the drag. In the little canvas tent that housed the press near the line, the South Americans set up shop. They perched on flight cases bang in front of the TV screens. Microphones in hand, they took turns at commentating the race as it unfolded. As if they were in the helicopter right above the riders. No châteaux or fancy castles for these boys. Just the bare dramatic bike race. Screamed at full volume. Every move'n'attack was shouted down the mike. The folks back home in Bogota, grouped around their transistor radios, must've pictured these guys leanin' outta a car window, roarin' alongside le peloton, eatin' up the miles. It was a magnificent act.

The Brits were more reserved. There were only two main journos. The Fotheringhams. Brothers. They were like a pair of medieval monks with tonsures. Removed from the sphere of ordinary people and yet worldly. They presented themselves as the portal between the sanctified mystique of professional cycle racing and the uninformed public. To gain understanding of Le Tour, their readers had to be guided through sheaves of technical details. Machinery, rules, tactics, equipment. I'd read their stuff for years. They'd cornered the English market. They were very good at what they did. I'd always felt that they must cycle themselves. They only really wrote for other manic enthusiasts. An exclusive club with its own secret language. Not in the least concerned with attracting newcomers. Like monks, they were the only access link between Le Tour and Joe Public. God'n'man. On the evil mystical cult of doping, the Fotheringhams were obsessed with routin' out the devil worship of chemicals. I tried to talk to one of 'em about it. He blanked me in his plummy public-school accent. They looked like they'd be just as happy watching the rugby at Twickenham.

I didn't have to sit and write a newspaper column every evening. I was a flâneur. I'd also done my homework. 1951 was the year of Hugo Koblet. I was a big fan of the late great Hugo Koblet. He was a one-hit wonder, which I also liked. Hugo won Le Tour de France that year and fuck-all else. He won it in some style. He bears a comparison with Lee Mather's band, The La's, who made the most amazin' single, 'There She Goes', in 1988. Never to be heard of again. It didn't matter. One of those was enough. Robin Scott made 'Pop Musik', which tells everything. As 'M', he wrote it, sang it, played it, produced it, published it. He cleaned up. He'd knocked around in colleges with Malcolm McLaren. Obviously learnt a trick or two. No follow-up. It was perfect. So was Hugo Koblet. He was dubbed 'The Pedaller of Charm'. His ridin' style was so smooth'n'attractive. So were his looks. The ladies loved him. He put on a great show. In his cycling kit, he carried a comb, a damp sponge and a small bottle of eau-de-cologne. If he was winnin' and close to the line, he'd pull out his equipment, wipe his face'n'sweep his barnet off his forehead, smellin' pullable. What elegant arrogance! He sewed up that tour of '51 right here in Angers. In the time-trial, he was placed third behind Louison Bobet, the French fave, and Fausto Coppi, the Italian champion. Yet everyone in the crowd was certain that Koblet, a Swiss, was way quicker. No computers, no digital cameras. Blokes in blazers, fingers on stop-watches. All the paperwork was pored over into the night. Hugo sat up waitin' with faith. He knew he'd been flyin'. At two in the morning, the lost minute from the last kilometre was found. Koblet was the maillot jaune. He was starvin'. He went out and devoured a whole chicken. He won five stages that Tour, includin' an 80-mile breakaway on his own. He liked to take in the scenery as he pedalled along.

If a rival was on his shoulder, he'd do the Teddy Boy thing to demoralise 'em. Hands off the bars, sit up, comb the quiff. Hugo makes it into the Hall of Fame for his one-off win and especially because great hair is the root of stylish success. After he'd packed in racin', Hugo lived the Life until the dough run out. Like Marc Bolan, over the hill'n'gone to seed. In November '64, his white Alfa Romeo was wrapped around a pear tree outside Zurich with our man at the wheel. The broken speedo said 80 miles an hour. Popular thinkin' was suicide. Chapeaux, Hugo.

The little kids had their own set-up. Haribo sweeties were quite a noise on Le Tour. They threw out millions of tiny packets of joob-joobs'n'gummies. A prized catch. One time, a wrap of small strawberry marshmallows had rescued my dehydrated mouth. Beside the finish line, Haribo had set up an extensive kiddies' playground. It had a mini racetrack, roundabout, cycling-on-rollers competition and karaoke stage. Treat the children. They were here in numbers, too. Somethin' for everyone. Hook the next generation. This one's free. It most certainly added to the carnival atmosphere of every day. Made me miss my own kids, Polly'n'Ruby. I leaned on the bright red wooden fence 'n' watched the innocent fun. Squeals and shouts of joy. Earl laughed and filmed 'em. Back home, in our fear-drippin' paranoid culture, we'd've probably got pulled in as a pair of predatory paedophiles.

Gettin' outta town was tough. The roadies always moved in fast to dismantle barriers'n'buildings. They didn't give a fuck if they blocked a road. This infrastructure had to be up'n'ready in the next town down the road by dawn. The blockage was solved by drivin' down rue Gambetta the wrong way. When there's a big Tour sticker on the windscreen, cops love you, wave ya through. God knows how the Brief had found the

71

hotel. It was shrouded in mist, down by the river. It was deserted. He wandered in, calling politely. He was eventually greeted in bad French with a Thames Estuary accent — Essex side. We were the only guests. Our host was a big man. Many gold chains. He showed us to our run-down chintzy rooms in the annexe. Fuck knows who was in the main building. Charlie had been there a few years but he wasn't sayin' a lot. He was pissed off. The thrill of bein' an ex-pat had obviously worn off. My take was that he'd sunk his dodgy, ill-gotten gains from some blag into this dream. Gone on the run. Now Colchester Charlie was missing his roots. Or else he'd done a Kurtz. Gone up-river, gone native. In this Heart of Darkness, he'd forgotten who he was'n'where he came from. He seemed lost. He went through the motions in his rough Franglais.

'The restaurant's closed, Monsieur.'

It looked like it had been for some while. Dust, cobwebs 'n'stacked basket-weave chairs. We dined in the town nearby. Everywhere was shut, except one pizza joint. There was nobody on the streets. I'd've thought it would have been party night with Le Tour so close. I checked the place on the map later. It was just north of the Line.

The riverbank was still thick with clinging mist as the morning light came up. It could have been a burgher version of that beautiful scene in Coppola's film. Very coffee table. Colchester Charlie scowled us a farewell. Maybe he too knew the local story of *The Prince of Thinkers*. Jean-Pierre Bisset worked at Angers train station at the turn of the last century. He claimed to be a prophet, the Seventh Angel of the Apocalypse. He spent all his spare time wandering the marshes and riverbanks around Anjou. His one aim was to learn the language of the frogs. A Monsieur Bisset was official timekeeper to Le Tour. He had the most elaborately coiffeured comb-over I have ever enjoyed.

I had to buy a comb. I wished to award a prize to the rider with the best hair: the Hugo Koblet Award. It had to be a decent comb. Took a bitta shoppin' but I came up with a black beauty in a green leather case with a green leather fob. The fob made pullin' the comb outta the case a smooth job. I was so delighted with the prize I awarded it to myself. Vladimir Karpets won the award. His long stringy fair hair looked dangerous'n'mean. A touch of the Romany; a man to have on your side against the odds. I couldn't get near him in Paris to tell him he'd won. I'm sure he'd have been thrilled.

Brittany is weird. Not properly part of France. In Texas, I used to see these bumper stickers with 'Secede from the Union'. Armstrong was asked, one time, where he felt most at home.

He replied, 'Texas, er, um, the USA.'

The Basques, straddled across the western Pyrenees, yearn for a homeland. Like the Palestinians. Brittany ain't quite so desperate. Like the others, it does have its own flag — on every street, in every punter's hand. Black'n'white. Shades of Juventus. Their own language; all road signs confusingly doubled. Their own nosh; crêpes. 'It's very similar to Cornwall,' said the Brief. The Celtic connection. I played at being a proper journalist. I spotted Mark Scanlon, an Irishman, the only rider from the British Isles in Le Tour. He was doin' all right in the rankings. It was drizzling. I marched up confidently to him in his AG2R jersey, blue'n'white hoops a bit like QPR. I stuck my Dictaphone close to his mouth. 'Johnny Green. London. This weather must suit you, Mark.'

'I live on the Côte d'Azur,' he said.

I slunk away. The goin' was getting' tougher by the day. The bad weather didn't help. Sunshine was badly needed. We were runnin' outta conversation in the car. I was sick of baguettes. The sprint finishes and breakaways were becoming a little repetitive. The stars were hiding in le peloton. It was too early for them to show their hands. The craggy northern coast looked lovely on the postcards. I never got to see it. I'd been trackin' a group of cops. I'd read a chunk in the local Breton paper that a posse of English police were doin' an exchange visit, based on Le Tour de France. I asked Matthieu. He didn't have a clue. No one did. And then, Shaboom! – good ju-ju – there they were: five British bobbies marchin' crisply across the car-park. No guns, raincoats folded smartly over left forearms. I had a chat with them. As'n'when Le Tour ever gets to London was their agenda. I hoped that they would be as diligent as they had been during the miners' strike. They were informative but cagey. Fuck it. I was the press. I was even cagier. Old scars run deep. I've seen the inside of a cell or two. The old cracked rib, done by a standard-issue size 12, still gives me gyp on a cold day. This sample of the Met's 'finest' was stiff, formal, uptight. I had nothing to learn. Later on, as the music played for the presentation ceremony, I was backstage, standin' on a pile of pallets. It was a good view over the heads. The French crowd was goin' mental. Little Tommy Voeckler was grinnin'n'wavin' as he put on the yellow jersey for the third day running. Pays for all. A much-needed, long overdue national hero for their national sporting event. The roars matched the martial music. Every photographer was there. So were the bobbies. Such changed men. Standin' to the side, they were clappin', smilin' – I even saw one cheerin'. The chief, with braid on his peak, pulled out a camera 'n' moved forward to record a memento. Anglo-Saxon reserve melted. They didn't go quite as far as their French colleagues and light up a fag. The mood had got to them. The elite gendarmes, the Republican Guard, travelled with Le Tour. A bunch of 'em with scrambled eggs on their heads oversaw the daily deal. The local flics linked hands nervously into a human chain. The top brass swanned around. One of 'em was a beautiful woman of a certain age. Another Jeanne Moreau touch for Johnny. Grey hair elegantly cut in a Parisian salon. I had the hots for her. I trailed her round. I smiled at her, hopin' her lovely laughter lines around the side of her eyes'n'mouth would respond to me. Nah! What was this Tour doin' to me? Me, fancyin' a copper, stalkin' a fuckin' copper.

The night before Quimper saw us holed up in a family hotel on the north coast of Brittany. The woman in charge was tight-lipped, sharp, runnin' her fiefdom at double speed. Matignon was due to hold a Festival of Comedy. A poster was stuck on the front door. I asked the manageress if she had any details. I was in need of a good laugh. Le Tour was gettin' a little sombre. She looked blankly through me and rushed off. Her crab cassoulet was delicious. The Brief praised his wild Rouen duck braised in port. Earl drowned his steak au sang in ketchup.

No challenger wanted to stick a neck out. Young sprinters were keen to fill Cipollini's void. Big guns held back. The Brief analysed strategy.

'If a few teams put their tactics collectively, they could attack US Postal in waves of power before the race hits the Pyrenees,' he mused. 'Unsettle Armstrong. I think they are consciously racing only for second position. It's a terrible shame.'

I agreed. 'Yeah. It's grim, man, it's grim.'

The words of Terry Dene – my favourite '50s English rocker. He did his call-up in the army, went bonkers after a few weeks and ended up in a mental hospital. Unlike Elvis. Obviously he had a poor brief.

We had caught the sunset in the supermarket car-park. The Brief was purchasing walnuts'n'apples. I couldn't make my mind up between a CD of Jim Morrison singin'

'The End' and Yvette Horner playin' her accordion. This goofy French chanteuse used to squeeze out a tune from a flat-top truck ahead of Le Tour in the '50s. Some long gig.

After dinner, I watched the little town 'en fête'. A dance in the square opposite my bedroom window. The DJ spun. Nobody came. The organiser and his wife drank cheap Chardonnay from plastic cups. Not acceptin' defeat, they danced together to Gloria Gaynor's 'I Will Survive'. I could've wept for 'em.

For so long, Quimper had been the transitory destination. The sorta halfway house. In the motor, we sang 'Twenty-four hours from Quimper'. If we could make it there, we would make it the whole way. We sang, 'By the time we get to Quimper'. Quimper was the turn-round point. We got lost on the last stretch of road. The Big Book fucked up.

'Honestly,' said the Brief.

'Do you swear you tell the truth on it,' I said.

The printed directions were wrong. The arrows on the roadside vanished. Tour cars in front, cars behind. All gone wrong. All looked like desperate getaway drivers faced with a one-way street. As Earl stopped, backed up, three-pointed it, I provided helpful obscene curses. Lost'n'late? Never.

There was a last twist before the rest day. Drivin' up to the finish, I was crowd spottin'. Cycling is a big deal in Brittany. The region has produced a lotta champions. Bernard Hinault is one of the greatest – a five times Tour winner. He now shepherds sponsors on the podium. He's part of the gang. The bodies were deep on the barriers. Black'n'white flags everywhere. Earl was hittin' the horn.

'There. D'ya see it?'

'I saw it.'

'Fuck me. Foghorn Leghorn. Am I hallucinatin'? Have I cracked? One mile too many?'

'No. I saw it.'

I had to check the vision. The Brief had informed me that a certain provisional assessment for havin' a screw loose, sorry schizophrenia, was seein' a bee, large bluebottle or butterfly, particularly but not exclusively indoors. By yourself, naturally. At that point, strung out on tiredness, weary from the travel, hungry'n'cramped, I would've called Earl a fuckin' liar if I hadn't witnessed a giant Foghorn Leghorn wavin' at us outta the crowd. I'd have taken him on for his blindness in my most aggressive manner to prove my sanity. My reality was the most real. The result would probably have been that the Brief would have been called into play to deal with the Men in White Coats.

The road to great rock'n'roll is paved with spectacular crack-ups. It's fair risk. Musos'n'roadies alike. The harder they come, the harder they fall. No one matched Mal Evans. Mal was road manager of The Beatles. When Beatlemania started takin' off, The Beatles took on Mal. August '63; Mal was well glad. He was a married man with kids 'n' a mortgage. He was a telephone engineer, but he did a spot of moonlightin' at The Cavern in Liverpool. He was a rock'n'roller. So roadie was the perfect job for Mal. No band had ever hit the road like The Beatles. Non-stop for years. Mal was with 'em every step of the way. Along with his oppo, Neil Aspinall, Mal invented the role that every roadie, includin' me, has copied ever since. He blazed that trail. But how do you follow that high? With The Fabs washed up, Mal ended up in Los Angeles, kickin' round the music biz, chaperonin' any spare Beatle in town. He lost the plot in his bird's flat. She called the coppers. Mal had a Winchester 303 in his hands.

'Put down the shooter,' they said.

He swivelled it at the cops. Not a good move. Six police

bullets killed him. It was the end of the road for Mal Evans. It can make ya crazy long before your time.

The rain of a whole week had eased to a drizzle. The arrival of the riders was some way off. The giant public screen showed a breakaway group that included Jakob Piil and Ronny Scholtz. Come on Ronny, my son. I set off down the course the wrong way. It was hard goin', swimmin' against the tide. After half a mile, I could see him. A large Foghorn Leghorn doll, being held up by a little man with a creased face and schoolboy fringe. Foggie was wearing a black'n'white cycling jersey.

It implied, 'Think you're whacky? Check this.'

I love cartoons. I have no time for Hornby OO-gauge model trains. Foghorn Leghorn is my all-time favourite cartoon character by some distance. He's a large white rooster who loves practical jokes that unfortunately rebound on him. He's a Confederate gentleman with the gift of the gab at high volume, a loud-mouthed schnook singing 'Camptown Races'. With his high-steppin' strut and his puffed-out chest, he has all the charm of a Southern diplomat at a church picnic. He is a creature so certain of himself that things always go wrong. Foghorn Leghorn is the best by far of Looney Toons, a brilliant lesser-known team player for the famous celebrity stars like Bugs Bunny and Daffy Duck. He came outta '50s America, an era of dazzlin' creativity. Jackie Martin took Foggie all over France to selected finishes of Le Tour. The shirt was local with the black'n'white stripes. It belonged to Bernie Hinault's first youth cycle club, here in Brittany. I was in the presence of powerful ju-ju. We smiled at each other across the barrier. We shook hands as fellow obsessives. I reached into my pocket 'n' pulled out my key fob. I carried it everywhere. It bore a small enamel Foghorn Leghorn. The journey to Paris via the rest of France looked promisin'.

Le peloton went like the clappers and caught the breakaway. Ronny Scholtz was swallowed up before he could find fame on the finish line.

Chapter 5

It was the day off. On the dot-to-dot circular map that is Le Tour de France, there are some gaps that are hard to join up. This first major gap day was between the rocky coastline of Brittany and the smooth volcanic hills of the Massif Central, from the north-west tip to the centre. We had 500-plus kilometres to drive. The teams and biggie-wiggies flew from Quimper to Limoges. I loaded up Black Magic, revved it up, and legged it down the two-lane. The Brief sat at the side, piles of books and maps on his knees. He peered ahead and above at the road-signs. He claimed to be a lousy map-reader. It was true that he'd got us lost in Liège on the first day. I'd thrown a loud wobbler, clipped a car wing and driven away without reporting the accident. What the hell! I had my defence right alongside me. One time, I had gotten nicked in West Texas for drunk driving. It was a fair cop and I'd admitted so. When the appointed lawyer arrived in cowboy boots to bail me out, he'd asked me: 'Did you come clean?'

'Yeah,' I said.

'Fool,' he said. 'If you walked into your own bedroom and found me naked in bed with your wife, I'd jump out and deny it.'

Since Belgium, the Brief had done a good job at pointing me in the right direction. We had the Big Book to guide us.

Usually a motorway run is done in a bubble of isolation. On Tour runs, the game is to spot others with the official stickers, fore and aft. Orange (us – meaning off-course), pink (Caravan) and blue (officials), green (hot press), grey (VIP), each sub-section had its own numbered colour.

Each group of car-passes had its own marked parking area, with coloured arrows beaming 'em in. On the open road, the repetitive sighting of the same vehicles induced a sense of belonging. 'France 2/3' drivers figured they ruled the roost. They cut up, cut inside, across, whichever way. They double-parked with an insolent stare. They flashed and hooted. Obviously their act was on a different mission to the rest of us.

It was some strung-out convoy down the road. Team buses were a colourful joy to overtake. More like speeding art installations. Orange Lettrism for Euskatel, royal blue dignity for US Postal, sky blue with bubbles for Gerolsteiner, flaming red Team Saeco always flash as fuck. I'd once ridden down the Pacific Highway in California on Dolly Parton's bus. It was done up like a Mexican bordello. All twenty-one teams used their buses to ferry their riders to and from the starts and finishes to the hotel, often some distance away. The buses doubled as mobile dressing rooms. Seeing them, I knew I was on the right road, going the right way with a sense of mission.

Then there were the cheery familiar sights by the side of the road. Mr Bricolage, a plumbing retailer, E. Leclerc, the supermarket that recalled the cod Franglais of 'Allo, 'Allo' with 'It is I, Leclerc' as the resistance man revealed his disguise. Of all the instant transitory one-night-stand motels like Formule 1', the chain of Mister Bed was my favourite. And, of course, the red roof of Buffalo Grill. The night before I had fulfilled a dream – I had dined at one. A culinary experience surprisingly not listed in *Larousse Gastronomique*. I have driven past the red-roofed buffalo-horned logo so often and salivated. I'd done my homework on the gaff. This French chef, Christian Picart, moved to San Francisco, like so many in the late '60s. He opened a French restaurant to turn on the Californians to boeuf bourguignon. It didn't quite work out. He fell in love with the hamburger and decided to export it back to his homeland. He opened his first Buffalo Grill in 1980 at Avrainville, on the southern outskirts of Paris. Now they're all across the country. I love French food but I'm a sucker for a Big Mac, like any dad. The two don't combine well, though, as José Bové, the gourmet freedom-fighter, demonstrated by smashing up the joint at McDonald's. Add a silly name and I'm in the door. The waiters stood self-consciously in red cowboy threads, Wild West sketches on the walls. Bison chilli sound Brum, so did burgers et frites. It was noisy and family-friendly; children crawled on the floor and climbed the walls. The décor was refined Wild West. The menu was meat. Muzak floated around. I love country music. I can't have too much Hank Williams. There is a tacky side to Nashville that also appeals, much like my infatuation with Margate. The sickly steel guitars belonged in this quasi-restaurant. I went into shock when Joe Ely jumped out of the speakers. Joe is real: hard-edged, meaningful, ornery, wistful and mean. He's wonderful and obscure. I had spent a year managing him up and down the high plains of West Texas, in'n'out the honky-tonks. He does not belong to the world of whining 'Baby, baby, you've done gone left me'. He ain't wallpaper music. Sting is, so is Phil Collins. But I hate it when I hear great rockin' music that I love floating quietly over the supermarket check-out. I finished my 'Denver Coup de Glâce' and left the building.

On the long journey, Earl was keen to learn more about Le Tour. 'I'm starting to realise that cycling's a much bigger deal than one man winning one race,' he said.

The Brief was keen to help. 'It is hugely popular over here on the Continent. Lots of people ride competitively as well as spectate. There are many more teams than those that take part in Le Tour de France. It is akin to the Football Leagues at home. We are watching the equivalent of the final stages of the Champions' League. There are dozens of lesser races throughout the season, all well supported. Furthermore, those outfits run large squads of riders comprising several teams. A good performance in Le Tour will enhance a cyclist's chance of a transfer to a better team.'

'I see,' said Earl. 'So the selfless anonymity can pay off.'

'Literally,' replied the Brief. 'There are prizes for the Best Team. Each team has its own agenda and target.'

'Is that where the different coloured jerseys come in?'

'To these fans, there is far more going on than just the yellow jersey, le maillot jaune. There are races within the race. Green and polka dot are rewards for consistency. Day after day, points are accumulated. Yellow and white are for winning, i.e. for getting round the course in the shortest possible time. Youth is valued here and encouraged, hence the Young, i.e. under-25, Award.

'If it's a three-week event, why is there so much excitement around the day's stage winner?'

'In the overall scheme of things, it is not significant. Winning a stage is invariably by a small margin. It doesn't affect the final outcome. That is why lesser riders do well. It's their opportunity to stand out and excel. The exception is on big mountain finishes. The gap will often be some number of minutes. You will notice that it's always on these that Lance Armstrong wins. He limits his supreme efforts to mountains and time-trials, where he can create the largest gaps in time from his rivals.'

Earl said, 'I notice that his team-mates never win stages or jerseys, even though they're brilliant in their own right.'

The Brief agreed. 'The strategy of US Postal is simple. It's to get the best out of their leader and prevent any serious opponent from breaking away. When Armstrong isn't challenging at the front, the team's job is to keep him out of trouble.'

'OK,' said Earl. 'Tell me this. If no other single rider is good enough to take on Lance, why don't the others get together and gang up on US Postal? They could burn him off relentlessly before he gets to the high mountains.'

'I don't fully understand that myself,' said the Brief. 'Perhaps there's too much inter-rivalry, with too much status and money involved in achieving second and third positions. These chaps are professionals after all.'

The symposium continued as I swung around the Limoges ring road. The Brief counted down the slip roads. The convoy split up to find their hotels. I headed for the country. It's no mean feat to book a room when Le Tour's in town. Block booking takes every bed going. Teams, officials, media, technicians; throw in the many spectators who do a chunk or the whole enchilada – it's grim. The Brief had got the *Rough Guide* out, but he'd picked some tasty places to stay. This gaff had a covered swimming pool, grounds and a restaurant. Positively deluxe. The annexe of Le Beau Site was a one-room cottage with veranda for one only. It marked the arrival of Ronnie Ronfler and Mr Ping-Pong Balls. Sleep is a vital part of good road-craft. I have followed the Keef Richards Path of Positive Insomnia. It doesn't work without large quantities of illegal stimulants. It induces extreme psychosis. It can't last for twenty-three days. The right pillow is important. A bolster will not do. I had unsuccessfully urged the Brief to pack his pillow of choice for survival not indulgence. I had failed to warn him about Earl's snoring. Darkness fell to rural full-pitch in the wooded valley. The bird-song fell silent. The river gurgled in the distance. The lights went out. They arrived. Ronnie Ronfler first. Mr Ping-Pong Balls later. Earl and I were up in the gallery, on twin-beds. His gentle sleepy breathing was like a summer's breeze. It ran through the power of a tropical storm into a full-blown hurricane in minutes. I swear the windows rattled. The inside of my cranium rattled. God it was loud. 'I can blank it out,' I thought.

Wrong. I leaned over and nudged his arm. Useless. Again, harder. No good. By now, the snores were vibrating with the intensity of Acker Bilk's clarinet and the volume of Motorhead. I am no stranger to violence. It has had its uses in my life. I whacked Earl in the side. He rolled upright, spluttering.

'In French, "ronfler" means to snore. Your alter ego is Ronnie Ronfler.'

'What are you on about?' I heard him say as I drifted off to sleep.

Moments later, someone smacked me hard on the shoulder.

'What the fuck ...?'

'And you, Father, have been snoring for half an hour. I can't sleep. You are making the noise of blowing ping-pong balls out of your mouth.'

In my half-awake state, I had a vision of a puritan Thai hooker. And so it went. All night. One on, one off. At least we both got some sleep. Down in the bed below, the Brief endured this Laurel and Hardy act in wide-eyed silence. He looked rough in the morning.

'Never again,' he muttered.

He managed to avoid sharing a room for the duration of the trip. Ronnie Ronfler kept his distance from Mr Ping-Pong Balls. Occasionally they would be seen arm in arm. A gentlemen's agreement seemed to have been made.

The next three days were spent buzzin' round the Massif Central. I liked this chunk of France. So do the French. It's not a regular destination for foreign tourists or Le Tour de France. The volcanoes are not as chocolate box as the Alps or as ethnic-calendar as the Pyrenees. They're smoother and smaller. I needed uplift. Any gradient would do. In gigging speak, the support bands had done their job. The sprinters had warmed up the crowd. It had been a difficult gig under the conditions. The venues had not been at their best. The top two dazzling faces had pulled out. 'Musical differences'? Crashes everywhere. Blood, grazes and scars all over the shop. I clocked a Japanese fan wearin' a T-shirt sayin', 'Scars are Tattoos of Better Stories'. Angel Viciosa, our Sid Vicious, personified the damage. Bandage and plaster covered the leaking skin on his face after his early smash. He was a nobody, except to his mum. I still thought he was a hero. He pushed himself for days in obvious agony. One day his name was scratched from in the runners and riders list. I missed looking out for his damaged head. Now this pause while the roadies set up the main attraction. For sure, it would take a few days before the power chords were bursting the beat. But the main musos had left the dressing room. The band was on stage.

This start was St Leonard de Noblat. A small medieval town with corbelled turrets on a hill in the area known as the Limousin. As well as being Earl's birthday, it was a special day for Raymond Poulidor. He was one of the greatest cyclists of his day in the 1960s. 'Pou-Pou' has a special place in the hearts of the French public. He wanted to be nicknamed 'Pouli' but failed. 'Pou-Pou' feels good to shout. It means 'doll'. It comes out the lips right. Sound, not meaning. I heard a huge crowd chanting it in Dax last year. Terrific. Goes on and on like the Pompey Chimes. Pou-Pou failed at everything. He is a Beautiful Loser. He had ridden in sixteen Tours and never won. He had never worn le maillot jaune. He famously duelled with Jacques Anquetil down the '60s. The one year that he didn't ride, leaving the way open for Pou-Pou to win, Anquetil pulled some behind-the-scenes jiggery-pokery.

Lucien Aimar won, Pou-Pou was third. As Anquetil lay on his death-bed, he croaked to Poulidor, 'I have beaten you at everything, Raymond, even death.' So Jacques was flash but cold, Raymond was a warm-hearted man of the soil. Down to earth, like the rest of us.

This itsy-bitsy place was home to Pou-Pou. Le Départ at St Leonard de Noblat was a reflection of the huge popularity of the man. He is portrayed as rural. I got close and looked hard for soil under Pou-Pou's fingernails, engrained earth in the palm of his hand. Not a sign. He does have a ruddy complexion, but the outdoor life and a glass of wine can work wonders. He is a senior ambassador for Le Tour. He has a great head of white hair, with the fringe and parting where his mama first put it long ago. They'd call him a Good Ol' Boy in Texas. I never saw him ride a tractor to work, though I remained hopeful, given how often the papers called him a farmer. He drove a corporate-sponsored car with his name down the side in trendy graphics. His boss, bankers Crédit Lyonnais, had him wear their colours. A yellow shirt. I thought that was taking the piss.

Pou-Pou was unaccustomed to public speaking. He wasn't about to lift his profile on his day of days. His giant mug-shot was all around the place. His voice wasn't. At a presentation on a small bandstand in the village, he was fêted by a bugler and the Butcher. He looked shy and embarrassed. The cameras zoomed in. He smiled sweetly. A local artist stepped up to present his work. Pou-Pou unwrapped the canvas and held it up. It was a hideous caricature of himself. The artist looked smug behind his goatee. It was all I could do not to cry out in horror. Or laugh. This art had all the deftness and lightness of Tony Hancock in *The Rebel*. Pou-Pou reacted graciously.

Food is never just nosh at a French event. It is a manifestation of local pride. It is the figurehead of regional distinction. It's what a lot of people come for. The trays of finger buffet circulated. These were good. Beef and nuts. Cakes too, big cakes. Coconut was popular. What made the spread special was the caterers. The mystic chefs. They had orange and purple gowns, sweeping to floor. Their silver-and-white hats were conical with some cabbalistic symbol above their eyebrows. As a tray of vol-au-vents was proffered, I felt fixed by a look of knowing instinct. To prepare and cook this food, I felt, was to know the true nature of all existence. Delicious grub. The mystic chefs were to reappear in different gear in a few places. Never less than top-notch elevenses − a perfect antidote to the day-in, day-out sponsored saucisses, Brie, brioches, crêpes. Maybe it was dressing-up day for the Rotary Club. I go for the other take. The mystic chefs were the esoteric. Far out!

All ways round, the atmosphere was becoming zip-a-dee-doo-dah. The early riders in the village had smiles and a spring in their cleated step. As I finished elegantly stuffing my face, Earl sidled up.

'Let's talk to him.' He pointed out a large black guy. He was a motorbiker, a mobile time-keeper, who hovered around le peloton. We called him Mr Happy because he was. 'Ask him why,' said Earl.

I did. His laugh boomed around the paddock. It was infectious. So was his smile. He had LA teeth. His answer was simple and enlightened.

'Le Tour is so great. Everybody is part of it.'

Of course. A Zen moment. I looked over at the mystic chefs. What ingredients were they using? Were the riders allowed to eat it? Would it show up in the dope testing? I wandered through the twisty streets. Perfect for spotty youths to burn up on their pop-pops. Past the tiny Rex cinema, showing *Spiderman*. That film was getting pumped up round the nation by three floats in the

RIGHT What race?

BELOW Le Grand Départ: formality in Liège, Armstrong in the green

Me 'n' Earl 'n' Black
Magic, about to stick
five thousand miles o
the clock

The crowds greet the
publicity caravan –
absurdity on wheels

The Devil gets excited at le peloton (*Empics*)

Very little disturbs the riders' concentration (*Empics*)

TOP Two old lags remember the best of times – Cipollini and Bettini

ABOVE Always meet your heroes – me and Le Beau Mario

OPPOSITE, FROM TOP Roadies to the rescue – Mario Cipollini's time-trial outfit b
the rules

ABOVE Cyclists, like jockeys, are the strangest of shapes

TOP Ripped 'n' torn, Bernhart Eisel lets it all hang out **RIGHT** Bloody crashes – Kurt Arvensen keeps going (*both Empics*)

Aquarel hostesses show
their love of ABBA

A rich variety of French
life follows Le Tour

LEFT TO RIGHT

Thor Hushovd puts down the hammer to leave Le Village liggers standing

Just hangin' around – Alessio-Bianchi team bonding

Full stretch on the line

LEFT TO RIGHT

Grit your teeth, clench your jaw – backstage relief

How loved is little Tommy Voeckler, race leader in the yellow jersey

Garcia-Acosta – that timeless look from down the years

LEFT TO RIGHT

Virenque – the French housewives' darlin'

Ullrich can't wait for his roadie

Basso swamped for a sound bite

American fast food meets French gourmet cuisine

It's a long way round France, whatever the vehicle

TOP LEFT Big boss man Jean-Marie Leblanc – 'The Pork Butcher'

TOP RIGHT Jean-Louis Pagès, Director of the Course – the heart 'n' soul of Le Tour de France

LEFT The press room – massed journos in front of massed screens

BOTTOM By the time we got to Woodstock . . .

Lance Armstrong
– a magnificent an
unstoppable cham
. . . from start to fi

Maximum intensity from Lance

It takes a team to get Lance to no. 1 – Floyd Landis rarely leaves his side (*Empics*)

Old Glory in celebration in the fields of Flanders (*Empics*)

A winner (Karpets);

a loser (Nazon, knackered);

a nutter pushing himself just a
little bit more (*Empics*)

Unless stated otherwise, all photography © Earl and the Brief

Caravan, giant masked figures on wheels entrancing rural kids. Back in the sporting world, the cyclists were massed, ready for the pedal off. Little Tommy Voeckler rolled up late, as befits a star. He was wearing the maillot jaune. He had become a national celebrity, plastered on every page and screen, just for being French and Number One. The crowd rip-roared and little Tommy wore a big silly proud grin. I liked him lots because that old feeling had really got to him. It was why I was there. The mayor wasn't there, though. He was due to wave the flag to start the day's race. An ASO woman, Agnes, ran up the hill with the mayor in tow, double-breasted suit jacket flapping. His puce face indicated a high level of ligging. To be this late on a day such as this was impressive. I've seen Paul Simenon amble onstage best part of an hour late in LA to join The Clash. Bill Graham, the promoter, slapped a whopping contractual fine on the band. He was a hippie. I've seen B.B. King strike up the opening chords three hours late for a gig. His bus had been stuck on the motorway. He played the blues on into the small hours to make up.

But they weren't in a race. I was. I watched the rear wheels leave town. Team cars, buses, officials were hot in pursuit. I legged it to Black Magic. The bonnet was pointed out for a Le Mans getaway. Cops smoothed the exit. The Brief wanted to wander. He chose the back lanes in his own company. It's hard graft, stuck in the car for hours every day, grinding out map directions. He didn't drive of course as he was serving out a ban. He knew the law. Throw in bad breath, the same bad in-jokes, high revs and lack of sleep. Pressure. He wanted to be alone, yet to mingle with the locals. Long trestle tables buckled with grub. Sunday best was worn. Shoes were polished. The bunting was out. St Leonard de Noblat was 'en fête'.

I had no wish to stroll it. Foot down to the floor on the

motorway is one kind of heaven. Earl stuck on a CD. He'd burned it off his laptop especially for me. Aw! Just like my own *Desert Island Discs* but without the pain of decision-making. Keef sang 'Happy', Mick Jones did 'Protex Blue', top Clash and Rocky Burnette was 'Tired of Toein' the Line'. My perfect custom-made soundtrack while I lived the exciting movie of my life. Earl was filming me at the wheel with a camera that fitted into the palm of his hand. I sped past empty team buses in a line on the inside lane. T-Mobile stood out in pink. Someone knew what they were doing. So did the young Elvis lean'n'mean. His first car had been pink'n'black. Synchronicity. Outta the speakers blasted Warren Smith's 'Red Cadillac and a Black Moustache'. Another fave rocker from the '50s Sun label. Cruisin' along a dog-leg of two autoroutes, I realised the doctor was right. I'd been to see her before I'd left. I told her I wanted a check-up, MOT. This was a long haul. I wanted to know all working parts of my body were in order. That was the opening pitch. What I was also after was any pharmaceutical assistance she might give me a script for. No dice. She knew my historical background. I was figuring: if it's good enough for the riders it's good enough for the followers. I was thinking: liquid testosterone.

I understood that quote of Herman 'Moby Dick' Melville: 'At my age and with my disposition, one gets to care less for everything except downright good feeling.' As so often, I pulled off the road on the shit side of town. I sailed up the rue Eric Tabarly. A nice touch crediting a famous round-the-world sailor hundreds of miles from the sea. I knew Matthieu would be impressed, being a nautical bloke. He had already told me that he was missing his regular trips under sail.

Matthieu was to be found on the wrong side of the

tracks on this day. Railway tracks, a level crossing away from the razzamatazz. Throw in barbed wire and sentries with cradled automatics. The press centre was remote, a vast warehouse with platforms slap-bang in the middle of a military base. I steamed into the cool gloom, immediately picking up the screens. A nod to Matthieu brought a 'Salut' in reply. I was chuffed at the familiarity. He called the shots here. The renewed contact with the race, even televisual, was becoming an old-time buzz. I checked out who was doing what, or not. The riders were two hours away from where I was standing. There was movement in the air. Journos were drifting around the hangar-like building. A few crummy tourist posters failed to lift the atmosphere. I walked out into the light, in need of uplift. I needed shades, the sunshine was so bright. The look was complete. Hefty mountain boots for the rough terrain. Excellent for kicking a space around me in a tight crowd. Australian roadies with TV crews have long appreciated that they get the edge on poncy Poms in trainers, sneakers, sandals and flip-flops by treading on them. Shorts, 'cos we're south. Hawaiian shirt to make a mark against mediocrity, dullness and corporate logos. I have no time for smart-ass captioned T-shirts that are so amusing in the bathroom mirror, but no one else bothers to read unless it's on the front of a great-looking bird. 'FCUK' is not rude and radical. It's naughty school-kid bottling out.

A poster in the dazzling entrance indicated a bus-ride to the buffet lunch. 'How far?' is the question. Across town? Was there time to commute and dine and get back for the day's live action? No one was owning up. I boarded the coach hesitantly. A few others were dotted speculatively around the seats. It set off at a crawl and went round two corners to the rear of the same building. Armed squaddies watched our backs as we got off. A journey of 200 yards. The threat of violent Islamic fundamentalism in the vicinity of visiting Texans was being taken seriously. Or maybe the French army didn't welcome investigative journalism out for a stroll. Either way, it cramped my style. I was getting used to free access to France with the green laminate round my neck. The spread was delicious, in particular the tender 'poêlée de boeuf'. Seconds were called for. Which left no room or time for pud. It was a surprise to be presented with a cake in a gutter. The piece of guttering was made from a brown porous roof tiling, 2 feet by 1 foot. The large soft cake proudly proclaimed itself as a 'Le Creuse'. It was a regional speciality and was handed over with a dignified ceremony. I cradled it on the short bus journey back. I nipped back to the car-park and stuck it in the boot.

There is something deeply satisfying, known to advertising agencies the world over, about getting something for nothing. A great cake in a gutter was a trophy. And so it remained for several weeks. I bought a wooden-handled Opinel knife to slice it up back at the hotel. I lugged it in and out of hotel rooms, every night all the way to Paris. By then, the cake itself had become totemic, even assuming slightly mystical powers to enhance my ju-ju. It had come to a point where I was afraid that a knife would desecrate its powers. So I lugged it back home to England. Triumphantly, I offered it to my kids explaining its lineage. 'It's stale,' they said. 'I think the walnuts have gone a bit mouldy,' said Nesta.

I flashed my pass and eased past the security. The back-stage at Guerrat was novel. A long thin white marquee ran beside the road. It was sectioned into units. Each had a huddle of chairs around a table which held pistachio and cashew nuts, crisps, chilled rosé wine. Each gaggle of smart casuals had a sign with the name of their company. Corporate hospitality, Tour de France style. Only inches separated the liggers from the road where the action would shortly be. Someone had neglected to order the camping model with the see-through plastic windows. Instead of a clear view, there was a television screen. I walked on and on through the canvas tunnel. The noise of the crowd outside grew. I came out the other end, bang level with the white line across the road and Monsieur Pagès. A bank of earth rose beside me. It was the most perfect viewing spot I have encountered. Across the road were the press, timing officials, announcers and Earl. He was wedged underneath a heavy-duty TV camera. The operator had warned him to duck when the riders zipped past. He would swivel the camera to follow them and it might break his neck, or at the least concuss him. He figured it was a fair risk for good spot. Mine was loads better. In the din, we signed to each other incoherently. We were both delirious that, as on every day, we were in the premier vantage point to witness the most exciting sight in sport. A bunch sprint finish of a stage of Le Tour de France. And we hadn't queued since dawn. The giant screen above told that the coming was nigh. All the usual mania crossed the line. Then the helicopters. The collective roar of the open mouths. It comes upon you so fast: the headlights of the cop-outriders, the blur of colour, the tiny cyclists up the straight bearing straight down at you. You're yelling and screaming before you can think, before you can organise a coherent word. Just roaring from the depth of your being. Consumed. It takes a few seconds to pass but in the intensity of those seconds, time has no meaning. In being swept up by the biggest wave, you become part of the wave. It is the purest rush.

It gradually settled. The brain returned. The pecking order was sorted. The giant screen was consulted for replays. Names were bandied. It had been a head-down wheel-to-wheel wobble, elbows jostling, shoulders heaving, eyes bulging fight to the death. Aussie Robbie McEwan, already in the green jersey, got it by the hair on a spider's leg from Thor Hushovd in his Norwegian-flag shirt. All the tough guys were in one terrifying flat-out judder.

I was still yakking breathlessly about it to Earl when we got back to the hotel. It was an hour and a half later, and we were still coming down. The Brief had returned from his day of rural contemplation. He calmed us with a tale of a restaurant – more a shack – by the river. Ducks quacking all along the bank, up tails all. The menu at the tiny unassuming place was all duck. He loves duck. He was sorely tempted but had come back. Today being Earl's birthday, we didn't dress for dinner, though I borrowed an iron to press my best yellow Hawaiian shirt. Got to keep up standards, even with road weariness. We ate in the hotel, too knackered to search out 'The Fat Duck'. I wanted to check out Madame. She was an ageing rock chick. Blonde hair piled high, though stringy. Not a spare ounce on her. Tight leopardskin leggings. Jimmy Choo's. Several kilos of Oriental bangles about her. Luxurious mascara. And a sour mouth turned down with lips that she painted before nine o'clock in the morning. She talked up the house specialités. Her old man was the chef. I only saw him, finally, as we left. Splayed out in the foyer, drunk. I was impressed. I fancied he'd once been hot stuff in the French charts. Maybe a Plastique Bertrand of his day. Sunk his royalties into this country hotel. He could drink and he could cook. Earl had steak frites and I had a beef pie with nuts. They stuck in my false teeth so I put 'em in my pocket. The Brief said, 'I think I'll try the magret de canard.' We sauntered back across the dark car-park. It was sealed off with accident tape, full of navy blue Disney vehicles from the Caravan: giant figures on the roofs, Goofy, Donald Duck, Mickey. Ripe for anti-American terrorists. Eurosport TV crew too. The place was full of valuable Tour equipment. Two cops pulled us up.

'We're "house",' I said, pulling my pass from my pocket.

I've long thought it poncy to wear a pass when it ain't required. Check out Tony Blair at a conference or Sven Goran Eriksson in the dug-out. We got nodded through. Back in the room, I sucked the last of the almonds from my gappy teeth and felt for my plate. Gone. Panic set in. I double-checked. They must've fallen out of my pocket, flashing that pass. I re-traced back to the cops, having first researched my dictionary. 'Les dentiers'. The main gendarme looked highly suspicious as I outlined my predicament with barely contained hysteria. That plate was titanium, as light in its way as Lance Armstrong's bike. It would cost an arm and a leg to replace. A large halogen torch shone under Mickey Mouse vans. I scrabbled in the gravel. So did the other cop. Nothing winked back at me. I felt doomed for the next fortnight. No more cool smiles. Just a Shane McGowan impression. I knew the mistrust that would greet me as I sought to mingle with le peloton. I ranted and raved to the Boy and the Brief. We three squashed into one bedroom. Ten days of on-the-road pressure poured out of my mouth. They told me I was impressively scary. The next morning, I reached into my washbag for a razor. A shining metallic smile greeted me. I must have put the falsies in there, safe, without realising when I came back in the previous night. With delight I skipped barefoot across to the car-park. The cops looked tired and bored in the early light. I flashed them a winning grin. I pointed to my teeth.

'Look, I've found 'em. Les dentiers.'

Their stare in return said, 'He's fucking bonkers.'

I was up early to steal a march on the race. There are two ways to get from start to finish. The standard is 'Hors course'. This involves parallel roads to the race route, open to the public but well notated in the 'Big Book'. These roads are mostly fast. They are usually further in distance: 360 km against 237 km for the cyclists. The stage for the day was over the top of the Massif Central. Proper mountain climbing at last. It had been a wait. The orange pass on the windscreen would allow us to go way to the rear, way to the side or way out in front. I was in need of scenery, crowds and passion. On Le Tour de France, mountains are where it's at. Black Magic purred off soon after breakfast; that is, two large pots of espresso coffee brewed on a camping gaz stove in the bedroom. Maximum caffeine, just short of horizontal eye-wobble.

As Lou Reed said of drug-taking, 'Know your metabolism: know your drug.' I'm a big man. And, as William Burroughs said of drug-taking, 'Protect your source.' I always carry it with me. I never run out. The substance of choice may change but the rituals don't.

We were getting blasé with our second wind. The Brief flipped through the maps.

'I suggest a short-cut. Miss out the start in Limoges. Go cross-country. Join the route here.'

He jabbed his finger. I didn't bother to look. I was busy adjusting my wobbling eyes to the small road.

'Good idea,' I said.

We were running just over an hour ahead of the publicity Caravan. The crowds were already bunched restlessly on the roadsides. Village squares were filling up. The road was closed to punters. Yet still they stopped to argue the toss at the barrier.

'My old mother has urgent need of her medication. Please allow me through.' It never worked. It just held me up, got me cross, gave me another excuse to thump my horn.

Were one to be delayed by such, one might get embroiled in the Caravan. Were one to overtake an authorised Tour vehicle in an unauthorised position, the resulting punishment would be dire. Wrong time, wrong place meant getting the boot. I had seen this close-up the year before. One writer had got the chop by ASO for cutting up others. He neglected to mention this in his book. He didn't refer to it at a book-reading that I went to. I thought it was a pity to be so shy. I stood up and told him so. He spluttered and turned bright red. I couldn't see the problem. Some journalists watch the race on TV in a hotel room.

I took great care to keep a distance. The mid-stage sprints were being erected, banners'n'barriers, for wannabe green jerseys to nick a few points, or 'bonifications'. The road was rising all the time.

Just being on the route was a thrill to quicken the heartbeat. Joe Public and his kids waved. I honked back. Simple pleasures. I spotted the Relais Étape at Anglards-de-Salers a hundred kilometers from the Arrivée. More white canvas marquees made me pull the motor over. More sponsored ligging made me drive on. Every day that Le Tour hits town is special for the locals, whether Rotarian or petrol pump attendant. It's the same thing for a band on tour. Everyone's waited for this day for a long time. Party time. Time to let it loose. For travellers on the inside, it ain't quite the same. Not ennui exactly, but excitement is paced. Having a good time is observed with a slightly jaundiced eye. Keep on truckin'.

The day was hot, the drive long. A scenic piss call was made. We piled outta the motor at a lay-by on a sharp mountain curve. On a stone wall, two golden lizards were motionless, basking in the heat. Below us was a green and beautiful uninhabited valley. The sun shone on the thickly wooded slopes. Bird-song filled the air. As we finished our call of nature, two women cyclists freewheeled into the lay-by. I zipped myself up quickly and carefully. One of the women took off her helmet and turned to the other, who had a Stars'n'Stripes pennant on her saddle. In a rich American voice, she said, 'Wait till you see Vermont.'

The final slopes of Le Puy Mary were above the tree line. As smooth as a bald man's head. The distant views were panoramic. The near perspective was dominated by three things: hundreds of cyclists, keen to notch a first category climb; hundreds of Yanks outed in Stars'n'Stripes, optimistic that Lance might make his move; thousands of French waving red dots, certain that Richard Virenque would go for it. He did. How right they were, though I doubt PMU, the national Ladbrokes, was offering good odds. King o' the Mountains goes to the rider accumulating most points in climbs. Every year, Richard Virenque breaks away on his own at the first sign of up. Every year he's allowed to by the rest. Every year he has it sewn up. Seven at the last count. He is the darling of the French. Women of a certain age adore him. He is eternally boyish in a Cliff Richard meets Edgar Allan Poe kinda way. He has the freedom of the Champion Supermarkets, the sponsor. I call him the Weasel-faced Rent Boy. I have seen that calculating innocence in the back streets of King's Cross and Piccadilly.

Richard does his limited thing to perfection. He doesn't mess about. On this day, he'd once more gone for solo broke. He had a whopping lead on the bunch. Yet he was no threat to Armstrong or Ullrich. I looked forward to his adoration.

As we cruised to the summit of the volcano, I braked hard behind a group of stationary cyclists. They looked terrified. On the road were two young bulls with sharp horns. They were puffing'n'pawing, having broken through fencing. As I weighed up the limited options, feeling glad I wasn't in shorts on a bike, an old bloke strolled down the hill. He waved his arms, gave them a look and spoke. He might have been dealing with a naughty puppy. The bulls scampered up a bank, through a fence and into a field. On we all went. Nothing stops the Tour de France. French bureaucracy is as inflexible as concrete. The French gendarmarie allows a certain idiosyncrasy. Cops might pack shooters, but they can smoke, laugh and dance the two-step. Handy for them when they're guarding a road all day. Annoying for me when I needed their assistance. I wanted to park the car on the top, my first this trip. Earl wanted to shoot some film. Make some art. He'd blagged a state-of-the-art Mini-digi camcorder from his nice dentist Ashley.

'No deal: keep moving.'

For a moment, I considered my mother's medication. My fall-back position was to roll a couple of hundred metres. I dropped Earl and the camera. I aimed to park lower down the mountain and walk back. Half a mile further down, sensible road-craft kicked in. It was a long haul down to the car-park. Double that on foot. Throw in thousands of similar spectators. Plus their camper vans. It would be solid for hours. A pass was meaningless. This was the Wild West, away from the privilege of the stockade. So soon had I forgotten the massed crowded madness that is Le Tour. The Brief was dispatched to fetch Earl; twenty minutes later we got the hell out of there.

Yet in the spirit of public integration, I laid out the tartan rug on the grassy verge lower down. It was busy. French families shoulder to shoulder, waiting for their man. Their radios told them he was coming. First thing you learn is that you've always gotta wait. We passed the time eating dirty great juicy peaches. The jovial merchandising of the Caravan passed me by. The garishly decorated advertising floats were throwing out free samples. I picked up a Disney key fob to give to a little boy. I waved at Father Leo, an actor on the Aquarel float, a float the shape of a church. I don't think he noticed me. He looked stir crazy. So did the bloke in the rubber duck. The whirr of the 'copter blades foretold the coming of St Richard. It was hard to pick him out coming down the rise. It was hot. The road shimmered with mirages. A battalion of cars and motorbikes surrounded the spindly figure. He was going like the clappers. His pointy nose identified him but I double-checked his race number – yeah, Virenque, 101. How creepy is that? Not for the French all around. They went mental. Orgasmic national pride. It was their race and he was their man. Never mind that, in the great scheme of things, he was an also-ran. No matter that he milked cheap publicity as relentlessly as Bono. Draw the curtains on his dishonourable crocodile tears when he was caught, bang to rights, doped up to the eyeballs. I didn't give a fuck about his drug-taking. He was a squealer.

'It wasn't my fault. They made me take them.'

Pathetic. 'Never a grass be,' my old mother said to me. How right she was.

A Gauloise later, the rest came down the road. More helicopters, half a dozen now that the natural backdrops were dramatic. Out-riders, lights and … action. A blur of coloured lycra and le peloton was gone. Le peloton is the main pack. It's the biggest bunch, where the top boys hang out safely when they're not goin' for glory but they don't wanna risk losin' time. The team members gather round their leader to pace and protect him. The space between them is negligible. I had my list of runners'n'riders in my hand. A fat lot of good it did me. I spotted one or two, a few. The trouble is that I like obscurity. I favour the ones nobody else goes on about. Humble team men like Ronny Scholtz and Vicente Garcia-Acosta. Little Tommy stood out in yellow. That's why it's the maillot jaune. He too was hoorahed, being French. The back-up vehicles zipped through, spare bikes piled high on roof-racks. I waited until the broom-wagon passed. These days, the Voiture Balai is a transit van. It picks up desperados out of steam, fallen angels who've quit. I knew my place. The regulations allowed me to tag behind. Earl drove. I lounged in the back seat. I watched the beaming people. The race, as always, had come to them. No stadiums. No tickets. It was the sport of the people. This was their day of days, 14 July, Bastille Day. In honour of the storming of the Bastille. The prison was demolished. A block of stone was sent to each major town and city as a reminder. When the people took to the streets of Paris in revolution, the red, white and blue tricolour made its first appearance. It is still waved wildly here; 215 years on and still going strong. Dr Joe Guillotin's new 'humanitarian' invention appeared at the same time. Named after him, like the Biro and Hoover. There'd be fireworks tonight across the land. We started the day with a short cut. We finished with one. The nearest hotel we could find was 50 miles away from the finish. We headed over hill and over dale. The main drag into Aurillac was lined with cheap motels. One of 'em was ours. Every forecourt was already full of Tour trucks. The scaffolders were getting an early kip, ready for their pre-dawn start. It all came back. I had passed through this medieval town one August bank holiday with Nesta and the kids. We had run right into the best festival ever. Street theatre. Living statues on every corner. I remember an all-afternoon tableau of 'The Burghers of Calais'. Human green stick-insects, frozen in tree branches. Dwarves with devilish grins running round my knees, splashing wine. Towering stilt-creatures in bright flowing cloaks. There were giant kinetic installations. Too many jugglers to mention, except that some were using chainsaws. Aerial trapeze bullets across ancient courtyards. It had all been so unexpected and magical. It was on every street and every corner. It was hard to tell who was performer and who was spectator. The joint was rockin'.

Not now. It was a ghost-town. Our shoes echoed from the cobbles. Tables round the main square were empty. While Earl squirted tomato ketchup on his steak Roquefort and the Brief stared at him with a gourmet's horror, I went walkabout. Without its revelry, I hardly recalled the town. It's the old gag:

'I didn't recognise you with your clothes on.'

Seemed like the Burghers of Aurillac had bussed the population to some park for compulsory celebration of Bastille Day.

The next day was to be a long run for the big hills. The decision was made to catch the finish down the road at Figeac, then drive through the evening dusk down to the Pyrenees – an autoroute push to get in position. A move to get ahead of the game.

I went swimming first thing. Earl was already floating in the chlorine-scented hotel pool. My getting in made it crowded. It wasn't designed for exercise.

'It's decadent,' he said.

'What, this?' I answered.

I flicked my memory back to Chelsea Hotel, NY, Château Marmont, LA, any Holiday Inn with a band and road-crew at three in the morning.

'Yeah, loafing about. Not rushing off in the morning.'

He was right. We hadn't idled in hot sunshine since we hit Belgium. It did feel perverse, as if we should be busy someplace. Perpetual movement and habitual restlessness had become our way of life. I fidgeted out of the water.

'It's the Terry Waite philosophy. Ten days,' I said.

'What's ten days?' said Earl.

'Getting used to anything. If you can last out ten days you can last any length of time. Doing anything.'

Terry Waite, the beardie Christian hostage, was handcuffed to a radiator in dark isolation. For fatty yonks. He lasted the pace. It's an attitude of mind. Three-month tours of the USA with a stupid broke rock'n'roll outfit is the same principle, though hardly in the same league.

'Perhaps we've fully acclimatised to life on the move.'

As he stretched out on his sun-bed, I said, 'Shall we go?'

The Brief zeroed us into a top-notch parking slot. Black Magic stood on the outer track of Figeac Rugby Club's pitch. It was right alongside the finishing straight of the étape. Two helicopters sat in the middle of the luscious turf. Earl stretched out on it on his back in the sunshine. He leaped straight back up yelling:

'Aagh! That grass is spiky as hell.'

I bent down to check. It was industrial grass. A woman journo pulled her car alongside, ignoring the 'Keep off the grass' signs. A row started. Two stewards told her that she must keep on the track. They wore fluorescent orange plastic tabards. I never understand why officials wear those when the visibility is excellent, they are standing next to you and it's baking. Maybe it is my anorak-phobia, being wrapped alive in plastic. The stewards pointed and shouted. The journo was desperate to quit. She gave as good as she got. She didn't bother with phoney feminine charm. Another figure joined the group, almost floated in, like Jesus in the Garden of Gethsemane. It was Jean-Louis Pagès, the Site Director. I had not seen him arrive. The stadium was huge and empty. We were all at the far side opposite the entrance. He was ghost-like in crumpled clean white cotton. He stood thoughtfully, listening to both sides ranting. He held the main steward's hand and spoke quietly. He stroked the woman's wildly gesticulating arm and looked into her eyes. This tenderness from a man who could rip off the head of a police superintendent in front of his constables. The woman moved her car onto the track.

Figeac was on a hill, looking out at vineyards. Like Aurillac, it was one of the string of medieval towns that shuttled pilgrims to Santiago de Compestella, all towers, turrets and twisty cobbled lanes. I went walking, soaking up the heat and atmosphere. It had been the home of Champollion, the man who deciphered Egyptian hieroglyphics. He was a linguist who stared day after day at the Rosetta Stone, bagged from the sands by Napoleon. In September 1822, he shouted, 'I've got it.' Like Little Richard. A transforming moment in history. Any clues to the outcome of this Tour were unlikely to be deciphered on this day. David Moncoutie won on his jacks by a couple of minutes. The contenders were all keeping an eye on each other. I looked for a pyramid in the market square. No sign, but there was loads of action. We dined at a kebab shop in the absence of a press lunch. As I placed the doner order, a madman ran in. He let off a sonic blast from an air-horn. We all jumped in shock. He laughed manically and legged it out to join his cackling mates. They were dressed up for the occasion. A pirate, Tin-Tin, a knight, Zorro, a Viking, Astérix. Amongst the dozen or so who'd made the effort, there was a distinct lack of a lawyer. I looked at the Brief but he shook his head. He hadn't brought his wig. They were wheelin' around on strange, brightly decorated (with flags and washing lines) bicycles. As they bashed into bystanders with gusto, I saw that they were lacking the precision of professionals. The pros can turn on a Euro, in'n'outta tiny spaces effortlessly. A pro on a bike in a crowd is a revelation. It is fluid movement, no braking, judged so casually to the millimetre. Machine and human are one organic whole. Metal and flesh joined, like the Alien created by H.R. Giger. This lot were rank amateurs having the time of their lives. A brass band with bagpipes and a big bass drum nearby played ABBA songs. They weren't too hot but the cacophony was the perfect soundtrack to local madness.

It was approaching finish time. A short-cut to the line zig-zagged straight up the steep hill, like a model village copy of Alpe d'Huez. Each mini-hairpin bend bore a mini-Christian shrine. Stations of the Cross meant good ju-ju. I contemplated gettin' down on my knees for a moment, or puttin' small sharp stones in my boots. Fuck that! Jesus might've died for someone's sins, but not for mine. I staggered up, sucking hard for oxygen and cursing every single Lucky Strike I'd ever smoked. Spiritually refreshed, if knackered, I entered the Technical Zone. It had been transformed. The white camper-vans were no longer huddled against the cold and rain. In the heat, a courtyard had been created. It was full of tables, chairs, recliners even. Parasols offered cover, awnings were stretched between the roofs of vehicles. Empty plates, wine glasses were abandoned. The catering crew from Le Gourmet Périgord were the only people moving. Roadies dozed in the shade. One smart bunch had filled up a kid's paddling pool and stripped to their Y-fronts to keep cool. The blokes on the blue Aquarel truck were shifting great shrink-wrapped crates of chilled water. It was marvellous to watch the whole entourage spreading out at last in the burning heat. I threaded my way past makeshift TV studios and radio booths. I avoided tripping over electrical cables as thick as an anaconda. It got to be like Hampton Court maze at times. Trucks and vans parked so tightly in the limited space that cul-de-sacs were created that had to be backed out of. There was no clear way of passage.

Jean-Louis Pagès was back in position on the finish line. His eagle eye took in every detail, from exact number of photographers to a dropped sweetie wrapper. Anything that might affect the smooth conclusion was under his scrutiny. He was under mine. It was a joy to watch a man at the top of his game.

The sweat stung my eyes as le peloton came in several minutes behind the solo breakaway winner. Everyone was dripping with sweat, not just the riders who'd slogged the 164 kilometres. Everyone was sipping whatever cold can they could grab to rehydrate. I took a leaf out of the American book and drank iced tea. I had noticed Floyd Landis had a taste for the peach flavour. Iced tea is a curious hybrid. Americans obviously feel the need to twist national tastes. Chop suey isn't really Chinese. It was created by Chinese cooks for American pioneers running the railroads westwards across the Rockies. Mexicans invented chili con carne in the south-west to suit Yankee taste buds. New York pizza is just that, it's not from the Bay of Naples. The iced tea was spot on, but I couldn't see it going down well with Victorian planters in Darjeeling.

Same sort of thing was going down with this Tour de France. Everyone was waiting for Lance Armstrong and US Postal to impose their decidedly American way of doing things on it. They had no use for transitory success. It was the Big One or nothing.

'If the contenders don't pull their fingers out sharpish,' I said, 'they'll hand it to the Yanks on a plate.'

'This is not a proper contest,' said the Brief. 'There is far too much caution in the approach of the other teams' tactics. There is too much at stake. I am very disappointed but not surprised. This is the nature of modern corporate sport.'

Meanwhile, little Tommy Voeckler was still stepping onto the podium to swap his red Brioche La Boulangère shirt for the yellow. His wide grin reminded me of The Beatles when they first hit the USA in 1964. You should be so glad. Ecstatic disbelief.

Chapter 6

I've got a thing about the Pyrenees. To judge by the thousands on thousands perched on the mountainside of the Col du Tourmalet, I'm not the only one. These were heavyweight followers of the Tour de France. They were not the 'catch a stage or two, throw in a bit of shopping in the hypermarket, channel ferry home' brigade. This wasn't a 'chilled glass of the local rosé in a café under the shady chestnut' group. It was a hard-core, busta gut, serious-planning crew. For France, the Pyrenees is roughshod and wild. It's the end of the world. The perfect place to catch the fine spectacle of grown men at the end of their tether.

We are not alone. Henry Russell had a thing about the place. His 'thing' was a fanatical obsession. He was born Comte Henri Patrick Marie Russell-Kilhough in 1834. He travelled the world, from Alaska to New Zealand, but this was his spot. The Pyrenees was his spiritual base. Here, God was a 'Presence palpable' to him. Henry Russell was a ju-ju man.

His top peak was Vignemale, a few miles to the west of where I stood under the Pic du Midi. He loved it so much he climbed it thirty-three times, the last time when he was seventy. In August 1880 he slept on the summit, having got his guide to cover him with scree, with only his head sticking out of the stones.

His affair with the mountain was not casual or moderate. Like the Velvet Underground and heroin, he referred to Vignemale as 'my wife and my life'. He dug three cave-homes high up and furnished them. He gave dinner parties there with fine wines served in crystal glass on damask linen tablecloths. Like a Tour winner, he was not a man to do things by halves. The local council gave him a 99-year lease on the summit, where he built his last cave, using explosives. He insisted that his guests get out of bed to watch the sunrise spectacular whilst sipping hot punch. This should be a legend to inspire millionaire rock stars – those who retired to become country squires, like Roger Waters in Hampshire, Roger Daltrey and his trout farm, that bearded bloke on one leg from Jethro Tull in the Highlands of Scotland. They should've been adventurous visionaries. Instead, they've kept their heads down in safe luxury.

I was looking for kicks and danger. Last year I'd been up the top of Luz Ardiden, across the next deep valley from here. Armstrong was head-to-head with his rivals, Ullrich and Mayo. In the final make-or-break sheer spurt, Armstrong had gotten his handlebars entangled with a boy's bag on the roadside. He went flying, picked himself up, slipped on the pedal, catching what's left of his balls on the crossbar. This would be unfortunate down the high street. It could well have been disaster for him right then and there. It should have broken him, would have sabotaged the winning chances of most anyone. Lance's eyes went on fire. He doubled his effort. He burnt off the opposition and arrived through the summit mist – alone and champion. His legs buckled as he was helped from his bike by his twin minders. I stood alongside him, trying to look into his eyes. They were locked onto infinity. He had proved that he could push himself more than anyone else. In his presence, I felt humbled and exhilarated. For me, it was worth the long journey.

That was the Centenary Tour. Full of honourable repetition and memorable reminiscence. Here they come again, mm-mm-mm. Catch us if you can. The Tourmalet tightens and tips higher up. By the time the riders eased over the line, the road was so steep that they had to be pushed up to their buses. Ste Marie-de-Campan, the village at the base of the climb, was a mad house. Everyone claimed priority. On foot, on a bike, four wheels. Life-size dolls, made by the villagers, stared at the manic fun. On doorsteps, in windows, the village was full of Worzel Gummidges and Aunt Sallys. They seemed the only ones that were calm. People leaning on the stewards, pleading with gendarmes, crashing the barriers. It was the place, fabled in Tour legend, where Eugene Christophe mended his bike. He walked 10 kilometres, carrying his bike with broken forks. It was 1913 and already the rules were tight. No assistance was allowed. He had to do the blacksmith repairs himself. A boy pumped the bellows of the forge to help him. A brutal fine came from watching officials. Christophe had the nickname of 'Cri-Cri'. His trials and tribulations, not to mention the injustice of his treatment, made him popular. He looked mean and moody with a big droopy moustache. He was, apparently, a happy man. He never won Le Tour de France but he is far more famous than many who did. Perhaps his popularity was down to his ability to keep milkin' it. He broke his forks again in 1919, en route to Dunkirk. Fans chipped in to make up his lost prize money. He ended up quids in. Three years later in '22, he smashed his forks once more on the Col du Galibier. Perhaps he was pushing his luck and his credibility.

The Col du Tourmalet lends its dark presence to stories like this. This was why I was drawn to it. Henri Desgranges too. It was not the obvious next move in 1910 to bring Le Tour here. Some would say that if the point of the exercise is a race between men on bicycles that the public can watch, stick it in a stadium. A velodrome in a big city. Huge velodromes like the Bernabeu, San Ciro or Shea Stadium. Pack 'em in, like Bernstein and Epstein did with The Beatles. Expensive tickets. Get rich. The Rolling Stones in '76 was the turning point for me. I had travelled a long way to see that band. From up north, down motorways, to London. I did the last bit on foot, with a pretty girl on my arm. Thousands of us, a throng. That record, *Exile on Main Street*, was always on my turntable. I was up in the balcony – 'upper tier' would be more accurate. I liked the support act plenty. The Meters had me groovin' with their Louisiana rhythms. I did notice the postage-stamp tiny piece of stage they were given in the pecking order. Plus the crappy sound mix. A wait and the lights dimmed. Earl's Court is a vast auditorium. All eyes were fixed on the stage, out of the hush came Charlie's cowbells. The intro to 'Honky Tonk Woman', Keith's jagged Fender chords. All I could see on the stage, without binoculars, was a Red Indian teepee. As the song kicked in, the tent went 'Whoosh' up into the air. The crowd went 'Roar'. There stood the Stones. Halfway through my roar, I stopped. The band were tiny dots, like Subbuteo figures. Giant inflatables filled the stage. The crowd was impressed. Not me. It was all smoke'n'mirrors. An illusion. As a youth, I had been through Beatlemania live. The screaming hysteria of Hammersmith Odeon with The Beatles had been mine. I came outta that rock'n'roll hall a transformed person. It was wonderful, vibrant, thrilling. Stadium rock turned it into a passive sterile day out. The expectation was wonderful. Little was delivered, except I could say I'd been there. It took the intimacy of punk rock to shake things up. Le Tour had flirted with this direction. Jacques Anquetil and company finishing the day by sprinting round the track of a velodrome, cheered on by the massed banks of urban spectators. Like a marathon in the Olympics. All the hard work was done on dusty roads out in the country. The conquering hero returns to acclaim. A lap of honour, even at speed, is a non-contact sport. It is so crucial to see the whites of the eyes. To get close, to touch even. It is possible at Le Tour de France to get an interchange of power-drive directly from a player at source. A look, a vibration in the air, or good old flesh on flesh. Sure, it's ju-ju. When it happens, I don't even know if the player is aware of it happening. But I am. I can feel the charge. I immediately recognise the transformations in me.

The setting figured strongly. Huge whale-backed ridges, dark forests on the lower slopes, bare crags ending in sharp rock needles. It was a long steep slog up to La Mongie, the ugly concrete ski station short of the summit. All around the finish line, the trucks, vans and cars spread out like mercury to fill every patch of half-level earth. Parking was a desperate matter. The stress of the journey up here boiled over in the car-parks, engines and people. At least there was a tarmac road for the tyres. A stony track carried the first cyclists back then. Desgranges had figured the tougher the better. I was still with him to a point. The first man, Octive Lapize, cresting the first Pyrenean top had waved his fist at the organizers. 'Assassins,' was all he said. It's still tough, though punters stagger up in stilettos, carrying babies and cool boxes, dogs on leads. But it's not so dangerous now. I've yet to see a wild bear or a wild boar, though the mouflons have pretty curled horns. In the '50s, the brilliant bird-like Federico Bahamontes, a Spaniard with hot-crimped backward wavy hair that is now extinct, hit his first Pyrenean col solo. The prospect of descending on his own scared the shit out of him. So he stopped on the top. He ate an ice-cream cornet and waited for the bunch to catch him up. He needed company. I bumped into him last year. He was doing a personal appearance on the Centenary Tour. Old heroes were wheeled out all over the place. I asked him if that story was true.

'Yeah,' he said.

He still had an elaborate barnet.

These days, the route is a jam-packed jamboree. The flags of all nations united the crowd. Team banners were popular bunting. French red for the Baker Boys (Brioche etc.), German sky blue for the Water Boys (Gerolsteiner). T-Mobile were always militaristic in presentation. Even their road-markings were done with a giant stencil. Uniformly impressive. Clusters of fans plumped for one rider. Home-made posters caught my eye. Lance, Jan, Richard, all the big-hitters as expected. 'Nicholas Portal: The Fifth Musketeer' warmed me up. Fifth? Portal was a favourite. For starters, he had a tasty looking mum. I was at the back end of the second week of my enforced celibacy. I saw a photo of her in a paper, one arm round her boy. Ever since I saw the French movie, *Viva Maria*, with my school mates, I've gone for that knowing mature woman look. My mates came out of the Ritz salivating over Brigitte Bardot. Too mainstream, too young for seventeen-year-old me. I wanted Jeanne Moreau. And so it has remained. I did keep an eye out in my travels for Mrs Portal. I saw a number of classy birds with the stamp of experience on them. In her absence, I adopted Nicholas. He failed to set the world on fire with his athleticism. I checked out his performance. He did stand out, though, at odd moments. His unexpected appearances from the depth of le peloton aroused my amusement. His name conjured up strange wobbles in the space/time continuum.

So, 'There's Portal, I don't know why, but he's wearing a First World War helmet,' and 'Portal's out in front; he was stuck at the back just now; remarkable!'

Left-field heroes for a day were dotted on roadside signs. Most of the 189 riders got a name-check at one time or another, by poster or road-graffiti. A welcome familiarity. I wondered if they saw, in the heat and speed of the race. It certainly livened our car up as it crawled upwards in low gear. Good signs got a blast on the horn, a wave and a shout out of the window. Every day, we saw the same signs and recognised familiar banners. They centred us in our rootlessness. Our perpetual movement was given substance. Each day, parked on the road verge, would be the Van from Sedan. A big hand-painted sign, proud of its roots up on the French/Belgian border, told us so. So too did the Floyd Landis Appreciation Society, the Friends of Jens Voigt, and many more. The complicated logistics of movin' on and getting into position day after day with no privilege made me shudder.

I stood inside the white canvas marquee, dry. Around me were dripping journalists. Outside the rain poured down, as heavy and ridiculous as film set fake rain. The pathways were torrents. The sky was as black as sin. Lightning flashed. Watching the stack of television monitors, le peloton was still down in the sunny foothills. It seemed a civilised world away.

The Brief had chosen this as a good time for a stroll. He followed a trail to the higher slopes above the busy heliport. He wanted a panoramic overview of the whole valley. He was also after carvin' out a rare piece of solitude. He wanted some freedom from the claustrophobic wind-ups that Earl and I used as release valves. I stood looking outta the porch at the electric storm. What a time to choose! Earl had thrown in the towel and retired to his laptop, surfing the net.

For a moment, we three seemed to have run out of road. We were as far away from home as we could be. Our small team had separated in different directions. The Brief had lost interest in the race. Armstrong was poised to win. His US Postal team had it in the bag, ferrying him to the foot of the climb. There were no serious opponents. I thought back to the names of riders held up on the roadside. One name was shouted from the void. The name of the last winner before the Age of Armstrong. Marco Pantani. Boy, was he good. He had taken off like a Harrier jump jet, straight up the mountainside. It wasn't the performance alone that grabbed me. It was the style. Marco looked the part. He was small and weedy, but he worked on his head. He shaved his skull long before builders down the high street did. He covered it with a knotted bandanna, which he would throw down at the foot of the climb. A stylish challenge. This flagged his Roman beak and sticky-out ears. An early goatee was grown. More Italian flash. A big earring completed the look: 'Il Pirata'. He walked the walk. He was no fey pantomime Adam Ant. He won Le Tour that year of '98. He had already won the Giro d'Italia the month before. It was the rare kinda triumph that only the truly greats like Eddie Merckx manage. Lance Armstrong has never done both but he's never tried. His focus is single. Pantani was a front-page superstar in Italia. Throw in his argument with a Land Rover in 1995. He'd been looking good, winning stages, stepping on podiums. Bosh! Multiple fractures and traction brought his rise to a standstill. His recovery to become Numero Uno brought all the more adoration. And he was cool. The stuff he said to journos stood right out from the usual dull mumbles. Like:

'We are all imprisoned by rules. Everyone longs for freedom to behave in the way they see fit. I'm a non-conformist, and some feel inspired by the way I express freedom of thought. I've never been meticulous or calculating, on or off the bike. I ride instinctively, responding to the moment. There's chaos in everyday life, and I tune into that chaos.'

If the very best rock'n'roll is heart'n'mind, a ju-ju mix of intellect'n'gut reaction, Marco had it. He was rippin' his homeland up in '99, leading the Giro with two days to go, when a piss-check caught him out. Tongues wagged about EPO. The matter was turned over to the briefs. In 2000, he rode the Le Tour de France. Up Mont Ventoux, the airless oven that had done for Tommy Simpson, he alone tracked Armstrong. Lance in yellow was recognisably human. Marco in the pink, veins standing out on his sun-polished cranium, looked from another species. He nicked it on the line. Lance said he let him, outta respect. How fucking patronising is that? Marco took it bad. That duel in the sky was his last superlative. The weight of the courts got heavier. Pantani seemed to be going down the Lenny Bruce road. Police on his back like Jim Morrison. He ducked outta my sight apart from the odd, smug paragraph about him being in some rehab clinic. He died on St Valentine's Day 2004.

In the gloom and the rain, I set out for a stumble round town. It didn't take long. Maybe ski stations look pretty in the snow, icicles covering the block concrete. Perhaps you ain't supposed to notice the grim tenements, only gaze up the peaks and gasp. The chair lifts were shut down. This was a shame. I fancied climbing aboard one for an aerial movin' view as the riders chugged up the last kilometre. I guess these tele-seages were closed to prevent al-Qaeda terrorists fire-bombing le peloton. Jean-Marie Leblanc may have feared Fathers 4 Justice muscling in on his event of the year with another high-wire demo. God knows, he'd seen it all before from farmers, actors, electricians.

As I stood in the now easing drizzle, I wondered if the Pork Butcher didn't fear a swashbuckling interruption from 'Il Pirata' fans. They were pissed off with hypocrisy. The Weasel Rent Boy, Virenque, was forgiven for blatant doping. Turned into a Champion national hero. Sweet Marco was heavy-dutied by the law.

'Richard? Well it was a slip,' went official-speak.

'Marco? An out'n'out druggie. Look at his death.'

His body was found in a cheap hotel room, in the out-of-season Italian seaside town of Rimini. White powder on the bed-side table. Alone. Unloved. Coked out of his eyeballs. Out of control.

'That's what happens to unrepentant drug-cheats,' is the line.

Le Tour organisers had nominated the next, second day in the Pyrenees as official 'Marco Pantani Day'. To their credit, they hadn't tried to brush it under the carpet. Sure he had won the stage up to the Plateau de Beille before in '98, the year the Butcher publicly thanked him for saving the Tour from a riders' strike against police dope raids. I looked up, down and around for the signs of celebration in his memory. Not a thing. It takes more than a nod of the head. And the place? A long, long way from home for the vocal 'tifosi'. The Alps were Marco's stamping ground, where he'd left his rivals for dead.

I was thinking about Gram Parsons. A rockin' country boy, who jumped across musical barriers and touched everyone he met. The Byrds, Dylan, Emmylou Harris, Keith Richards and the Stones. Actually, Keef touched him in the end with his bad boy ways. Booze, smack, cocaine too, of course. His body was found in a cheap motel, the Joshua Tree, in the Arizona desert in 1973. One year after *Exile on Main Street*. Like Marco, Gram had apparently overdosed. Unlike Marco, Gram had ice-cubes stuck up his arse by some chick to revive him. Well, of course it's a shame. Sad and tragic? No, it's hardly surprising. Rock'n'roll runs a dirty great list of young death from Eddie Cochrane and Buddy Holly through Jimi, Janis, Sid, Kurt; hell, justabout all the Ramones, up to dear Joe Strummer. Indeed, I had an appointment with Jim Morrison at the end of this Tour. Back in Paris at Père-Lachaise cemetery.

In the aftermath of the thunderstorm, I raised a glass of cold Coke to the memory of Marco Pantani. In the winter before his death, he'd been running wild in Cuba. Rumours had his running mate as Diego Maradonna, the Hand-of-God footballer with wicked, wicked ways. Stories of hand-cut glass fruitbowls brim-full of glistening white crystals. Expensive bikes and watches given away to Havana street kids. Ripped out pages of passport scribbled with paranoid psychosis. The autopsy said 70 per cent pure gear. I should hope so. The man was well in at the top end. I wouldn't have been surprised if Marco was once on Pablo Escobar's Christmas card list. They had a lot in common. Colombia loves cycling. Then again, over half of the seizures by UK Customs in 2004 were of 79 per cent purity. And in six months of 2003, only seventeen people in Great Britain died from cocaine use. In other words, our man was no dabbler. He was flash. He was flush. He'd got through eight grand over the weekend. He had gone full tilt for everything. That was why he was so magnificent. Even in death.

Remembering Marco Pantani on his Day of Days didn't mean shit. Burghers are solid folk. They cut off sharp edges. They smooth things down. They polish things up. Nothing should jar or disturb. They wear double-breasted suits. They run the show. And now is now. The Armstrong team steamrollered on up the rough steep climbs towards the Spanish border. Such was the power of Lance that his second place, yesterday on the Tourmalet to the young Italian pretender Ivan Basso, was whispered as 'deliberate'. The burghers always want safe and well-organised. Trouble is, as Henri Desgranges knew well when he first sent Le Tour up here, it sits uneasily and unpredictably with drama and excitement. Mind you, the Plateau de Beille was alpine pasture. High, sumptuous, luscious. Great mountain scenery backdrops for the helicopters to film. There were loads of helicopters. 'Shoot the choppers,' I instructed the Brief. He got two rolls of stills before complaining of a stiff neck. The photos didn't really have the impact without the whirr of the rotor-blades. Live, the noise, movement and vibration in the air heightened everything. The place was packed as usual. The finish line was adorned with camera and commentary booths. The VIP clubs that I'd once lusted for and now walked on past were entertaining busily. Pros showed urgency. Lance was comin'. I was waitin' for him. So was Sheryl Crow. The American singer had dropped in by 'copter to catch her man. She'd flitted around the race early on in Belgium, but was back for the main action. She must've thought he would look good in yellow. So as not to upstage Lance, she wore a woolly and jeans with minimal make-up and jewellery. She looked cool'n'demure, playin' second-fiddle. Stars get edgy when they step outside the beam of their spotlights. She was flanked by US Postal minders. She was positively un-rock'n'roll compared to a chick nearby in a pose that was all pink sparkly hipsters, shiny bangles up to her shoulders, pink lipstick, patent Jimmy Choos and a tiny furry dog-ette in her arms. I struck up a chat with her, as casual as could be with wire fence between us.

'Oi, Sheryl.'

She looked over at me.

'Miss Crow is not giving interviews to the media at this moment in time,' replied her press bloke.

'OK. Right. Oi, Sheryl, I'm from *Mojo*,' I continued. *Mojo* is a classy music mag. It was edited by Pat Gilbert, who'd given me plenty of journo tips to get me to this juncture. Pat is one of the good guys, with a sharp brain and a big pumpin' heart. I figured I was on safe ground.

'Oh, wow! *Mojo*. What are you doing here?' said Sheryl, shoving past her attaché.

Her eyes were bright, her face alert as she talked to me through the mesh.

'Same thing as you, I guess. Tryin' to catch the buzz,' I said.

'Yeah,' she replied. 'Cycling is like what rock'n'roll probably used to be, say, when The Stones were in their heyday. Now, rock'n'roll, or music, has become sorta silly.'

I nodded. I was impressed because I knew she'd done a world tour as support to The Rolling Stones not so long ago. She'd even cut a live version of 'Happy', Keef's signature tune, with the man himself on Fender guitar.

'I can tell you,' she continued, 'that cycling is more edgy and has more amazingly cool personalities than rock'n'roll these days.'

I was finally beginning to feel understood in this world of anoraks.

'I like the way there are great personalities in this sport and you really get to know who they are. You start to follow them and get very dedicated and emotionally committed. That's probably how it used to be in my world.'

'How do ya deal with a romance in such an open place? There's no back-stage privacy.' I wondered.

'I guess when you were around, it was some real back-stage scene. I don't care what's captured on film. I'm just happy that he's safe and that he's got where he wanted to be. It's the nicest thing to be a support and not be competing,' she said.

I brought up the old wisdom that taking your bird out on the road was the kiss of death. How did she find this macho world?

'It's amazing that Lance has included me 'cos it's a very male sport. The women don't come out. It's very kind and generous to include me in all this. For me, it's a real kick.' She laughed. 'I'm gonna drag him out on the road with me.'

I figured she'd have more time to share, knowing how completely driven Armstrong is.

'Yeah, he's blown out from performing and he's switched right into getting the job done. He'll go home, get a massage, eat dinner and crash.'

The press man by her side had tried to stare me out. He'd bared his teeth at me in a fake smile. He moved her along as other journos arrived.

'Ta, Sheryl. Bonne chance and keep cool.'

'Yeah. I'm probably more nervous about it than he is.'

Now that Lance Armstrong was a global celebrity, it made a lotta sense to have a bird who understood Lear jets, especially one with her head screwed on.

The punters without passes were staked out on Henman Hill. This grassy hillock was perfectly poised, above the last hundred metres of road-track. It made a natural grandstand. The giant screen was bang in front, hence the Wimbledon comparison. The mood was peaceful, pleasant, even jolly. It got called Henman Hill as well because of its nationalistic overtones. The French so desperately wanted their own winner at their own national sporting event. It had been a long wait. All the flags were out in the sun. Yank, Frog, Kraut, Spic, Dago and Belgian. It's hard not to side with Lenny Bruce when individuals get pumped up about their homeland. Too many stupid wars have started from small-time rivalries. Basques didn't have their own country on the map, but it didn't stop them being out in force. I could hear 'em comin' some ways off. Pipes'n'drums. Marching music with a loud, firm beat and flutes that pierced the air for miles. A raggle-taggle army would tramp over the rise in bunches. Orange was the colour, berets followed by shirts. The Euskatel Euskadi team announced their plan to cover the mountainside in orange by giving away thousands of free T-shirts. They did good. The vague attempts to keep in step seemed to be hindered by undisciplined consumption of booze. Perhaps it was the hooch, but for a while, I swore that The Pogues had re-formed for a one-off. Mad and wild and swirling round the car-park went the music. Celtic? Yes, no. Hispanic? Yes, no. Electric? Folk? I couldn't tell. I went looking. Instead of Shane MacGowan, I found a bunch of orange-clad Basques with instruments and bottles. They were beltin' it out deliriously and infectiously amidst the Julie Andrews scenery. It was with a spring in my step that I watched the finish. Jubilant yee-haws told that the American presence was swelling daily. Dirty looks came from the rest. I could see heads going down.

'Lance's cleaned up,' seemed the unspoken thought, 'and that's all his fans care about.'

Sour grapes maybe. Bitter lemons perhaps. It was the first time I'd seen a rift in the idea, 'Le Tour is bigger than any individual'.

Getting off that mountain was a nightmare. Ain't it always the same? You drive in keen and considerate. Stacks of stewards usher you clearly down wide driveways. The lines are executed with mathematical precision. Care is taken with each door opened. You have arrived safely at your goal. You feel expansive. Come going-home time, things have changed. It's every man-jack for himself, 'contra mundum'. Eyes are narrowed, lips tightened, teeth bared. Engines are revved higher than necessary. Move up to the bumper, an Asperger's foot on the clutch. Under no circumstances let another motor in. Cut across lanes. Wind the window down. Start swearing. This is the moment the uncool lose it and resort to the horn.

Plateau de Beille had been a terrific place to hang out for such a day. In the vast network of grazing meadows that were doubling as car-parks in the sky, the place lost its appeal. Every one of us, and there were thousands, was intent on regaining tarmac at all costs. The way up was now the way down: a single-track B road. It took a long time. For starters, the riders had to get off. Mini-buses shuttled to the big team buses with all the trimmings dumped in the valley below. A few riders freewheeled on their own all the way downhill, wrapped in cling-film for protection, and pulling on unfamiliar brakes. Jan Ullrich, supposedly a number two, had been riding for days like a turkey. Now he looked like one. Every day he would announce how powerful he felt. Every day he'd come in behind Armstrong. He was a fat German boy. He supposedly loved the Californian high life. His taste was for choux pastry. Someway down my list of decadence. I had taken to edging close to him as he slowed over the line. In the crush of press, I would say, rather than shout, 'Ullrich, you wanker.' Not that I was after a fight, it just needed saying and no one else was. Earl said I'd bottled it. He was right. I wanted to hang on to my pass. In the yards of column inches, Ullrich was daily talked up as a serious contender, but … nah. For my own honour and peace of mind, the word 'wanker' had to be spoken aloud. The cyclists were strung out in all senses. They took a while to sod off.

It then became a free-for-all at 2 miles an hour. French TV claimed priority but no one else agreed. As the traffic squeezed slowly into a single lane, I got talkin' to the next car. The passenger was that rare breed, an American with humility. He revealed himself to be a cameraman with OLN, the US TV network. While the race was on, he sat, or rather stood, on the pillion of a motorbike. He balanced at speed with a heavy camera on his shoulders, swivelling alongside the riders to catch close-ups. I was well impressed. I've seen them lean over the side of the motorbike and hold the bulky camera just above the flashing road. All to get a shot of spinning spokes and spindly ankles. That is some tough gig. Long hours of aching gymnastic and mind-searing concentration. This one had just finished his day's shift, yet he was relaxed and detached. Without fellers like him pushing it, Le Tour would have no intimacy in the sitting room. These kamikaze drivers were hard men with inscrutable faces after their helmet visors were lifted. They never seemed fazed. They hovered around le peloton like tick birds on a rhino. They kept to each other's company.

The rest of us inched off the mountain. Then the evacuation ground to a halt. Dusk fell. The majestic peaks of earlier now seemed threatening. Views of the valley far below were annoying. Pedestrians overtook cars. Fans in jesters' hats with bells on were no longer funny. A group of Dutchmen dressed as Friesian cows trudged past the windscreen.

'It's not big, it's not clever, and it's not wanted here,' was the best I could manage. Competitive snarls of drivers turned to yawns of boredom. Pissed-off cops lounged at intervals, waiting to be picked up. And there lay the nub of the problem. There were no gendarmes on duty, vigorously sifting the traffic into haves and have-nots. Passes, that is, on the windscreen. All the punters who spent days on the summit or parked beside the road for a good position were allowed in at the same time as me. Too much too soon. That old rock'n'roll motif was our undoing. It was three hours later and dark when we hit the main road. One cop blew his whistle, waved his arms and told me to hurry up. I was so numb, I couldn't manage an obscene retort. It was so rare to see Le Tour organisation fuck up big-time that I couldn't quite take it in.

How different from twenty-four hours ago. It had been

the same old number. Watch the winners getting their bouquets on the podium. Feel the stirring winners' music deep, deep in my heart. Pick up the sheaf of papers, the updated daily lists of order. Scramble. Getting off the Col du Tourmalet had been a doddle compared to this. That road went through La Mongie, on up for a couple more kilometres, over the top and down. Through traffic. The last bit hairpinned up to a café with art. The Brief had his camera out. I suggested a coffee-table book: *Views over a Hot Chocolate from a French Summit Café*. This one was a cracker. He ignored me. A huge bike on a plinth dominated the scene. I didn't know if it was an installation. I never do. This was a massive tip o' the cap to Jacques Goddet. He was the second great Tour directeur. Jacques' style was modernist. His dad, Vic had stumped up the cash for Desgranges' first Tour de France in 1903. Young Jacques took control in '36 and ran it through to '87. He swanned it like a big-game hunter, all khaki with a pith helmet.

Jean Cocteau called Goddet, 'The last of the troubadours, who sings Le Tour like an adventure novel.'

His style spoke of his view that this race was a battle. Like Henri, he kept Le Tour lean, mean'n'dangerous. Reluctantly, he allowed the use of gears on the bikes for softies. Goddet started *L'Équipe* right after the Second World War. It's still some legacy. A full-time daily sports paper is, to English me, an outrageous indulgence. I love it. The pages of *L'Équipe* nourish my brain first thing every morning on Le Tour. Jacques Goddet had a dodgy reputation. It is said that 13,000 Jews were held for Nazi export at his cycle track in Paris. Just whistle that Maurice Chevalier song. Then again, this Great White Hunter was a Romantic.

He is a major reason, this far down the line, why Le Tour de France is a heroic legend and the French Grand

Prix is a race.

As he said himself, 'It's necessary to keep the inhuman side to Le Tour. Excess is necessary.'

The descent went past in a blur. I ignored sightseeing pleas from Earl in the back. I had the steering wheel between my teeth. The car behind started honking. Now we all love a honk as we trundle along to get a wave from an excited kid or a smile from a pretty girl. This honking was manic. I took a look in the rear-view: a small grey battered Fiat was driven by a youth. He looked like a young Ken Dodd – wild hair, goofy teeth, wild eyes. He was acting loopy too. Leanin' out of his window, shoutin', laughin', honkin'. The line of getaway cars got up a head of steam. We were experienced at leaving the scene of the crime. This guy was a natural. As I pushed down my foot on the pedal to keep up, the guy with the clear, sticker-less windscreen was right up my arse. His jubilation was infectious. He'd pulled it off. I couldn't stop lookin' back at him. Even though I was kosher for this privileged policed-escort exit, I felt the exhilaration of speed and freedom. It was that Dean Moriarty moment in *On the Road*. That long engine-off, driver's-tyre-stuck-to-the-white-line, no-brakes, Rockies-to-Promised-Land descent. This mountain road was clear but narrow and twisting. The convoy, plus gatecrasher, was going at a lick. It must be something else on a bike. How fast? 50? Does it matter? Faster than is sane or safe. No cheap shell of plastic headgear is gonna keep a stone wall outta your brains if you crash. Fabio Casartelli had bought it in '95 near here, exactly like that. Descending on a bike is like drug-taking. A few can handle the come-down a lot better than the rest. Floyd Landis was great. He'd tow his team-mate Lance to the foot of a climb, get left behind but fly down so fast that he was back in position to work for Lance again up the next hill. Specialists leant so far over they must fall off. Bernard Hinault had trained on a slope, aerodynamically, with one arm behind his back. The long day was almost over. And still they tried it on. One or two motors, such as France TV2, were edging, peeking, trying to overtake at some risk. Just pushin' it.

There is a fateful photograph, taken on Le Tour of '57, that shows two bodies lying on white boulders. Their mouths are gawping open. Their limbs are splayed awkwardly. Their shoes are dumped alongside a wrecked motorbike. A group of bystanders stand forlorn, arms folded, resigned. The two men's bodies look like broken dolls on the rocks. Alex Virot had been reporting the race from the pillion of René Wagner's motorbike. He was a big-name journalist. They were a renowned double act. Virot carried a large 'lucky' stopwatch on his chain. The bike had slipped on the gravel, high in the Pyrenees, flipped over a small wall and tumbled down a gulley.

These blokes weren't trying to save the world. It wasn't the Battle of the Somme. Just tellin' the world about Jacques Anquetil. They had a disregard for death and ran outta ju-ju.

'Flip, flop'n'fly, don't care if I die,' sang Elvis.

It had been a happy memory of the day before. This traffic jam cock-up made it rosier. I turned to the Brief. 'No duck tonight. Nothin' open at this time. Just think of the cake on a stick.' We had finally pulled off, the evening before, hungry in Luc St Sauveur. A stall by the side of the road had an elaborate barbecue. A bloke was pasting sugary dough onto a rotating spit. It turned and spat and sizzled and cooked. It was shaped like a pyramid, and it was delicious. A local speciality, gâteau à la broche. Earl leaned over the seat to watch the Brief move methodically into action. Out came the squirrel bag. This was a grey canvas shoulder job that travelled everywhere with the Brief. Out came small brioches, crisps, cashew nuts, inch-cubes of cheese, mini-packs of plain biscuits, salami, apples, bruised peaches. Every day, the Brief visited a variety of buffets with the future in mind. At odd moments, Earl or I would catch him sliding his hand into his bag. 'Got to keep up the blood-sugar level,' he'd mutter. He was seriously getting into endurance psychology. When the riders ran out of steam, they called it 'the bonk'. Like 'hitting the wall' for marathon runners. To keep their legs pedallin', they kept nibblin'. So did he. How right he was now. He passed the freebies from his squirrelling raids around. It did the job, washed down with free Aquarel water. Finally, off I sped.

There was more energising needed before I could leave these hills. More death to tap into. Midnight found us parked in pitch black. Ours was the only Tour vehicle. No Moussaka boys, no Nobbys, no Disneys. Nothing had a sticker. It had been a long haul. I was knackered. My eyeballs stood out from staring at black roads. I slept the sleep of the smug. No chemicals coursing through my veins. I was no drivin'-cheat. And Ronnie Ronfler had his own room tonight.

I needed that espresso in the morning, though. Two pints of home-made in the room and I was movin'. A courtyard outside was shaded by chestnut trees. This auberge was tranquil, with a few guests. Tourists were sipping fresh orange juice, eating croissants, smiling, having pleasant, soft conversations. The barely contained hysteria that accompanies Le Tour wherever it goes obviously hadn't made it this far. I wasn't surprised. I'd picked this gaff outta the *Rough Guide* a couple of days ago. We were miles off the route. For a good reason. I looked up and across the valley. Above the rows of low grapevines in the soft morning light were limestone ridges. On the most difficult of accessible points, north and south, were great ruined castles. The Cathar châteaux of Queyribus and Peyrepeteuse kissed the sky. (Yeah I know this next bit sounds kinda hippie, but stay with me.) I hadn't gone way off track just to do a spot of sightseeing. I didn't need postcards; they're free like everything else in Le Village. I don't pack a camera. I wanted to plug in to that energy that makes people remarkable. This place had witnessed plenty back in the thirteenth century. Great swathes of this area, the Languedoc, held the Cathar faith back then. It nestled alongside the orthodox Catholicism of the rest of France. The Cathars were inclined towards pacifism, vegetarianism, re-incarnation, sweet vibrations in the air. They had no strict hierarchy. Their Elders were called 'Parfaits', or Perfect, and could be men or women. A bit ahead of their time. They were big on medieval expression, art and music. The travellin' troubadours came from the Cathars. Men wearing tights, pluckin' a lute and singin' sweet ditties to a lady on a balcony has gotten turned into a soft cartoon. The winners write the history. I prefer to see this bunch of musos on the road as the pioneers for Elvis'n'The Beatles. The big idea that the Cathars had goin' for 'em was that this material world was evil, created by the Devil. God was another space, not on this Earth. US soldiers in Vietnam, 'grunts', wore jackets with the legend 'I'll go to Heaven when I die 'cos I've served my time in Hell'. Pure Cathar, from 700 years ago. Pope Innocent took all this personally. The 'heresy' was spreading. Always does when there are rumours of 'free love' and wild, wild sex. The Catholic troops were sent in under Simon de Montfort. There's a gig in Leicester called De Montfort Hall in honour of his murdering. The mass slaughter of the Cathars was called a Crusade. It began in nearby Albi cathedral. Great stone blocks with no windows on the ground floor. It reminded me of Paddington Green police station, where they take IRA 'terrorists' and dodgy-looking Arabs. De Montfort's squaddies were told at Béziers, 'Kill the lot. God will recognise his own.' So the Cathars holed up in these castles. But patient siege tactics won out. The choice for the defeated Cathars was the sword or the Cross. A lot chose death. Bravo! It was heroic. This earthly life meant little to them.

The ju-ju stone in my pocket had to be fully re-charged. As I threw the bags in the boot, I saw the headlines on the Brief's paper. Usual stuff about Bush and Iraq, 'For us or against us', Axis of Evil, suicide bombers. Nothing changes. I thought of Marco Pantani again as we left the Pyrenees behind.

'It is, it is a glorious thing, to be a Pirate King,' wrote Gilbert and Sullivan.

Yeah, but it doesn't come with a guaranteed room in the old people's home. The start of the day's stage was at Carcassonne. The battlements of this medieval city are perfect, beautiful in a Disney kinda way. They're fake. Restored a century ago from ruin, and now home to tourist boutiques full of home-made fudge, olive-patterned curtains and coffee-table books. The burghers have done a splendid job in creating 'Cathar Heritage Country'. It was perfect as a visual backdrop for the riders' pedal-off. Le Tour, as usual, was perfectly placed. I gave it a miss and hit a dog-leg for Nîmes. The coastal motorway filled up with familiar friends flashing their credentials. I was running parallel to the riders' road. The étangs to the right, limestone to the left, it was straight across the coastal plain. On until the signs said 'Stop'. Now and then, there were no signs. Roundabouts would fill with circling Tour cars as they tried to get their bearings. My response was loud cursin'. The Brief buried himself in the pile of maps balanced on his knee. Team-work helped in keeping the car cool. He would flick on the air-conditioning as the sun beat down. I've caught too many colds in the motels of America from A/C. I liked open-windows, the rush of air. The Mediterranean was a strong blue pull across the hard shoulder. It would have been so refreshing to run down the beach into the sea. A timeless, weightless float would have been ecstasy. To break away from the rushing diesel fumes. As if this was a holiday! The tunnel-vision of the itinerary meant that day-dream never got off the ground. Le Tour de France hadn't always been so regimented. Back in 1950, on a similar hot day by the side of the Mediterranean Sea, the riders had climbed off their bikes. They'd waded out into the water and splashed about like kids. Just to take the heat off. Jacques Goddet had been horrified at their irresponsibility but had been powerless to stop them. There was running chaos that year. French crowds were pissed off at Italian domination of the race, so they did what any bigoted nationalistic thug would do: they pelted Gino Bartali with stones and bottle-tops and knocked him to the ground. Goddet got the Italian team through the ruck by waving his stick. So they pulled out and went home. The route was immediately changed to avoid riots in San Remo. That's how le peloton came to be frolicking in the Gulf of St Tropez. And narrow-minded mean-spirited people now chew out Cipo for choosing the beaches of the Adriatic over northern pavés. It's impossible now to conceive of such 'carnival antics', as the director Goddet called them. Like 'café raids', wherein riders would jump off and run into a roadside café. Any drink, booze or soft, on the bar would be knocked back, glasses proffered, bottles stuffed into jersey pockets. It was a raid, so no charge. The landlord made the dosh back through local prestige.

'Well sure, honey, Le Tour de France came right through this very bar.'

But, like swimming, a maverick stunt like a raid takes time. It causes chaos. I wish I'd witnessed them. In these days of ear-piece instruction and tight tactics, there is too much at stake. With all-day TV coverage from the moto' right alongside, every move, every gesture is beamed around the world. Messin' about, hell, having fun would give the wrong impression. People might say, heaven forbid, that Le Tour ain't bein' full-on. Riders are not allowed to use mobile phones during the race. Mario Cipollini was spotted sitting up in the middle of the bunch, chattin' with his mates on the beach.

'Fine him, ban 'em. F–U–N? No sirree.'

Cycling is a serious business.

Nîmes has the best-preserved Roman buildings outside Rome. Aqueduct, amphitheatre, temple. The press centre was an impressive and spacious concrete warehouse in the modern style. It was right out on the ring road. I walked a couple of miles to the Finish, past car-parks and high-rises. The helicopter's cameras get the classical Roman architecture, the roadside cameras get the breakaways, the leaders and the flaggers on rue Gambetta, the motorbike hand-held cameras get the facial ticks of Lance, Jan and Ronny Scholtz. The way that all the angles are covered and spliced is what makes great television. Smoke'n'mirrors. The television producer acts like the Wizard of Oz. For three weeks, there is no need to follow the yellow brick road, just sit back and watch it all on the telly. For detail, it can't be beaten. But I need a buzz. I need live. I love to be behind the goal at a football match. To see the ball coming at the net. Players' faces and shouts. Not just the man with the ball. To shift my attention where it chooses. To take in all the pitch, everything. I love to be part of a football crowd. That's why I pay an arm and a leg for a season ticket at Gillingham. I belong. They may be a crummy team, compared to the exotica of the Premiership, but they're my crummy team. In the crowd, feelings let rip. Passion is shared. I can let loose the caged beast within me. When I watch football (it ain't 'footie') now and then on the box, it's like watching the Royal Ballet. I'm not there, involved. I'm passive. As dynamic and meaningful as that bloke in Essex, '76, who kicked in his TV screen when the Sex Pistols swore on the Bill Grundy show. Oh sure, Arsenal v. Liverpool shows the moves from every side, over'n'over, beautiful patterns is all. And there's a man tellin' me what's goin' on. I can see what's goin' on. I may not be sure of a player's name right away. I might not know his background; how much he cost from Dynamo Kiev or that his girlfriend's pregnant. I do know that when the man shouts, 'It's a corner,' I can fuckin' well see it's a corner. I do not need a commentator to stoke up my emotions. This is Disney thinking: enforced enthusiasm, contrived passion. Barry Davies as the priest, the crucial link between God and Man. The same thing is happening with music. Glastonbury (it ain't 'Glasto') beamed live to your fireside. 'You can be there.' I don't think so. It's one-way traffic. To be at a gig is to be a molecule in the body of the crowd. To lock on to the band. The band plugs into the crowd. It only happens in person. As a rule of thumb, the bigger the security pit in front of stage; the worse the show. It was at Glastonbury a few years ago, that Joe Strummer bundled a TV cameraman off the stage. He'd been strollin' around like a beachcomber, inches from Joe's mouth.

'They've made the effort,' shouted Joe, pointin' into the crowd. 'This is for them.'

I joined the crowd in Nîmes. It was Sunday afternoon. Sunday is special in France. It's Big Cake Day. Patissiers pull out the stops to create gâteaux that look like hats at Royal Ascot. Even their boxes are splendid. It's a regular deal to trot out on a Sunday for Big Cakes. I walked past windows that winked back at me. Full of colours, fruits, chocolate and mountains of cream. Choux pastry to go crazy on. I felt an outsider. For a second, being on the road meant being out of touch. These are not cakes to munch on the hoof. It ain't street food. It's elaborate and messy. It don't travel. I've tried. A box of Big Cakes on the hot back-seat of a car is soon a disaster. The chilled cantilever structure soon collapses and melts. Appearance is almost everything.

The locals were dressed up to the nines. I was still wearing my size 13 walking boots. I hadn't taken them off since the Pyrenees. I might as well stick with 'em into the Alps for the next few days. For days, the world had been waiting for Lance Armstrong to make his move. The smart money said the Alps. Alpe d'Huez, to be precise. It was three days away. Until the race became make-or-break, there was a lot of puffin'n'blowin'. Jostlin' for position in the races within the race. Green, white and dots jerseys up for grabs. Every morning, over caffeine, I would look down the list of current placings of riders in L'Équipe. Every day, I would be surprised to find strange names jumpin' off the page. Cyclists I had never heard of had been milling around the starts'n'stops, yet I completely missed some. Young hopefuls, old lags, at the top o' the pile. Each had started in small time-trials, local outings. Winnin'. Each year, castin' his net wider. Takin' on the area. Winnin'. On to regional races and national events. Winnin' or close. A name in the paper. A silent scout in a raincoat'n'hat, notebook in hand, 'having a look at the boy'. The hours, days, weeks of painful, lonely training, put into makin' it. I don't know how talent is spotted in a young cyclist. I asked the Brief about how it worked in football. His lad was tasty at football. He'd been trained by a big club for a while. The talent in a kid, he said, is down to two things. Ball-control, trapping; that is, what does the kid do when the ball comes hurtlin' at him. The other is: what's his attitude when he's clattered. Does he get up and get on after a heavy tackle? And does he keep keepin' on time after time? Football coaches reckon everything else can be taught. I remembered that story about the great Stan Bowles, who liked a flutter, 'If only he could pass a bookie's like he can pass a ball.' There's more to making it in sport than technique.

Try this. Choose a bumpy road with loose gravel, preferably a steep hill. Ask a mate to join you. Pedal down it full tilt. At a point unknown to you, get him to bash into you so that you go flying. Pick yourself up, lick off the blood, bite off the loose skin, having picked out the loose stones in your raw flesh. Now cycle back up to the top. And do it again. Six times.

Le Tour de France is above all about endurance. There were riders fallin' off the back, leakin' down the grid, or just staying in bed. Angel 'Sid' Vicioso had given it his best shot but called it a day on the Massif Central. Others limped away. It was staggering to stand next to a bruised and bloodied cyclist, flaps of ripped lycra hangin' down his legs, and know he'd most likely be back in the saddle next morning. Dogs on playing fields are an amusing interlude. Footballers stand hands on hips until a copper or a goalie grabs the animal. Sammy Dumoulin rode for the AG2R team. A Frenchman in a French team, he was young, lively, jovial, friendly. I'd see him around often in the mornings. It wasn't difficult. He stood out, in an inverted way. He was a dwarf. Big head, massive chest. I like dwarves a lot. Circuses, always: David Rapaport and the 'Time Bandits.' Whether Sammy had a modified bike, I don't know. He was fuckin' good enough to ride in the greatest bike race on earth. But he wasn't quick enough to avoid the dog that ran out under his wheels during the race earlier back in Normandy. The injuries from that crash had been savage enough to put little Sammy out of the Tour. What a cruel trick of fate. What terrible ju-ju! A year's preparation down the plug-hole because of no dog lead.

Tyler Hamilton was fancied. His name was on the board as a possible Tour winner, if Armstrong got hit by a dog. He'd been a US Postal sidekick of Armstrong. He'd done real well, movin' on to lead team CSC. On a stage into Bayonne on the Centenary Tour, he'd done a breakaway on his jacks for over a hundred miles to win the stage. It was the kind of impressive solo victory that Le Tour loves. One man against the rest. Contra mundum. Yeah, and a man with a broken collarbone. A big deal was made of Tyler's strapped-up broken body every day for a fortnight after he'd crashed on the second day. Poor Tyler. Brave Tyler. To win like that was the stuff of Tour legend.

Tyler was rattled enough by talk of conspiracies to produce his X-ray. When Walter Godefroot, T-Mobile boss, stood up and said of the X-ray, 'It's certainly a fractured collarbone, whoever's it is,' Hamilton was outraged. Like many cyclists, he has a strangely stunted body. His head also has unusual dimensions. How appropriate that he should hail from the town of Marblehead. A man might do anything to get away from a place called that. I am fond of silly place names and America has some corkers. Truth and Consequences in New Mexico; Happy in Texas. This year, Tyler was head honcho for the new Phonak team in lurid yellow'n'green. Great things were expected. Sadly, his dog died. The death of his labrador, Tugboat, put him right off his stride. This, coupled with a gippy tummy, meant that Tyler had to quit mid-race. The same summer, Tyler came up against the dope testers. Twice. In the Athens Olympics Time Trial, Hamilton won gold. His first dope testing was positive for a blood transfusion. His follow-up test, to confirm his guilt or innocence, got frozen in the wrong part of the fridge. This made the test invalid. Tyler kept his winner's medal. No mad Irishman rushed out to knock him off his bike. A month later, in September's Tour of Spain, Hamilton retired with a gippy tummy. He then tested positive, both samples for blood transfusions. His team, Phonak, suspended him. Blood transfusions are cool and of the minute, now that EPO is spotable. Take a bit of clean blood out, your own or someone else's, stick it back a coupla months later, chock full of energy rich red corpuscles. Tyler Hamilton was caught by the blood-transfusion testing equipment in Switzerland. Plus ça ju-ju. He swore on the grave of his dog that he was innocent. The US Anti-Drug Agency rejected his defence. Hamilton was found guilty and banned for two years, pending a possible appeal.

I walked away past roadies winding up miles of thick cable. Two blokes were working the crowd. One was dressed as Mickey Mouse with a Tour sticker. The other had a Polaroid camera. They were selling an instant memory. In between marks, Mickey's furry head came off. Its owner was flushed and sweating cobs. I noticed his Disney suit was threadbare. The Tour pass belonged to a bygone year. He looked done in. His mate shrugged at me. I hoped they'd earned a few bob. We all need it.

It was a rest day, but the conspiracists were hard at work. Little Tommy Voeckler was keeping the maillot jaune warm for Lance Armstrong. His fresh face was everywhere on the magazine racks, two weeks in. He'd been out front since we'd left the spires of Chartres cathedral. Tommy had become a fixture, a reason for national celebration. He looked like he was really enjoying himself. Every place went mad to see him. He was happy to give back his time and enthusiasm. He stood around signing autographs, letting his new fans drape themselves around his shining jersey for photos. He was refreshing to be around. But the dark word was that he was allowed to keep the jersey. It suited the big-hitters. Armstrong would claim it when he was ready, in plenty of time for the Champs Elysées. There was no one to give him a serious challenge, so all the contenders were manoeuvring for second, third and fourth. Hence, Voeckler was a safe interim choice. It was great for Le Tour to have a new face. It was wonderful to give France a sense of pride. How can you tell? Ain't that the beauty of conspiracy theories? They provide conversation on dull journeys.

Chapter 7

Vaison la-Romaine is a pretty town. It's the kinda town that Le Tour de France loves to show off. Elegant cafés with wicker chairs and awnings were dotted around a square of plane trees. Wide pedestrian streets made sauntering attractive. The shops were full of home-made fudge, olive-patterned tablecloths and coffee-table books on Cathar castles. There was a lot of local home-made nougat about. Down the road was Montelimar. Nougat city. I love the stuff. I was brought up calling it 'nugget'. It was a shock in life when I met people who said 'Noogah'. There were plenty of them around here in the streets and cafés. I inspected one of the nougat stalls. Arty boxes, 'belle époque' paquets, red and white boxes in the shape of an old French mile-stone. As I was dithering, I saw down a side alley: an old pikey lady, quite capable of giving you the evil eye, was shovellin' nougat from an industrial box into itsy-witsy gold'n'silver cellophane. Rubbin' my ju-ju stone, I bought a couple. A solid stone bridge ran over a river. It linked the town with medieval citadel, wound around a hill. The arches through the walls had been tight for Black Magic. The twisting cobbled streets had threatened the wing-mirrors. It was so atmospheric, we couldn't find the hotel. I started shouting. It worked. I left the motor where it was and walked into reception. La Roche du Columbier was small and classy. Key fob in hand, I went out slowly to get the bags, admiring the tapestries on the walls. An American couple in their thirties, all designer sports casual in shades of blue, were staring disapprovingly at our car.

'I guess they had a parking problem,' he said to her.

'So the road is blocked. So what, honey? This is Le Tour de France, baby,' I thought.

'Fuck off,' I smiled.

The trickle of transatlantic tourists was startin' to gush. The creeks were on the rise. Earl and I were sharing a twin in the West Turret. The Brief was on his jacks in the annexe. He went off to inspect his pillows. I was surprised that he hadn't brought his own deluxe pillow from England. He was a man of taste, precision and ritual obsession. It helps to have things in common with a travelling companion. The heat was still up as night fell. Earl hadn't shifted since he'd flopped onto his bed. We stared blankly at the television. White-line fever dropped away, leaving an exhaustion that we'd ignored for a long time. The programmes were disturbingly familiar: *It's a Knockout*, *Who Wants to be a Millionaire?*, *Treasure Hunt*, the one where a randy cameraman chases Anneka Rice's bum. In French, naturally. I've never come across activists having a go at global televisual blandness. Coca-Cola, McDonald's, the military-pharmaceutical corporate network all get it regularly in the neck. Banking, of course. But the same old shit on the box, whatever frontier you cross? Maybe satellite TV has made protest irrelevant. There's a BBC channel for business people overseas. I gave it a try. Dull crap. Even if you were considering investment in Malaysia, why would you stay in your claustrophobic hotel room to watch a programme with some droning suit telling you what you already knew? And if you weren't in that line, why the fuck would you tune in when you could be enjoying some woman hysterically climbin' into a helicopter in her hunt for treasure? Shouldn't you be out on the town with an expense account?

'Étape of the day' came up. The day's Tour highlights. All the bits we'd missed on our motorway dash to Nîmes.

Soundbites galore and in-depth interviews along the lines of:

'Well, the ball came over, I stuck out my foot and in it went. The points are handy.'

Cyclists always say they're fit and confident for tomorrow. Team bosses say that it's goin' to plan with a few hiccups. It sure looked pretty though. A long line of multi-coloured lycra going through fields of waist-high sunflowers. It's the classic shot. Never fails to please. I wondered if ASO ordered up the planting when they announced the next year's route. ASO has an outfit that checks, repairs and resurfaces dodgy roads in advance of the Tour. That's progress that old-time riders would disbelieve. Pot-holed tracks transformed into smooth gleaming tarmac. I saw roads in the mountains a foot above the drainage at the sides from constant resurfacing. Now and again, it screwed up. Coming off the Col d'Izoard near Gap in 2003, Beloki crashed heavily, breaking lots of bones, when his tyre stuck in melting tar. At the same time, Armstrong shimmied around the crash, across the fields on foot, pushing his bike, cutting off the loop of the bend and keeping his race position. You had to applaud the wag for a dynamic instant response.

As the TV and lights went off, the noise from the hotel garden below lifted up through our window. Braying laughter, shouted conversation.

'Hey, let's party,' I said to Earl.

'I've gotta better idea,' he said. 'Let's not.'

Outside, the talk turned to a detailed intricate analysis of Tour tactics and prospects. 'D'ya reckon Lance'll do it tomorrow?'

I couldn't identify which of the fifty-odd states the party came from. Noisy as it was, it's a fair bet that Ronnie Ronfler and Mr Ping-Pong Balls gave as good as they got.

A rest day on the road is a state of mind. Earl took it literally.

'It's the pool for me, dear Father,' he announced.

The Brief had picked this hotel as a notch up just for a day like this. A bit of a lazy treat. Once it would've been drunken chaos. Now, for me, this was laundry day. How else do you keep up when you ain't near a launderette, haven't got a spare few hours, and are permanently movin' on? Especially, I needed the dazzling yellow Polynesian shirt with the big nudes on. There's no excuse for adopting the look of a shy tramp or an English journalist.

Leaving Earl to turn himself into a bronzed Adonis, I strode down the hill. A spot of shopping. As I strolled between the Provençal knick-knack stalls, I realised that I just couldn't hack it. Nor could I be bothered trying to hack it. I couldn't slow down. Couldn't stop the flow of adrenaline. I didn't want to. Furthermore, I felt my hackles rising at the arseholes in straw hats and flip-flops. Gettin' in my way, slowin' me down just to buy lavender soap. I speeded up in a straight line, barging ladies in olive-patterned sun-frocks, elbowing balding men in cargo shorts. I was mutterin'n'sweatin'. Something had to give. I walked into a pharmacy. I bought a box of the heavy-duty high-strength codeine that you can't get any more in Puritan Britain. I washed a handful down with ice-cold Coke at a pavement café. I waited the seventeen minutes for the drug to kick in to my bloodstream. Oh, nicotine, why have you deserted me in this hour of need? I could've murdered a fag. As I sat tight, a beautiful thing happened. A woman in white calico walked past. I watched her and noticed how well she fitted her surroundings. Another woman passed in front wearing denim'n'lace. I felt the corners of my mouth lift. I looked across the square. There were a lot of gorgeous women out in the sunshine. As Ronnie Wood once said, there's nothing wrong with a spot of window shopping. As I settled the tab, I found myself staring hard at a woman in a red suit at the next table. Walking along the rue Gambetta, I couldn't stop my head swivelling at the female flesh comin' at me. There was loads. My eyeballs traced the outlines of a thong under thin cotton. Bare midriffs sucked me in. This was gettin' outta hand. A simple pleasurable glance had turned into lustful mania. The sight of all those bulging tits, tight arses and strokeable shoulders was doin' me in. In all the headstrong charge of keeping up with Le Tour, I had forgotten sex. So consumed had I been by men on bikes, I had ignored my mounting celibacy. At this rate, I was gonna be needin' the Brief in a professional capacity. I legged it back to the room, thinkin' about hotel chambermaids.

I didn't go creepin' along hotel corridors in the dead of night. I couldn't say how the riders deal with this. Lance met Sheryl now 'n' again. How polite they were while the race was won was their business. A rock'n'roll band on the road ain't short of bed company. Lotsa local inhibitions go out the window when a band hits town. Plus the regulars. I'd spotted Eric Zabel, the German champion sprinter, waiting motionless on his cross bar for the daily start. The front of his handlebars was adorned with a blonde, very rock'n'roll in leopardskin, grinding her pudenda against his chrome. I saw her with him often. Their eyes met. Cheesey Moreau had a beautiful young wife, Emilie. He took coffee with her every morning at the Crédit Lyonnais stand in Le Village. She worked there, as elegant as a *Vogue* model in her yellow sleeveless shift dress. When the Brief first spotted them smiling'n'canoodlin', he whipped out his camera. He thought he'd hit a paparazzi kinda moment. It wasn't quite in Bill Wyman territory. Old Bill had married a young teenager called Mandy Smith. It ended in tears, but not before Bill's son had linked up with Mandy's mum. I'd be shocked if there weren't groupies around Le Tour. Power and fame are strong aphrodisiacs. Ask Henry Kissinger. In days when armies marched to battle, like Waterloo, groupies set up tents behind the squaddies, out of the line of fire. Camp followers. Even milkmen have groupies. On the road, it's a perfect end to an enchanted evening. Everyone concerned knows the score. Maybe that was why Tommy Voeckler's mum had flown in from Martinique. To protect her boy. The top dog was gonna get talent. Hang on a minute, maybe that was why Sheryl had flown in … no, no. That would be getting too close to the bravura of Fausto Coppi.

Coppi was an all-time great. He won the lot in his time, badly interrupted by spending the Second World War as a prisoner of war, including the Giro d'Italia and Le Tour together in 1949 and again in '52. He looked awkward and angular, all elbows, knees and aquiline nose below blackened come-down eyes. He rode as smoothly as a perfectly oiled machine. Off the bike, he was a city slicker. He enjoyed the perks of his fame. It all came to a glorious head with his Woman in White. Like John Dillinger's Lady in Red, Giulia Locatelli did for her man. Coppi didn't care. She was the kind of looker he could never have pulled if he'd stayed as a butcher. She chanced into her lover because her husband was a big fan. Dr Locatelli was a man of few words and great reserve, ex-army. Cycling was his passion. Giulia tagged along one time, in ignorance. Stuck in the traffic, right next to Coppi's transport, she was intrigued and magnetised. It was beautiful ju-ju. She trailed the star and pulled him. This was '50s Italy. Fausto had a wife, Bruna. He had a Pope, Pius XII. It was a major scandal, with the lovers on the run from the paparazzi. A midnight police raid on their villa looked for stains on the sheets. The Pope himself asked Coppi to return to his wife. He refused to bless the Giro. Serious pressure. Coppi shrugged. He rode it out. He was the Campionissima.

I don't know what Raymond Poulidor's reaction would have been if a chestnut-haired naked beauty had come a' knockin' on his door. He seems a private, cautious man. His nemesis, Jacques Anquetil, let his knob run riot. Like Coppi, he was The Man of his era. He was a five times Tour winner, four of 'em on the trot from '61 to '64. He also liked the high life. Jacques was a sharp dresser from a humble background in Rouen. When, as a teenager, he met Coppi at his peak, Anquetil took great care to dress down in old gear. Smart. Perhaps he'd been after pick-up tips for doctors' wives, because he pulled the same stunt. Mrs Janine Boeda was married to Jacques' doctor. After a bit of to-ing'n'fro-ing, Jacques jumped on a plane from Cannes and whisked her away into the night. She was wearing a fur-coat over her nightie. It didn't do him any favours with the French public. They never loved him. He wasn't bothered. He had other fish to fry. Like his affair with Annie, Janine's daughter from the doctor. That gave Jacques a daughter, Sophie, from his step-daughter. When you've been King from your efforts, conventional considerations must be meaningless. Next up was Dominique, fifteen years younger than him. She was married to Alain, Janine's son. Dominique moved into Jacques' château and had their son, Christophe. Phew! The sex drive of Jacques Anquetil was worthy of a soap opera. It's the drive of a man who was Champion of the World. It ain't 9 to 5. It's the stuff that gets you up mountains in first place.

'Fancy a spin?' I asked the Brief.

I knew right then I had to keep rollin' all the way to Paris. Earl split to spend the day with Ambre Solaire. We went lookin' for cyclists. Out came maps, brochure, guidebooks. You can't miss Mont Ventoux. It is a big mountain all on its own to the eastern side of the mighty River Rhône. As Le Tour got ready to hit the Alps, I figured a few teams might fancy a training ride up its flanks. I was wrong. The road was packed. Maybe everyone was tryin' to burn off their excess testosterone. Too much anything is fair enough for me.

The little town of Bedouin lies at the foot of Mont Ventoux. It was lunch time on a very hot day. We found a boulangerie and filled a bag with those little savoury tarts. The sort of quichette, size of two thumbs'n'two fingers. Eggs, cheese, ham, cèpes even. We sat in the shade outside on a wall. There were several cyclists nearby doing the same thing. They noticed the official logo on our motor, heard us talking. 'You are English? With Le Tour?' I nodded, mouth full of grub. 'What about David Millar?' said a fit-looking Dutch hippie. He mimed banging a works into his left forearm. I thought that was a bit rich, coming from the land of free soft-drug use. I've worked the Paradiso in Amsterdam. I've gigged a lot in Holland. I don't smoke dope. Soft drugs for soft people. I've seen the best minds of my generation turned to cabbage water with that muck. I used to be a class A man, a child of the pharmaceutical society. I fuckin' hated those Dutch clubs full of chokin' spliff smoke. Always a smug little cunt inside the entrance fiddlin' with his dope scales. I'd punched a bloke in the lip one time in the Melkveg club for persistently foisting a joint onto me. Marijuana is a proselytising kinda drug.

David Millar was a fair point. Everyone I met in the three weeks, once they sussed I was British, wanted my take on the matter. Millar was the best British rider, he was the only fucking British rider. Now he's gone, gone, gone. Caught bang to rights. Singin' like a canary, and all the rest of it. Two used needles with traces in a hollowed-out book on his mantelpiece. Straight outta Le Carré. He'd been lifted out of a restaurant in his adopted home of Biarritz by police and made a full confession. He'd been a professional for half a dozen years, always threatening a breakthrough but never quite managing it. He was rated as a time-trialer. He was liked as a pleasant young man. 'Oh woe is me. It was a foolish mistake,' was the sorta thing he came out with. He wrung his hands and fooled no one by wearing a white collar and tie. EPO was his drug of choice. 'Join the club,' thought Joe Public. 'He shouldn't have got caught, very sloppy for a pro,' I thought. The press went mad. 'Drug cheat', was the pious sanctimonious chant from the front pages.

The road wobbled through olive groves towards the mountain, a shady anti-clockwise loop up to the flank. Dozens of bikes tucked into the kerb, heads down, cautious, steady. I cruised past carefully, leaving a fair gap, polite, considerate. It seemed only right. These enthusiasts had gone to a lot of trouble to put themselves on two wheels on this hill. There were no towns nearby, no train stations or airports, the roads were country crappy (terrific surface, though). What better holiday if you wanna watch the pros one day and pretend you are one the next. Like kids on a Cup Final day out the back alley with a football. Or all the tennis courts fully booked during Wimbledon. Some of these fanatics wore the costume and rode real racing bikes. Not as well: one look at the speedo told. Others had mountain bikes, a few panniers covering every eventuality. Tandems showed a sign of commitment. There were a lot of Americans. I could tell. They were very proud of their flag. My daughter, Ruby, has a long dangly pole up off her rear axle with Nemo on it. The fish, not Georges. This lot had Old Glory. Not a cool ragged tattered one, like in the

Robert Mapplethorpe photo. And I could hear 'em talkin' through the open windows as I eased east. I couldn't figure how they could talk as well as breathe'n'pedal. The Ventoux has a reputation for airlessness. Tour riders have long identified a lack of oxygen as a problem here. I knew it as a place where people lost it big-time. A bloke in front a way wobbled on his bike and crashed to the floor. The oozing tarmac broke his fall. His friends stopped and stared down at him. I pulled over. His mate was wearin' a Foreign Legion hat with the flap on the neck, made from the Stars'n'Stripes. It used to be taken as an insult by American conservatives if the flag was used incorrectly. Jerry Garcia of the Grateful Dead went into hiding in the '60s for that. Jagger knew the score precisely when he wore a top-hat with a flag pattern at Altamont. The Armstrong Fan Club had made it patriotically cool. I offered the man with 'road rash' grazes a lift to the top.

'Where ya from?'

'Montana.'

He turned it down with a puzzled look. And he was still in the shade. The madness comes higher up. Chalet Reynard marks the point of no return. A big café on a tight bend. The trees stop. The landscape becomes lunar. White rocks bounce back sunlight'n'heat. No streams, no vegetation. It's bleak, man, it's bleak. There is nothing to distract the eye. To ride a bike all day must be mentally tough. To end up here at the end of it must be mind-destroying. There were no spectators on the roadside. There was no race, except in the minds of these rest-day cycling tourists. By now, most looked desperate, hangin' in there. The memorial to Tommy Simpson, a couple of kilometres short of the summit, was the only relief. Like a gravestone on the white rocks, it received a jumble of mementoes. A bouquet from Le Tour and a doff of the cap from riders, down to a kite, a bike wheel, and the scribbled prayer on a notebook from fans. Tommy was that rare creature, a top-notch English cyclist. In the '60s, he'd cracked the European circuit and won big races. On 13 July 1967, while The Beatles sang of love, Tom went for broke on the Ventoux. Le Tour de France was everything. His heart blew up. He zig-zagged into the rocks, mumbling, 'Put me back on the bloody bike,' to his roadie, Harry Hall.

A kiss of life, an oxygen mask and a helicopter lift to hospital didn't help. Nor had the speed in his body. Tommy had good gear. Tubes of laboratory amphetamine in his jersey, more in his hotel room. There was a wailin' and a gnashin' of teeth at Tom Simpson's death.

No one quite said, 'Dirty little drug cheat got what was comin' to him,' but a doping crack-down was launched.

Commentators said wisely, 'If only he'd calmed down and behaved more sensibly.' Calm, sensible people don't win Le Tour de France. Speed works in the head by telling you that you're fuckin' invincible. It makes you push that bit harder, that bit longer than the next bloke. Yeah, it kills you if you get it skew-whiff, but if you are seriously competitive, that's a fair gamble. It won the war. All those pilots chewin' manically on long raids over Dresden, or back-to-back Spitfire sorties in the Battle of Britain, were heroes. Speed-freaks, with the medical officer as dealer. It was part of the culture. The Stones sang of 'Mother's Little Helper'. Uppers to get you through a tiring, tedious domestic existence. Millions shipped on scripts. Factory workers. Was an athlete any different?

'Wanna stay up all night dancin'? Swallow these.'

'Three-week endurance race round France? Why not?'

The Beatles got a great laugh when Lennon said to Harold Wilson, on getting some award, 'Thanks for the purple hearts,' as they were handed a golden heart-shaped trophy. Takin' speed was no special deal. Fuck it! The

Beatles got great by playing all night, every night, in the Star Club, Hamburg. 'Prellies' (Preludin) were their inspiration. Tommy Simpson, like all of us, knew what he was doing. He took a common risk. If Tommy died for someone's sins, it wasn't mine.

The summit of Mont Ventoux has an observatory stuck on it. It looks weird and isolated. Got great views across to where we were heading – the Alps, snow glinting. There's a café. I drank Fanta lemon and waited for the Brief. He was testing the gradient against his calf-muscles. At the next table, a northerner was holding court. He was dressed for a sponsored walk in Scarborough. A bunch of exhausted men and women, wearing red and white striped shirts, very '50s, with 'Shropshire Wheelers' on the back, hung on his words.

'Many, many thanks for the loan of the cycle,' he said. 'Now I will be able to say on the programme with authenticity that I have ridden on Mont Ventoux!'

How they laughed. The Brief eased into the chair next to me.

'That's Mike Smith of Eurosport,' he said.

I listened on to a patronising put-down of Smith's predecessor, David Duffield.

'It's a modern sport now. Technical. Tactical. There's no room or need any more for flowery rambling.'

Pity, I thought. Ain't that why I and so many loved old Duffield. Rattlin' on about châteaux, appellation controlée, battles, recipes. He allowed us to see how Le Tour, in the widest frame, fitted into what's going on in the area. When I'm watchin' Le Tour on the telly, there are chunks when not a lot is happening, except everyone is truckin'. So that lovely château, tell me about it. What has happened there? Those fields, what grows in them? Satisfy my curiosity at quiet moments. Because as sure as eggs is eggs, I care not what poxy gear ratios are used, or what the tension of the brake cable is, or the fibrous compound used in the shorts. That's for engineers. Previous race statistics are another blind alley. OK, tell me who's done what before. A track record, or palmares, can flesh out an understanding. Keep it brief. As Steven Spielberg said of movie pitching: 'If you can't say it in twenty-eight words, don't bother.'

To hear a commentator rabbit on'n'on with statistics is awful. That's for mathematicians. It don't tell me what's happening now. It don't help. Sidekick analysts confuse with their simplistic deconstructions. There ain't that much to tell. Let me sit back and watch. Let me figure out for myself, you smart arse. Cut the moral crap. 'It's a disgrace,' as a comment on a sportsman's behaviour. 'Disgraceful' when fans go on the lam. I have no wish for extraordinary people performing extraordinary actions to carry on with ordinary timidity. I just knew that if I were to switch on Eurosport tomorrow, I would hear him say, 'I had a cycle up Mont Ventoux yesterday.' I took a photo of the Brief on the very top, next to a sign that said '1909 metres'.

In the gift-shop, I almost bought a musical didgeridoo that doubled as flame-blower for camp-fires. This place seemed to fan up madness. It had hit more than Tommy Simpson.

The very idea of having a finish on the summit is crazy. To see every tiny inch of space crammed with the Technical Zone machinery and people is a wonder. All in a day's work for this crew. The first winner on Ventoux was Charley Gaul. Charley was from Luxembourg, not noted for its mountains. Perhaps it was the unknown that caused Charley to froth at the mouth when racing. He won the whole race that year. Apart from the froth, Charley was loved by the ladies. He was getting 609 letters a day that year. His team-mate, Marcel Enzer, on reading the outrageous ones, swore he would never marry. Charley liked his nickname, 'Angel of the Mountains' but the crowd went for 'Monsieur Pi-Pi'. He'd stopped for a piss in the Giro when his rivals took off without him. It didn't happen to him again. He perfected pissing from the saddle on the move. Where the '50s blurred into the '60s, Charley Gaul was a great rider. He had the rare ability to leave other greats, like Bobet, for dead. He stood out from the crowd. And so it should be. His inability to mix with le peloton, to show some emotion, came through after he quit. He ran a bar back home, briefly. He identified with Jean-Paul Sartre; 'Hell is other people.' He did a Harry Roberts, living in the woods as a fat recluse with a grey beard. He traded in his wife for Pock: a dog. No phone, no electricity, no running water. It took him twenty-five years to re-surface but he joined the ageing stars at the Centenary Tour. I spotted him there, looking stunned at civilisation. I shook his hand.

I wanted to ask him, 'Where did it all go wrong, Charley?' I felt sure he'd answer, 'Mont fuckin' Ventoux.'

The north side down to Carpentras is short and sharp. Bikes were wingin' past me like bats. I was watchin' my rear mirror as much as the windscreen. A lot of these active day-trippers were met at the bottom by their courier and a bus with soft seats. Then whisked off to the next day's stage to become spectators. The US contingent were paying thousands of dollars for the deluxe tourist treatment. Some, like Trek, Armstrong's bike company, threw in guaranteed ring-side seats for their punters. The holiday was accompanied by name guides, ex-champs such as LeMond and Roche. Hey, way to travel, boy!

This was the stretch of downhill that had seen Ferdy's last Tour. Ferdy Kubler had won Le Tour in '50, come second in '54. He was top drawer. He was Swiss, so you'd reckon he'd know how to treat a mountain. The following year was his first time on the Ventoux. It is a freak. He was warned that it wasn't 'a mountain like any other'. Now Ferdy Kubler always spoke of himself in the third person, just like B.B. King and Roy Orbison. Never 'I'. Must be the mark of greatness. He replied, 'Ferdy also racer not like others.'

He took off like a man berserk. Soon, he was a 'bobbin'n'weavin' across the road, gurning like a village idiot and foaming at the mouth. His manager, Alex Burtin, urged him to take it easy. Red rag to a bull. Ferdy swore at him. He crashed a couple of times on his mad flying descent. As the road levelled out towards Avignon, he stopped at a bar for a cold livener or two. He got back on his bike and pedalled off in the wrong direction; some bloke pointed out to him that was the way he'd come.

'Stand back,' Kubler shouted. 'Ferdy's gonna explode.'

That night, he packed it in. He never rode in another Tour.

He commented, 'He is too old, Ferdy, he is too sick: Ferdy killed himself on the Ventoux.'

Crossing the baking plain back to the hotel, the Brief pointed. The sign said 'Chocolatier'. I swerved up a dusty farm track, across dry fields, pulling up in front of a modern bland bungalow. There were a couple of cheap plastic table, chair and parasol sets from the garden centre plonked outside. The icy blast of air-conditioning, turned all the way up to 11, dried our sweat in an instant. The Brief beamed. 'Aladdin's Cave,' he said. Chilled tiers of the most beautiful hand-made chocolates were displayed behind glass, like in a jeweller's. Hand-written calligraphy indicated flavours of the region, of the globe. This was the Asprey's of the confectionery world. A young man delicately spread his arms across his art. I was gobsmacked. Chocolate melts. Here we were on the hottest, quietest back road in France. We carried cornets of hand-made chocolate ice-cream out into the wall of heat. I ate mine very quickly. The brochure on the table told the tale. This chocolatier artisan made his sweeties for top restaurants and hotels, lifted outta here under cover of cool darkness by refrigerated vans. Pure madness. It was a great find.

I rescued Earl from the hotel pool. He'd turned a shade of cooked lobster. He winced as I slapped his back. He seemed relieved to escape his conversation with a young American couple. 'Oh, wow, the Tour de France is comin' near here? Can we get to see Lance Armstrong?' was the nub of it. Earl was shocked that anyone could travel so far and be so thick. We finished the rest day with a game of crazy golf. It was the most perfect course I've ever played on. It was built into the citadel walls, of the same stone. The hoops, ponds, mini-suspension bridges had the precision of a postgraduate civil engineer. The layout was intricate, obsessive. I told the owner how brilliant the concept and execution were. He swept each hole with a broom between each player. He took my praise with a serious manic gleam. I felt relieved that the Brief was nearby, with his wealth of experience.

Chapter 8

Twenty-four hours before the big set piece, everything was unravelling nicely. I stood alone, high on a hill-side, gazing down on chaos. I felt glad to be there. The Greatest Show on Earth had hit town with a vengeance. The operation had been comin' apart at the seams all day. It had grown too big for its roots. Tomorrow, across the Val d'Isère, there would be the individual time-trial at l'Alpe d'Huez. That would shake out the winners for sure. Monstrous crowds were predicted. It didn't bode well for this alpine warm-up.

The day had got off to a disastrous start. 'La Riste d'Aubergine Jean Martin' had been tepid. It was a stew, dish of the day, in Le Village at Valréas. The routine was re-established. A read of the papers over a spot of late breakfast, watching the riders flit like butterflies around the local Rotary Club. More mystic chefs, but they fucked up their slimy aubergines. Perhaps the strong ancient papal vibe of the town messed with their ju-ju. It felt wonderful to be back on track in the members' enclosure. The security men on the gate shook hands. Their tans were deeper. Their 'bonjour' turned to 'salut' in camaraderie. The super-models masquerading as Crédit Lyonnais receptionists smiled more sincerely. Journalists said hello to each other. The crowd outside the fence was cheering each and every rider as he stepped up to take the pledge at the signing in. The mood was of serious intent. Watching the faces, I was reminded of the beginning and end of the film, *Cabaret*. The distorted mirror, orchestra playing '30s sleazy Berlin music, blurred colours, Joel Gray as MC, converts to Nazi arm-bands and swastikas.

You hardly realise how the numbers in the audience have swelled. Here, it was Americans. There were a lot. The old square was heavin'. It was a slow and difficult walk back to the motor. I recognised the neck-flap.

'How ya doin', Montana?'

He swivelled. 'All right.'

He didn't recognise me. Car-parks emptied at speed, following the Big Book's instructions and matching arrows. Little children waved their new giant green PMU hands, so amusing when you first see them. Cops whistled us out of town, pronto. It's the feeling of the getaway driver. Stop. A small matter. A two-hour-long traffic jam outside town. There was only one road out. It was carrying more traffic than it saw on any other day of the year. Impatient, angry traffic. Some bright spark at the Council Roads Department had ordered major road works. With one-way traffic lights, tipper trucks, JCBs, the lot. The France TV2 cars tried the hard shoulder. Banks of gravel forced them back. The rest of us sweated'n'snarled. The Brief pulled out the squirrel bag. 'Cashews, anyone?'

We nibbled our way onto the autoroute. Earl started motoring. Everyone was hittin' 100 mph plus. It was like the Charge of the Light Brigade. Eyes on watches, signs for Grenoble. I lounged on the back seat, enjoying the views of the mountains. Le Tour de France does get you out'n'about, to appreciate the richness of the country, whether you're privileged or punter, full-time or weekender. You can just pick your spot, your special moment.

'I wonder if we'll see the Mentor,' I said.

The Brief looked over and nodded. 'L'Alpe d'Huez was his spot.'

We chewed over the memory of 2003. It was fresh, painful and near here.

It is a rare and beautiful thing, to see a man lose the plot completely. The day had got off to a flying start. Breakfast is the ugliest of meals. Puffy sleep-bloated faces, phlegm-filled grunts, eyes down to the tablecloth, shovelling food in gobs like farmyard animals. The Mentor loved breakfast best of all. Carbohydrates. As soon as he'd crawled outta bed and had a piss, he stumbled down the hotel stairs. He strapped into his dining place. Without further ado, he was off. Demolishing a pyramid of warm rolls, croissants, bread. Two-handed action in a blur. Crumbs were everywhere, notably in the huge grey bush of his beard. While his mouth was full, he would wash it away like his sins depended on it, with great bowlfuls of weak milky coffee, the colour of the gutter. Even as the liquid dribbled outta the sides of his mouth, like a fully satisfied breast-fed baby, he would cram in another fistful of warm starch. He shoved his chair away, rising on his spindly legs.

'Let's go,' he said. 'Blood-sugar level is satisfied.'

I was mesmerised, still gluggin' onna pint of espresso. The Brief sat to the side, tasting small spoonfuls of fromage blanc. It was still dark outside. I could just make out the looming shapes of big mountains. We'd travelled wearily over 'em the evening before. Stuck in a police road-block, high on the Col du Galibier, the Mentor waited patiently in line. I had raged. We had got through by pointing to our 'Access All Areas' pass. The Mentor had objected to such elitist treatment. Without it, we would still have been on the wrong side of the hill from Le Tour. Our hotel was in a small village. Madame was young and pretty. The Mentor gave his only grizzled gap-tooth leer of a smile of the day. She had served breakfast at this ungodly hour as a favour. There were two others, English cyclists from County Durham, Andrew and Michael, discussing cog-sizes and braking power. They yakked on technologically, regarding us as lightweights.

This was their day to match the pros. It was our day to get high. The Mentor was revving the engine, shoutin', 'C'mon, c'mon' outta the car window. The Brief was packing a considerable squirrel bag for his day. Breads, cakes, biscuits, nuts, fruits, an assortment of goat cheeses. He had ejected the Swiss chocolate after the early weather forecast had told of unbroken alpine sunshine. He was carrying a lot of mineral water.

'There'll be plenty of mountain streams,' said the Mentor.

The Brief did not reply. He continued to check his waterproof, sun-cream, camera, binoculars and maps.

'You need a bleedin' Sherpa,' I said.

'Survival is preparation,' he replied.

The Mentor put an apple and a small water bottle in the pocket of his safari shirt. I had fuck all. We headed west, sunrise in the rear mirror.

The plan was, hey, everybody, do your own thing. The Brief was clear what he wanted. To stride up the Col du Galibier and watch the race come over the top at its highest point, at 2,645 metres. He had his perfect spot chosen, on the first hairpin just below the summit. It would take him a few hours of puffin'n'blowin. He was on his own, but he knew the score. He claimed the Galibier as his main source of inspiration on the planet. So had Henri Desgranges. When he'd first sent Le Tour this way in 1911, he'd let it all hang out:

'Oh Sappey, Oh Laffrey, Oh Col Bayard, Oh Tourmalet! I will not shirk from my duty in proclaiming that beside the Galibier you are nothing but pale babies; in front of this giant we can do nothing but take off our hats and bow.' I noticed the Brief had his large-brimmed Mediterranean straw hat on the seat beside him. Desgranges' ode continued:

'Today, my brothers, we gather here in common

celebration of the divine bicycle. Not only do we owe it our most pious gratitude for the precious and ineffable love that is given us, but also for the host of memories sown over our whole sports life and which today has made concrete. In my own case, I love it for having taken my heart within its spokes, for having encircled a part of my life in its harmonious frame, and for having constantly illuminated me with the victorious sparkle of its nickel plates. In the history of humanity, does it not constitute the first successful effort of intelligent life to triumph over the laws of weights?'

I asked the Brief, 'Is that what you reckon?'

'Sort of,' he said.

I couldn't hear the Pork Butcher waxing so eloquent. How right that the Desgranges obelisk was at the Galibier, erected a week before I was born in 1949.

We parked up on the watershed of the Col du Lauteret. It was busy, even at this early hour. The glaciers shone and sparkled above us on Les Ecrins. A file of fans, hikers'n'bikers, were settin' out on the 2,000 foot haul up the Galibier. The Brief unloaded himself.

'Have either of you changed your mind?' he asked.

Not a chance in hell. My lungs were shot. Thirty Lucky Strikes a day and a recent dose of pneumonia have put paid to hill-walking for now. I intended to wheel it all the way to the finish line. If I could prise the keys to his family hatchback from the Mentor's grip. His plan was to be dropped at the foot of Alpe d'Huez. He wanted to stroll the course with the revellers. To pick a spot on the mountainside and observe closely the trials and tribulations on the profiles. He wanted to be anchored like a human TV camera, yet float like a bird above it all. Good for him. He was my Mentor.

'You're fuckin' mad,' I told him.

'We must remain in communication,' said the Brief. 'Let

me show you how to work your mobile phone. Did you charge it up last night?'

The Mentor's wife had given him a brand new mobile. It was still in its box.

'Not necessary,' he said.

His plan was to step it down to the main-road in the evening. He'd hitch a ride the 30 miles back to the hotel. It would be a doddle. Any of the expected 300,000 fans would be happy to give him a lift. The Brief shook his head and said, 'Ring mine if there's a problem.' Off he went. I was envious. It was the most amazing setting on a perfect day to witness sporting drama of Herculean proportions. Endurance and self-preservation are what it's about. We drove on down the valley, double-flanked with camper vans. The residents, German, Dutch, Belgian, were greeting the day groggily. They waddled as if full of farts, breakfasts in hand. An occasional wave at our official sticker. We were a forerunner of the event. No cops yet to seal off the road. I took in the white plumes of the Cascade de la Pisse, a thousand-foot freefall, and the Sant de la Pucette. Bikes were slowin' us down through La Grave. This was a serious matter.

'Are you sure about doing this on your own?' I asked, looking at his battered sandals. The Mentor barked, 'Stop fussing,' at me.

I did. He had mentored me for some thirty years, marking my academic card, filling me up with information from Hindu gods'n'Tibetan deities to modern conspiracy theories. He was a master of objectivity and professional success. He was always right. His musical radicalism seemed to have ground to a halt around the time of Ray Charles and Charlie Parker. We travelled in silence.

'If I spot the car at the end, I'll tap on the roof,' he said.

It seemed optimistic, but who was I to argue? Anyway,

he was fluent in French.

'What can possibly go wrong? I'll borrow a phone and ring you up at the press centre, if I need to, which I can't see,' he said.

We crossed the lake via a dam and pulled up. The crowds were massive, in jaunty colours, hats, with flags, banners. Everyone seemed to have rucksacks, bags and boots except the Mentor. He climbed slowly out of the driving seat.

'This is a day in which people will help each other,' he prophesied.

He seemed imbued with the spirit of Woodstock. Looked it too. I was thinking more Altamont. And then, he was gone, swallowed up in the mass. An American woman stuck her head through the window.

'Could you give me a lift to the top?'

'Sure, honey, where ya from?'

'Lawrence, Kansas.'

'Ah, the home of the great William Burroughs.'

'I believe there is a well known poet lives there,' she replied.

I left it at that, fearing a journey into further Dark Stuff. Burroughs made it to old age through a life of adventure, danger, endless curiosity and extreme drug intake. He was very good at self-preservation. The Mentor had a full knowledge of old Bill. In his academic career, he had accumulated huge amounts of interesting information. It made him good company at a dinner party, in the common-room or the front seat of the car. Trouble is, I wasn't convinced that he had translated it into practice in his own life.

At the end of the day, I was hot, bothered but elated by the race. I'd waited around the finish, watching the exhausted riders collapse into the arms of their minders. The heat was so great I'd had to keep dodging back into the air-conditioned relief of the press centre. I'd rehydrated in front of the TV screens, scanning the crowds for my mates. Closing time found me stuck in an elite traffic jam in the ski resort. Way down in the valley, I could see blue flashing lights, hear wailing sirens. A Swiss journo leaned into the motor.

'There's an accident down below. The cops are taking us off on the side service road.'

A long circular detour via a tiny back road brought me to the morning's starting point. The roads were jammed. I inched homeward along the valley floor. Three hours and 20 miles later, I crested the Lauteret and pulled over. An English voice shouted my name. The Brief was precisely where he'd said he'd be. His face was flushed with the sun and success.

'How was that?' I asked.

'The day lived up to every expectation,' he said. It showed. 'Any sign of the Mentor?' he asked.

'Nothing. In a third of a million people, I'm not surprised. He'll get back under his own steam. He was very insistent.'

We ate late near the hotel. The Brief was enjoying 'magret' after his long, strenuous day. I was tucking into my gratin dauphinoise, when his phone rang. He listened and put the mobile on the table without speaking.

'The Mentor said for you to pick him up.'

'What, now? It's eleven. It'll take hours to get back there. Where exactly is he?'

'He didn't say. He didn't give me a chance to ask. It was an order to you.'

'Fuck that,' I said.

Another round trip would do me in, take most of the night. With the Brief's logical guidance, we chewed over the pros and cons. An emergency rescue mission was out of the question. Our own survival was at stake. This was an endurance event. Rest was vital for recuperation. We figured the Mentor could bag a bed for the night in some nearby hotel, even a couch in a lobby. He spoke French. He had a pass. As we parted for bed, at midnight under moonlight, we did wonder what he'd been doing with himself all that time.

The Mentor rang at six in the morning.

'Where are you?' he croaked. He sounded rough.

'At the hotel. You'll have to sit tight,' I replied.

It was Groundhog Day all the way. The drive along the beautiful valley was a bore. I'd done it too often in the last twenty-four hours. The Brief and I had speculated all along the road. What could have happened to the Mentor?

'There he is,' shouted the Brief.

He was leaning against the same telephone box where I'd dropped him. He looked even worse than usual. His jaw sagged, his face puffy, with bloodshot eyes. His bedraggled long grey beard, so proudly academic yesterday, now gave him the look of a mad tramp. 'No one would give me a lift,' he wailed.

I could understand strangers recoiling from his manic advances. Even I didn't want him in the motor. He'd been on the open mountainside all night with heat-stroke. No hat, no water, no chance. He collapsed into the back seat of his own car, a first-time experience for him. There he lay, inert, groaning, all day. At last, at the next hotel, a charmless ski motel, he was decamped into his room. The Mentor took to his bed immediately. He was full of cold drinks and recrimination. He lay hirsute and naked.

'Just like Jesus,' said the Brief quietly.

'How could you leave me? Why didn't you come for me? You bastards.'

My explanations fell on deaf ears. He wasn't having it. The blame was on me, for not dropping everything in his hour of need. His alpha-male bullish independence of the previous day was forgotten, replaced by a pathetic self-righteous whingeing. I left him to it. I could hear the groans right along the corridor.

One year later, neither the Brief nor I knew the story. The Mentor had limped back to his wife, a broken resentful figure. Another road casualty, unlucky or inept. He had never explained. So savage ju-ju had caught up with him on Alpe d'Huez. Now we were due back there on the morrow. But first, a warm-up sideshow on the heights of the Vercors on the far side of Grenoble. The Big Book said take junction 13 off the motorway. As with the Bible, there was no point in interpreting the words. Literal or nothing. After 12 came 14.

'What shall I do?' asked Earl at the wheel.

I roared obscenities from the back seat.

The Brief said calmly, 'Take it.'

There were, increasingly, times that the written route seemed to have come from a computer. It seemed logical but didn't match up to the vagaries on the ground. Maybe this was like the numerical ju-ju of American hotels and lifts. Number 13 doesn't exist, so it can't bring bad luck. The error meant that a line of Tour cars was drivin' up'n'down the side carriageway. We were stuck'n'late. Lots of us. A bridge took us over the river. The convoy sped up a gorge that tourists must linger in and onto an alpine plateau of meadows and wild-flowers under limestone peaks. I was looking at my watch. Time was tight. The finish was charted on the far side of Villard-de-Lans. The traffic stopped dead. Nothing moved. Everyone got out, pacing urgently along the road. I could see where our road joined the race road, across the fields. The blue lights of the gendarme outriders would be along soon. It was a first real inch-by-inch, all through the pretty town, bunting and floral arrangements on a bicycle theme. Punters were delighted to examine the occupants of every motor. I was looking for Foghorn Leghorn. He said he'd be here. Somehow, it seemed flippant. Holidaying spectators were laughing. Pass-wearers were grit-teethed. Unless the last couple of miles were cleared real quick, le peloton wouldn't get through. Every day, we had soared through the barrier-protected road like avenging angels until we were whisked aside at the last minute, a few hundred yards from the line. Now, it was like the M25 on a Friday night. Smoke'n'fumes came from the front of Black Magic. Bystanders pointed.

'Yeah, yeah, it's diesel,' I muttered back.

All I needed was a burned-out clutch. I could feel the bile of panic rising in my throat. ASO officials were running up'n'down the line of cars, waving arms. Cops were frantically blowing whistles. Senior officials appeared alongside shouting, 'Allez! Allez!' OK, but where to? There was a car inches in front and one beyond that. A static line. A catastrophe was about to happen. After six urgent hours in the saddle, Le Tour de France was not gonna reach the line. I was horrified. So was every insider face around me. One of the great delights of Le Tour is the way that what seems to be a messy shambles can suddenly come right at the last minute. A silent click o' the fingers had always brought order outta chaos. It was one of the event's impressive yet inexplicable traits. I never tired of watchin' it come good. But this was a step too far. I could see no way out. The race gets bigger every year. More people follow it. More work in and around. Yet Le Tour stays true to its roots. It insists on visiting the small, the beautiful, the dramatic. This time, too many vehicles had hit not enough space. Yet I felt a contradictory delight that I was here to witness the past collide with the future. As if by magic, the sweetly contorting face of Jean-Louis Pagès was alongside my window. Looking elegantly casual, his manner was manic. His entire body urged me forward. I let out the dodgy clutch. He shouted me on. He puffed his cheeks until his eyeballs stood out. The line of cars dribbled onto a left-hand turn. His arms were like windmills, blowing the route clear. I could feel the momentum of his will. It worked. I parked high above the course, a zig-zag one-lane. Having got clear, we all pulled our keys outta the ignition and left 'em where they were. Most ran hell for leather down the line. I stood still, throbbin'. The Brief and Earl had jumped out earlier, rats off a sinking ship. And the blue lights came through, far below. An old man holding a dog offered me his binoculars. He tapped my pass.

'You need 'em,' he said.

He was right. Although I was curiously relaxed and detached, the desperate intensity of the day was still rockin' the race. Lance Armstrong roared round the last coupla bends as a man possessed. He spat out his rivals. His power vibrated right up the hill-side to where I stood. The old Frenchman smiled at me, nodding his head. I think I had been shoutin'. As the tiny cyclists wobbled in for lesser places, I walked down past hastily abandoned cars. It was like Godard's movie, *Weekend*. Some drivers arguing, most didn't give a shit. I stopped a man.

'Can I use your mobile? I need to find my friends,' I said.

'Fuck off,' he snarled.

I smiled. It does make things come alive when people are losing it all around.

I found Earl on a grassy knoll near the finish line. He was ecstatic.

'A proper race, at long last,' he said.

'Yeah, touch'n'go,' I said.

In the bus-park, team RAGT were sitting on the gravel with their cleated shoes off. They were knackered, slugging water, chewin' slabs of cold pizza. Desperate to find enough energy to stand upright. One rider was having his legs massaged. The public stood by them, starin' as if it was a road accident. Ain't no luxury or privacy for the small teams. This was survival. It wasn't graceful. It wasn't pretty.

It took several hours longer to cut across town and find the hotel. It seemed that everything that day, except the magnificently driven Armstrong and the beautifully manic M. Pagès, had imploded. It somehow seemed appropriate up here on the Vercors. The place had a dark past.

During the last war, this massif had been a hotbed of resistance activity. It was astride the main corridors for German troop movement. The 'Maquis' made the Vercors a stronghold. In July 1944, bang on sixty years ago, the Allies encouraged the resistance to come out in a show of arms. The idea was to take the German eye off the Mediterranean coastal landings. They were promised Allied support. It never arrived, but the Nazis did. They sent in loads, by parachute and glider. They meant business. Anyone suspected of resistance leanings was rounded up and killed. Even doctors and nurses. Women and children. Over 700 died. The graves and memorials were obvious; the bitter resentment less so.

We dined late. The only spare table in town was mugged up for us in a back room of the hotel. Shades of the TV boys, way back in Maubeuge, being screened away from the nice restaurant. There was no menu. We ate 'Madame's plaisir'. I was wondering if, on the morrow, Le Tour would be able to cope. Speculation had always been that the Individual Time-Trial would decide the whole caboodle. A million people were expected. Three times what I'd seen last year. That is a fuck of a lot of people with fuck-all resources. I don't know how many people go to Michael Eavis's Glastonbury shindig. I do know they have toilets. They've also got twig-tea, falafel stalls, shade and first-aid tents. On the 9 miles of Alpe'd'Huez, there's bugger all unless you carry it. Don't take my word for it. Ask the Mentor.

Traditionally, Alpe d'Huez has been the Dutch mountain. They've bagged it. Like the British did with Everest up to 1953. It's a tough one to figure out. Maybe opposites attract. Flatlanders need some relief. Maybe their eight wins did it, starting in '76 with the splendidly named Joop Zoetemelk. There would be plenty of Hollish up the slope. Orange is the colour; silly hats is the game. Shouting 'Hup-Hup-Hup Holland' strikes me as weird. There had been a large placement of American forces chanting 'Lance, Lance, Lance' as he powered home in Villard. Earl had hated it, football fanatic that he is. Said he wanted to shoot 'em from his grassy knoll. Said they were charmless, nationalist, styleless, blinkered, celebrity-driven, lumpy lunkheads. Actually, he just said 'Fuckers.' The US presence had grown to huge proportions. Alpe d'Huez would be the coronation. It was a good job that Holland is a nation of hippies. It might've been war up there, a conflict of national sensibilities. I'm not averse to a spot of violence. It livens up a good argument. Trouble is, hippies fall on the floor'n'curl up into a foetal ball. Kinda spoils the fun.

Chapter 9

I was tired, I was weary, but I didn't wish to sleep. I was elated. Driving along the Grenoble ring road in the early morning light. Big peaks all around. One of 'em, across the valley, was Alpe d'Huez. Even at that time, it was real busy. Earl had stuck Chas'n'Dave' on the speakers. I love drivin'. Black Magic purred. This felt like another Neal Cassady moment. One elbow out the window, lazy hand on top of the wheel, head swivellin', spare foot tappin'. Neal was the riskiest, most exciting and greatest driver of all time. It didn't matter that he'd dropped dead by the side of the railroad tracks in Mexico. It is not, 'He was only forty-six'; it is, 'Just reckon up what a life he crammed into forty-six years.' Kerouac knew and loved those fizzin', poppin', burstin' fireworks. He'd've dug the miles, the movin' on, the adrenaline rush of Le Tour de France.

That was until we hit the road-block at Bourg d'Oisans, Le Départ. I had decided to get on up that mountain as soon as I could. After what I'd seen yesterday, it was well possible that ASO would shut the road down under the sheer weight of numbers. Sure, they needed the press up top. The timid and the pragmatic would have been in place last night. Then again, a lot of these punters stick their camper-vans on the prestigious verges a week ahead of the race. The cops on the main road-block were having none of my sticker. Everything was being shunted through the little town. It had the hallmark of an over-the-top draconian response to the previous day's snarl-up. I followed a Belgian TV van along a pot-holed dirt track round the back of Bourg. Things looked grimmer when the road was barriered off. The newly created pedestrian zone looked like a cross between Cup Final Day and Harrods' Sale.

I moved the barrier, leaned on the horn and adopted an expression that said, 'I don't give a fuck if I break your fuckin' legs.'

Not for the coppers, though. They got the 'There's been a terrible mistake and I find myself on the wrong road. I am urgently required on official business at Le Tour HQ on the summit.'

It worked, but it took quite a while. Chas'n'Dave chugged on, lifted our edgy spirits with their music-hall rock. Just so English, but, for us, in no way nationalistic. Who gave a flying fuck about national identity? So David Millar ain't representing us? So what? What's so special about frontiers? The well-heeled sports tourists from the USA — the road was boilin' over with 'em, the flag everywhere. There were other flags, but the peoples mingled. The Yanks stood apart, in big clusters. They were here to see their man, Lance, win the race. The rest of us were here to see the race. More than that, to be part of the event. The twenty-one hairpins of Alpe d'Huez are stacked up like the tiers on a wedding cake. It makes for great viewing. The crowds fill the road, only parting right at the last moment, like the Red Sea did for Moses. It's almost as miraculous. The riders brush against fans. Some are given a helpin' shove. Riders end up with bruised backs. It's against the rules, but who's countin'? Water is poured over 'em to cool 'em down. The classic French stance in this proximity is knees bent, arms out pumpin' upwards from the elbow, faces gurnin' like a Somerset yokel. The Brief did an excellent imitation, shouting them on, 'Allez! Allez!'

It's a great and rare chance to pat and cheer your hero in action. The other side of the coin is malevolent.

Armstrong was spat at later in the day, sworn at as he ascended to his heaven. He'd taken the precaution of having armed police on motorbikes front'n'rear. It didn't stop the gobbin' from the many who resented his tunnel-visioned taking of the crown and the arrogant isolationism of his supporters' club. America loves winners and these American supporters had only come to see Lance win. They had minimal interest in the wider event. Maybe the cops stopped an al-Qaeda hit-man, though, over the thousands of miles, I could've come up with a location where he would've been more vulnerable and provided a clearer target. At the end of the day, Armstrong spoke firmly about the need to protect riders. He stated that ASO should seriously consider fencing off the full 9 miles. He added that spectators were interfering with the athletes' effort by being so close. I wish I'd spat at him now. He misses the fucking point. It ain't just a contest between fit young men on bicycles. It never was. The chaotic inferno of the course is a vital part of the contest. Stuff happens. It is a mountain that produces remarkable and unforeseen results.

In 1999, Beppe Guerini, an Italian, was in the lead when Eric, a nineteen-year-old spectator, stood in the road to take a photo. Now, riders are used to punters leapin' out the way at the last second. Eric, looking through his distorted viewfinder, misjudged the distance and timing. Guerini hit him and fell off his bike. He got back on and won. Eric melted into the crowd but had the bottle and honour to show up at Beppe's hotel to say sorry. Same thing happened with a gendarme and a camera and a rider on the Champs Elysées. André Darrigade killed a man in 1959. A security bloke stepped out on the track. Heads cracked.

But, hey, that's what makes it. The crazies are all that is remembered. In the Athens Olympics, a wild Irish rover in a plaid kilt, green waistcoat and beret joined in the Marathon. He ran'n'grabbed the leader, the Brazilian Vanderlei de Lima. Bundled him into the crowd. The athlete didn't know what had hit him. The madman was promoting the Bible. It's my strongest memory of that Games.

No one's saying, 'Let's run the marathon in a 26-mile glass tube. That'll stop hooligan intervention.'

It works the other way too. Vehicles charging through, hit and clip the fans who play matador. A little boy was killed by the Caravan in Draguignan in 2000. In '64, a helicopter assistance van ploughed into the crowd at Porte-de-Couze, killing eight. Hey, everyone knows the score. The intimacy is the deal. So is the danger. It's attractive. If it bothers you, stay home in front of the telly in your slippers. It obviously bothered Armstrong this year. He said it was getting dangerous. What was he thinking? The Brief also expressed relief as we drove into the final, protected stretch of road. He was feeling hemmed in by the thousands of touristes-routiers. The entire way had been solid with amateur cyclists. It made driving a precarious matter as they weaved'n'wobbled in exhaustion'n'pain. This stage in particular is about pain. It ain't no excursion on a bike. It is a Festival of Pain. There is no better close-up view of self-flagellation outside Iran than this. And no finer way to celebrate it than to dress up. I saw a man in a Nazi SS officer's tunic top with stockings and suspenders, drinking cheap Chardonnay with a nun. There were Disney and Looney Toons characters, though sadly no Foghorn Leghorn. The costume hire shops had done a roarin' trade. So had the paint shops. The tarmac from top to bottom was one giant canvas. Individuals right across le peloton got a name-check. From an Anglo-Saxon point of view, there was a distinct lack of painted foul-mouthed swear words.

I missed 'em. My favourite was a big spliff with the declaimer, 'Bloody Hippies'. I thoroughly approved.

There was a white van parked on one of the hairpins; on the side was painted 'Ciao Marco'. The simplicity of the farewell was moving. This was his spot. This was where Marco Pantani had made his finest mark. He'd won it in 1995. In '97 he went like a bat outta hell. He creamed off all-comers, setting the record at 37 minutes 35 seconds. He liked to throw down his bandanna at the first hairpin, like a gauntlet. It was a hard act to follow, for him too. After his death, I checked out his website. A cartoon of Marco in yellow Pirate King garb. He pedals up the dark mountain, lighting up the grey ridge. On reaching the summit, he keeps going, into the air, across the sky to a great yellow ball of a sun. He melts into its heat. It's a great tribute. The music is sombre synthesiser, muted'n'velvet. It's hands clasped, eyes down in the chapel. Reverential. It's poor Marco, abandoned in his lonely hotel room. It should've been rockin'. So Pantani got burned out. That's the name of the game. Heads up for the triumphs that he achieved. He lifted me and others. Live fast, die young. He was an inspiration. Anyone who pushes it that far is takin' some big chance. After being outta sight, the difficulty is returning to ordinariness. Marco was the best. Like Charley Gaul becoming a hermit, Marco Pantani didn't fit into normal daily life. It's not that people like him are trying to kill themselves, it's that they have a disregard for death. It don't matter. It's like the old tale of 'Blackbeard', Edward Teach, the eighteenth-century pirate. He liked to impress. He stuck lighted matches in his great beard and hat for furious effect. One time, drunk at sea, he suggested to his crew that 'We make a hell of our own, and try how long we can bear it.'

He and three others went down into the hold and closed the hatches. They filled several pots of brimstone and set 'em on fire. Blackbeard refused to open the hatches, suffocatin' them. He was 'not a little pleased' that he held out the longest. This is Keith Richards territory. There are high stakes being played for. Marco was looking to replace the buzz of being the best. Closing the hotel door, barricading the world out, is a fair option. Especially when, like Lenny Bruce and Jim Morrison, the hounds of the law have been set loose on you. Choosing cocaine as a best friend makes a certain sense. Losing your life, or even your mind, is just a risk. Riding Le Tour de France, especially aimin' to win, is a big risk.

Lance Armstrong did it in 2001 by trickery. Again, here on Alpe d'Huez he out-smarted his main rival, Jan Ullrich. Armstrong had trailed all day up'n'down the cols. He was looking in bad shape, suffering. As the two approached the first hairpin at the base of the Alpe, Armstrong levelled alongside Ullrich's shoulder. He turned to the German and gave him a serious eyeballing, then, Boof! Lance accelerated away like a fuckin' rocket. I was clockin' it on the box. I roared out loud. I was alone in the room. I couldn't believe what I had just witnessed. Out-psyched. It turned out that Armstrong's celebrity friend, comic actor Robin Williams, was in the passenger seat of the US Postal team car. He had been coaching Lance into the fooling role. Puttin' on the agony. There is a lot more work than pushing pedals. So much of success is in the head. Jan's brain was badly damaged that day. There are those who say he never recovered.

I was pissed off at missing the ju-ju stones. Stuck under one of the top hairpin bends are two black volcanic rocks. They are gifts from Colombia to mark that country's links with Le Tour de France. For what reason? Good ju-ju, like my blue pocket stone, I guess. They can't even be easily seen. But I felt their presence, as I swung round their bend, unable to stop in the gagging crowds. Obviously, the tragic fate of the Mentor was decided by his not having staggered that far. I tried to scan the mass of people for a sight of his beard. I figured he might just be stupid enough to return to the scene of his crime. Maybe to put things right in his own head. To convince himself that he was a hero, not a silly arse who'd confused business with pleasure. Getting round is what Le Tour is about. Anyone at all who makes it back to Paris is a Hero. The rest are Beautiful Losers. It was disturbing to read in the paper the next day that a body had been found. It was in a ravine high up and just next to Alpe d'Huez. The unidentified body was that of a man in his late fifties. The victim had tried to avoid the packed exit after the race by going across country. He must have slipped and fallen. He had died from injuries and exposure. Oh dear! This fitted the Mentor's modus operandi. Just the kinda blusterin' foolhardy stunt he might pull. He was a man, who after rollin'n'totallin' his motor, had declined a police lift back to his country home. Instead, he walked 10 miles over the hills 'to clear his head'.

'Concussion? What're you talkin' about?'

He'd got lost. After dark, his missus had called out a police search for him. He arrived home in the middle of the night. His wife wouldn't let him in for being so foolish. It took another day for a name to emerge for the dead man. It wasn't the Mentor.

I left Black Magic in the press car-park, over-heated. I'd taken four times as long as a man on a bike to slog up the hill; it was that busy. The clutch was slipping from too much heel'n'toein'. The trip was taking its toll.

Alpe d'Huez is ugly, very modern and functional. It bears something in common with the city of Hull. It's the end of the line. Folk don't go there unless they have to. The architecture is postmodern chalet. It doesn't matter. In Skisville, the days are short, the nights are long. Winter stuff. Buildings are for being warm inside. To congregate après-ski, mulling over a jug of wine. The stores are hire shops, alpine gear shops. Boots of Italian leather, the softest fleeces, the daftest hats, snow-proof one-piece overalls of fluorescent attraction. You need never be lost in a white-out avalanche. The souvenir shops were dear. Cow bells, thimbles, ornamental plates, digital thermometers. Your mantelpiece need never look empty. Crap T-shirts that cost an arm'n'a leg. I guess skiers have a few bob. The beckonin' boards outside the rows of cafés offered microwaved Savoy specialities. All-day full English breakfast was missing. This didn't seem to be a 'Brit resort'. Alpe d'Huez didn't seem to be a summer resort. There was an air of desperation about the joint that wobbled into resignation. A lone couple skated lazily, absorbed in themselves, on the outdoor ice-rink. Nobody seemed interested. Hardly surprising, with Le Tour de France in town.

All the action was on the main drag. The side roads were empty. Punters several deep waited patiently, leaning on the barriers along the route. The smart money had hired ringside apartments, especially if they had balconies. I watched parties starting on them, party food laid out. Early drinkers were hitting it from sun-loungers. Keen fans polished their binoculars. The best view of all was above the roofs. Layer upon layer of sharp grey granite ridges drew my eye. Snow still nestled in some of the gullies. Chair-lifts and cable-cars snaked up towards the tops. They were shut down for the day. The ski-runs themselves were marked out by poles, along the edge of bright grassed pastures, shorn of shrubs and trees. Across the deep valley that ran eastwards to the Italian border lay the massif of Les Ecrins. The jewels on that crown were huge hanging glaciers, sparkling and twinkling in the sunshine. The peaks were sharp cut-outs against the impossibly blue sky. It would be difficult to discover a more dramatic panorama for an event. When The Beatles decided to play live again after a few years off-stage, they scouted out locations. The Pyramids of Egypt were considered. Too corny'n'obvious was the reckoning. The American hippie outfit, Grateful Dead, picked up that crumb from the table some years later. A Roman amphitheatre, perfectly preserved in the Libyan desert, was favourite. It didn't happen unfortunately. The setting would have matched the magnificence of the event: the Fab Four back in the groove. They ended up, cheaply, on the Apple building roof at Savile Row. Yeah, it was good. It could've been great.

Le Tour de France does not lack vision or daring. It came to Alpe d'Huez for the first time in 1952. The owner of a couple of hotels there, Georges Rajon, offered a coupla grand for Le Tour to visit. Georgie wanted to expand. He needed to pump up trade. Jacques Goddet, the superior, was dubious. It was some risk. He sent his assistant, Elie Wermelinger, to case the place. He arrived in winter to find a rutted, pot-holed unbordered half-road/half-track. His guide's motor needed tyre-chains to reach the tiny primitive resort. There were no ski-lifts, chalets or shops. It was grim. But Elie was a visionary. What a stunning view! Either that, or old Georgie Boy gave him a stiff bunger. The man from ASO, he say, 'Yes'. The truth was that the timing was spot on. Le Tour needed harder challenges in the face of so many excellent riders. Hugo Koblet had creamed everyone in time-trials the previous year. A dirty great hill was a good shot. The majestic Fausto Coppi won that inaugural climb to seal the venue's reputation. Men on bikes, though, didn't return for almost a quarter of a century. Since '76 they've hardly missed a year. Those eight Hollish wins brought the partisan Dutch crowds. The '90s went Italian; Pantani's coups de grâce, so near his homeland. And now it is festooned in the star-spangled banner. Just like Jimi Hendrix playing in the dawn at Woodstock. In fact, the whole event is goin' down that road. A million people? For sure. America's a huge country. A lotta folk wanted to get back to the land, try'n'set their souls free. At least catch the bands on stage. Like here. There were those who came every year. It didn't matter which rider was in the lead. Being here was the deal. Joinin' together with like-minded souls. Goin' up-country to New York State was no easy matter.

Chapter 10

Bikes were being wheeled like pedigree dogs on leads. Machines at this level would set you back quite a few grand. Not for leanin' against a wall, Amsterdam-style. It struck me that these serious amateurs don't think the walkin' side of it. Modern cleated cycling shoes are wonderful, twist'n'click, for getting on and off the pedals. Brilliant in a fall to kick away from the dangerous frame. But strollin' nonchalantly around a dusty ski village, with calves like knotted hawsers, the cyclists resembled old crocked professional footballers. Or little girls in mummy's stilettos.

The racing bike came in within the memory of my generation. It's all in the handlebars. Drops with white plastic tape like puttees were impressive to secondary school me in the late '60s. They meant business around our council estate. Trouble was that business was just serious speed, just gettin' there. It was to do with puttin' your head down. Sure, the flat top could be held sittin' back in the saddle. It was OK. Flash was cow-horns. Stickin' up in the air like two fingers up at the world, cow-horns still meant fuck-you quiffed Teddy Boys. No attempt at measured performance. Arrogance above efficiency. Dad had a solid, Sturmey-Archer sit-up'n'beg bike. Mum's was solid too, but in pastel colours. No crossbar, obviously, to snag her frocks. Everyone had a bike. A car was exotic. In the mid-'50s, only Fred Field opposite our house had a bulbous navy-blue motor. The rest of us pedalled, walked or bussed.

I grew up in Gillingham, Kent. It was part of the sprawl of the Medway Towns, which included Chatham. Chatham had a big naval base and dockyard. You could hear the five o'clock hooters all across the towns. Klaxons sounded like an air-raid warning. This was the signal for the buses and the few cars on the road to pull over. Drivers turned off their engines and lit cigarettes. Out from the dockyard gates poured the army of dockyard workers, capped to a man except for nascent Teds. Most were on bicycles. They filled the main roads to Gillingham and Rochester like a swarm of locusts. Traffic lights were ignored. Right of way was assumed. Mothers shielded prams and held on to small children, away from the kerb. Actually no one in their right mind travelled at going-home time for the dockies.

Driving up Alpe d'Huez on Tour morning brought back that childhood memory. The town held little interest. The Brief beetled off, festooned with cameras around his neck like Sean Flynn in Vietnam. Earl and I practised walking like Americans. We placed our feet at 10 to 2 position, like Charlie Chaplin, pushed out our guts and waddled. Our ridicule went unobserved. I picked up a yellow 'Go Lance' banner in the shape of a table-tennis bat to get more into role. I blended even more with the patient static crowd. The amusement with pastiche was short-lived. It was time to go elite.

I walked along the course, which switch-backed through the little town to the far side. A 90-degree left-hander led to the line. The pantechnicons of the Technical Zone were wedged as tightly as ever in a triangle alongside. A narrow fenced dirt-track separated the zone from the helicopter landing field. Beyond was wilderness. High spires of rock with sharp buttresses. Natural cathedrals. This was John Muir territory. Muir was the great American Victorian pioneer who opened up California. He was a poet and an artist who loved nature. He would take off into the Sierras with his greatcoat pockets stuffed with nuts and dry bread. His mapping out of virgin peaks and valleys lead to the founding of the first National Park. He turned Teddy Roosevelt on to Yosemite. Hiked him up to a summit. Swung his arm around him.

'Look at all this beautiful wilderness, take it in. It belongs to the people. Don't blow it ...'

He pushed it. Standing in relative safety and comfort, I could see all around me what drove John Muir on. How perfectly brilliant of Le Tour de France to bring us all up here to appreciate this wonder. The whirr of rotor-blades was incessant. The choppers were working full-tilt, ferrying guests, VIPs, vital crew members, up to the top. Later, they would evacuate the star riders, by-passing the clogged roads. More shades of Woodstock, where the bands needed urgent transfer from back-stage to distant hotels. Those early festivals had got off the ground so simply. Bring the music to the people. Do it inna lovely place. Rollin' fields. Let everyone in who wants to come. A big fuck-you to the disembodied money-making distance of Shea Stadium and Wembley. Glastonbury got in on the groove. Over time, the old bourgeois twin peaks of order and profit took charge. Michael Eavis built a security wall to rival Ariel Sharon's anti-Palestinian 'fence'. And you couldn't see the whites of the musos' eyes. The master of ceremonies at Woodstock was a ludicrous figure, name of Wavy Gravy. Like Daniel Mangeas here on Le Tour, he introduced the performers, stoked up the vibe and relayed useful information. 'Watch out for the brown acid. It's a bummer.' Useful stuff. Ten years later, on the West Coast, I ran into him. He was wearing a suit with great wings on his back. Same gig, MC-ing the Monterey Pop Festival Revisited. I was working it with The Clash. Big events need cookies like Wavy Gravy to inject random thoughts into the collective mindset.

Traditionally, unbelievers will say, 'Why Le Tour? It just flashes past you in an instant, a blur of unidentified colour, doesn't it?'

Yes it does, compared, say, to a game of cricket. Today was not like that. An Individual Time-Trial puts each man under the spotlight. Setting off solo means attention can linger on each individual, normally anonymous members of le peloton. Atoms in one body. Names on the list of runners and riders become deeply personalised tortured souls. Cycling styles can be appreciated. Faces can be studied. The name'n'number of each rider, like a prisoner, was emblazoned on the following car. Emergency wheels, sprockets, god-knows-what intricate spare gadgets were on board with a team roadie. A motorbike, lights blazing, went just in front to split the bodies on the road ahead. The running order was biblical: the last shall be first and the first shall be last. The Lanterne Rouge was hotly contested. I nipped round to the back of the pits. A flashed pass got me through the rubber-necking punters. The ASO men on the back-stage gate hardly needed to examine the laminate. As a matter of good form, as well as ease of passage, I always took the time'n'trouble to shake hands and exchange a light word. The strip of road was sparsely populated. A few journos and photographers, officials. The team minders were professional in arriving bang on time. It was easy when the race could be calculated by television in the team bus. They were needed. Going full tilt up that unrelenting gradient, with no chance of coastin' for a second, meant that plenty of riders needed a strong pair of roadie arms to hold 'em up at the end. There was a lotta fluid needed replacing from the rehydration roadies. Each got his specialised treatment, away from the daily pack.

Joly was my man. He had been fighting it out tooth'n'nail for days for the coveted position of last.

Jimmy Casper was giving Sebastian Joly a ding-dong battle. They went off the ramp at two o'clock. The big boys wouldn't stick their cleats into the pedals until five o'clock. Three hours of non-stop action. The gap between riders is one minute. Ding-ding-ding until the last twenty super-stars get a two-minute space, just to up the drama. Those gaps are needed but some poor sods, goin' badly, get overtaken. The first ones in looked terrible. It stands to reason. If those boys are that far down the pecking order, they ain't much cop. Yet they've gotta keep the wheels turnin' in case they miss the timed cut-out. It's a delicate art being Lanterne Rouge, and much appreciated by the French. I wondered what contemporary American thinking made of that. I recalled slow bike races from my childhood. Going from one lamp-post to the next without puttin' a foot down on the tarmac. Last one in was the winner. I wondered if that perverse game was popular in Des Moines, Iowa. I doubted that such lateral thinking fitted into a winner-takes-all mentality. Nor would this bunch of no-hopers have been of any interest to the folks back home. I was fascinated. To stand next to burnt-out doubled-up wiry athletes, honkin' up spit'n'phlegm, coughing their guts up like thirty-a-day Capstan Extra Strength smokers, crawling beside their bikes on hands'n'knees. Fucked Jean-Patrick Nazon, of the French team AG2R, was particularly impressive. After a full work-out of bodily fluids while still in the saddle, he keeled over prone. His roadie helped him limb by limb into a state of dignity. He sprawled on the road, head between his knees. His hands held his head. A puddle formed on the tarmac below his down-turned mouth. His breathing sounded like an old bellows. His roadie placed a soaking wet white towel over Nazon's head. He did this move with such gentleness and love, adjusting the cotton edge minutely with his fingers. He cared about his man. I thought of Elvis at Las Vegas, his papal generosity to the faithful with white scarves. I stood next to the two of 'em just watching Jean-Patrick's suffering being tended. He was spent. Others swept past inches away. I felt privileged at such intimacy. And the intimacy that Le Tour de France offers all around is because there is little attempt at privacy.

And so it continued at one-minute intervals. The crowd politely applauded each rider. Many were hardly household names. Quite a few I had never heard of, and I'd been there every day for a good fortnight. A mid-afternoon break was called for, the equivalent of afternoon tea. A time to put up my feet, have a drink and watch the fun on TV. I retired to the press centre. I started to count the number of Dutch riders. Half a dozen. Michael Boogerd, Lotz, the elegant Desmond Dekker. And of those, I wouldn't have wanted to gamble a pony on any of 'em pullin' off a stage win today. Which was a pity. I wanted to hear the bells. The church of Notre-Dame-des-Neiges in Alpe d'Huez would ring its bells if a Dutchman won. It was a tradition going back to the early visits of Le Tour. After the Second World War, there was a lot of disruption and dislocation. A lotta people didn't have a clue any more where they belonged. Combatant or civilian. Drifters had no direction home. Jaap Reuten arrived at these mountains in the late '40s as a rep for a Dutch beer company. Welcome as he must've been, he figured that spirits were the answer. He became the priest. The church became the strangest press centre. Journos whackin' out their typed copy from the pews. It was basic back in '52, Coppi's year. So it went when Le Tour returned in the '70s. Father Reuten was delirious that the first winner back was Joop Zoetemelk in '76. He rang the church bells for joy at his countryman's success. The pilgrimage from the Low Countries was on. Three on the trot in successive years. Then more. Old Joop again. Maybe there is a load of bollocks talked about psycho-geography. Special happenings in special places at special times. Then you look at Alpe d'Huez. Perhaps the Dutch presence, wanting it to happen, made it happen. Whatever. The baton has passed on. Nothing lasts for ever. As for a great band, time is short. Like Eric Cantona, the knack is to quit while ahead.

The press centre is no longer divine. It's a sports hall, like all the rest. The coolest thing about the place is the air-conditioning. It was a good place to rest up on a long hot summer's day and take stock on the middle order. The unsung heroes had put their heads down through the race. Team players battlin' for their leader's glory. Stickin' their logoed shirts on the telly. To promote their sponsors' wares. A solo time run was great exposure. It was a big day for numbers men. Statisticians came to the fore. Times'n'distances, split times, projected distances. The numerical rolls on the banks of computer screens drove me into a torpid state. Of course, the statistics informed on the state of play. In terms of tappin' into the momentum, it's as relevant as a train timetable. Jack Webb in *Dragnet*. 'Just the facts, Mam.' No, no, no. I want the buzz.

I was refreshed by the television appearance of number 87, Ronny Scholtz of the German water-boys team, Gerolsteiner. 'C'mon, Ronny, my son,' I muttered. Someone's got to root for 'em. Back I went. I had the mountain boots on. I looked up at the majestic alpine peaks, not tiring of the view. A scramble on the ridge tops would have been great. There is that recurring feeling, while following Le Tour, of 'So near, yet so far away' (Billy Fury — great barnet!). You find yourself close to so many great places to hang around in. You don't have the time or relaxed   concentration to indulge yourself. Keepin' on track consumes you.

On the roadside, I bumped into a Welsh bloke on a bike. Daffyd Williams had a big red Cymru dragon on his cross-bar. I stared at it. He was red in the face, taking off his helmet. He stared at the press-pass round my neck.

'Did you cycle all the way up here?' I asked him.

'Yes,' he said proudly.

And he was off. He gave me a highly detailed account of the ascent, hairpin by hairpin, all twenty-one. He described variations in the gradient. I learnt of the condition of the road-surface. He talked me round his bike, pointing out cogs, spokes and chain.

When Daffyd said, 'The tracks of my tyres,' I replied, 'Smokey Robinson'. He stared blankly at me. It dawned on me that dear Daffyd thought I was conducting a formal interview with him. Well he would, wouldn't he? I was a gentleman of the press. I had a Dictaphone in my hand. I was just curious to look into his psyche to check out what kinda crazy diamond would do what he'd just done. If his reason was any more profound than George Mallory's on Everest, 'Because it's there,' I never found out. His motive was buried in a pile of technical detail of alpine proportions. Like the pro commentators.

Up at the finish, I met Earl. He'd found a dodge – a chink in the fence without a steward. It let us into a privileged stand on the last corner before the line. Even better, it was right under the giant TV screen. We stretched out in our chairs. This was the life. I could follow each rider's progress, calculate the lead, count the running times, watch each bead of sweat drop off the nose'n'chin. Until, *shazam*, the very same rider zipped around the corner right in front of me. The nature of reality was called into question.

Since before Le Tour de France had started back in Liège, informed and knowledgeable commentators had wisely predicted that the overall winner would come from this day. This Individual Time-Trial up Alpe d'Huez, an innovation, would decide the eventual outcome. Bollocks. Armstrong had it sewn up already. Ullrich, supposedly his nearest rival, plodded up a minute behind. I wanted to shout 'Plodder' but I was worried that I'd get found out for bunkin' in. I was having too grand a day. Vladimir Karpets had also had a brilliant day. The young Russian rider was timing his late run for position with perfection. There is a prize for best young rider. The day-by-day leader wore a white jersey. Skoda motors stumped up the sponsorship. Tommy Voeckler had held it since way back at Chartres cathedral. Now Karpets had the jersey in his sights. He'd stormed up the hill, finishing seventh. I'd given him my best shout as he'd leaned round the corner next to me. His time was comin'. I was pleased. In the midst of all the niceness and pleasantness, Vladimir Karpets looked fucking mean.

I watched Lance'n'Sheryl whirr up into the sky in the chopper from the field behind. Lance's maillot jaune shining in the evening light. I expect their teeth shone as well. It must've been an amazing flight down the mountainside, over the top of the million heads, knowing that he'd turned every single one of those heads with his remarkable performance.

Boof! Time to go. Time for me to get the hell off that dead-end mountain. Time to steal a march on the rest. We had no hotel booked. The Brief had drawn a blank in his preparations. There had been nothing doing anywhere near Grenoble – the place was swamped. The course road was impassable. It would be an all-night-long evacuation. There was a tiny service road marked on the map to pass-bearers. I checked with ASO officials to see when it would be in use with police escorts. I got dopey smiles and shaken heads back. 'Go and get yourselves a meal in the town. It'll be hours yet,' one senior bloke said. Much as I like Gratin Dauphinois, the regional speciality, I was in no mood to hang about. Road fever burnt through me. We three jumped into Black Magic. It had been some day. Let's fuck off. As the car jinked down the skinny back-track, the road forked. I hesitated. The Brief leaned out the window, politely asking two workmen stacking barriers in textbook French the correct direction. They jerked thumbs. I followed. A couple of hundred yards on, I screeched to a halt. Just in time. I had almost pulled back on to the main road down. It was one-way and chocker. If I'd done that, we would've been doomed to an all-night traffic jam. I slammed the motor round a three- (or thirteen-) point turn. Teeth bared'n'gritted, except for the stream of obscenities shouted. I was gonna kill those fuckin' workmen. I'd give 'em 'Only havin' a laugh.' I had blood'n'violence in my soul. I retraced the road. There they were. Still grinning. I'd teach the cunts to cast me down into the despond of punterdom. As I slowed alongside them, feeling for the six-inch lock-knife with the non-slip grip in my pocket, a surprising feeling of warmth and benevolence washed over me. I leaned out the window, shouting 'Yeah' and stuck my foot down on the gas pedal. Le Tour de France does strange things to you!

I flew down the darkening mountain like Armstrong had gone up it. The exhilaration at crackin' it, by-passing all the grief. No bad-tempered snarl-up to ruin a fine day. It was brilliant logistics by Le Tour organisers, ASO, to whisk us away so sweetly. It was an act of genius to remove all the infrastructure from a remote mountain top and have it all in place, fully functioning the next day. The small town of television studios, generators, platforms, gantries had to be dismantled and packed away. It had to be transported in the most massive convoy. Bravo to Nobby. Chapeaux to Norbert Dentressangle, the Master of Truckin'. His red'n'white trucks carried the lot, from time-judges' viewing platforms to vans of gaffa tape. How gingerly they must creep around the exposed hairpins with their precious load. Then up the motorway for a couple of hundred and into brand new positions, unpacked'n'plugged in. The nocturnal crew had deadlines to hit, elaborate layout plans to work to. French precision was impressive. Major bands on the road don't work this tight. For a start, two days off in twenty-three says a lot. One off a week in rock'n'roll is measly. A band the size of The Stones doesn't knock itself out like in the hectic days of the '70s. The old rockers are leisurely nowadays and the young 'uns are lazy with their giggin'. They've got MTV and the Internet to flash themselves across the cities of the nation. Big rigs also come in pairs. One stage set to bamboozle the fans. The other, identical, leap-frogs to the next hit. One up'n'runnin', one on the move. To Le Tour that is indulgence. One size fits all. This stage set rumbles through the night. It is in place with the dawn chorus.

The same motorway took us around Grenoble and northwards. There was no room at the inn. Earl drove. The Brief flicked through maps and guides. I lounged across the back seat. I was tryin' to stay in touch with my intuition. Not easy with rising panic. Earl stuck a few miles on the clock to get away from the bottleneck. The road was ominously busy, given the hour. We started scouting off the slip-roads. Campaniles, with chrome, Mercures with pine, Novotels, bland and green. Every hotel was full. Coaches pulled in; car parks were full. The Brief and I took turns at pleading with the concierges. Our prominent Tour passes on our chests cut no ice. Back on the dark multi-lanes to the next turning. Auberges in art nouveau, chambres d'hôtes, like sleeping at your Nan's. Full. As the witching hour approached, our voices had become strangulated. We had taken to running across the car-parks, dozens of 'em. Sleep was the issue. Survival was the game. The joke was a daily one we'd thrown around inside Black Magic on the long daily drives. I'd have the front wheels, the Brief would have the rear axles. We'd sleep under the car if the worst happened. Earl could have the back seat. He was the one with dodgy pins from his rickets. Oh how we'd laughed. It was a joke at the Mentor's expense. He'd said it for real often enough, fancyin' himself as some Nature's Boy-cum-raggle-taggle gipsy. It was starting to look as though some lay-by would be our bivouac. Which was ominous. Without a decent kip, you're fucked for the next day. And so on, domino theory. Le Tour de France is about endurance. Naturally enough for the riders. It applies to every one of us out on the road. Now the chance of a pillow was looking slim. The Brief was a man who knew about pillows. I had known him pack a favourite to take away on holiday. He usually made a pillow enquiry when booking a hotel. His particular loathing was for the French bolster. Earl had, on this trip, discovered the bolster and had taken a perverse liking to the sausage-shaped firm cushion under his neck. I didn't care. I just wanted to get my head down. Daylight was a distant memory. On the edge of Annecy, a lake-side tourist trap surely crammed with empty hotels, I pulled into another car-park on an industrial estate. It had a guard who eyed up our obvious desperation. I entered the foyer and marched up to the desk. All attempts at subtle charm had been worn away. A hard-faced old crone weighed me up warily. I looked into her dry piercing eyes. There was no compassion. Just euro notes. I pulled my wedge outta my back pocket. I fingered the money ostentatiously. Her eyes moved from my face to my hands.

'I need a couple of rooms urgently. I'll pay whatever.'

It worked. She went through the pretence of checking the reservations book, humming'n'haaing. It seemed two roomfuls of guests hadn't made it in and hadn't sent a deposit. The enormity of how many people one million actually is hit me hard. That mountain, Alpe d'Huez, way back down the road, would be clogged all night. I made this observation to Madame. The money talked. She almost smiled. With heavy key fobs in hand and sweet relief in my heart, I unloaded the bags. I opened the room door for Earl.

'Monsier Ronfler, Mister Ping-Pong Balls welcomes your company.'

Ronnie grinned back, exhaustedly. It was unlikely that either of us would be troubled by noise that night. The Brief's relief was tangible. He looked out of his window.

'Look. Guests arriving. A family with young children at this hour.'

I closed the curtains. 'Fuck 'em.' Survival was the game.

It was a refreshed trio that rendezvoused the next morning. The Brief is a healthy sort, a man of ritual. His morning constitutional had disappointed him. Here, in his beloved Alps, he had failed to walk beyond the confines of this industrial estate with its panorama of warehouses. He had been pleased to find a LeClerc supermarché. His squirrel bag was bulging with nuts, pain au raisins, apricots, crackers and packets of sweet biscuits with lurid artist's illustrations of contents that never remotely matched. He was pleased to be re-victualled, ready for our last day in high mountains. Earl sloped out of the hotel at the last minute. I was buzzing. Two pints of espresso. The usual. As a lapsed drug fiend, it's all I've got left. Hell, I'd given up the fags last winter. No booze, no gear. I'd made it to this fine morning, by the skin of my teeth at times. I have been no stranger to the de-tox ward and re-hab therapy. It's one way to last the course.

Chapter 11

Drug taking has been a tradition in Le Tour de France from the word go. I did not know that when I made my first connection in '98. Oh sure, the Tommy Simpson 'Heart done blown up on too much speed' story was familiar.

I just thought, 'Those mods!' 'cos Tommy had a razor-cut barnet'n'sharp Italian-cut threads. He looked every inch the pill-poppin' sort of mod who followed The Who.

He shoulda counted his purple hearts more carefully. I can remember being well-impressed by the cine footage of Simpson wobblin' up the Ventoux on his fuckin' bike, moments before collapsing dead on the roadside. For me, it was an impressive one-off.

I was into football. Watchin' it. My local team: Gillingham, Division Three lowlife. The occasional top-notch match: Manchester United, Chelsea. My lot looked like pints of ale men, the King's Road boys might run to a joint now'n'then with their Beaujolais. Drugs didn't used to figure with sport. Or so I thought. Russian shot-putters apart.

Although I was a child of the '60s, I was not a weedy herb man for long. I blame Keith Richards. In the '70s, he was dubbed 'The world's most elegantly wasted being', quite correctly: those beautiful Annie Leibovitz photographs of Keith draped in silk, shades and Tibetan scarves across hotel suites and bare dressing rooms. Out of it. He was ostentatiously consuming a cornucopia of pills'n'powders. At the same time, he was creating the most sublime rock'n'roll ever made. *Exile on Main Street* is the very best record, depending on your day-to-day mood. To combine the two to maximum effect has made Keith Richards a hero in my book. His longevity is an irrelevance. Keith would probably never have chosen an old man's wheezing fireside death. His best way out would have to be on stage, in the middle of a Telecaster power chord. It's a rarity to catch someone poppin' off in performance. Tommy Cooper dropped dead on stage. The punters in the stalls roared with laughter. His heart-attack was taken as a gag.

But it doesn't have to come to that. Keith has shown that taking drugs can enhance your sensitivity, derange your senses in Baudelaire/Rimbaud-style, or just plain get you through a tough day. It's all in the perspective. Sensational slagging is the New Puritan angle. No 'cheating'; no 'performance enhancing'.

As I watched le peloton down bikes and sit in the road on that Tour of '98, I twigged. The riders were on strike. They were protesting at police harassment. Drug raids at dawn. Hotel rooms turned upside down. Team managers, soigneurs hand-cuffed. Riders in cop cars, blankets over their heads like paedophiles. It was insulting and humiliating. I knew the feeling. When you travel the world with a rock'n'roll band, you get to expect that sort of reception. Cases opened de rigueur at every customs check. A lubricated rubber glove, if you're lucky. Paul McCartney busted for marijuana at Tokyo airport, if you're not (though his roadies got an eight-day all-expenses-paid holiday while he was in the nick). The only damage being done was to their own insides. That was their business.

It was messy, that year of '98. It all started with an own goal from Willy Voet of team Festina. He was a soigneur, a trainer. He got pulled on a country back road on the French/Belgian border. He was en route to the Grand Départ in Ireland. It is my experience that having an official motor gets you waved through rather than pulled over. It was a set up for a crack down. Poor old Willy had box-loads of dodgy gear. It was an exotic cocktail that is lovingly called, 'Pot Belge'. This is a mix of heroin, cocaine, speed, steroids and multi-vitamins. He had it in his own bloodstream too. Le Tour organisers twisted and turned. Leblanc, le Directeur, said there was no proof that it was intended for the riders' consumption. He'd been a fuckin' rider himself. The story leaked out over the days. The big deal was EPO, a handy drug that increased red cells in the bloodstream. This meant more oxygen. It helped muscular recovery. The bottom line was that your man goes to bed knackered, gets up fresh as a daisy, fit as a bullock for a hard day's pedallin'. Cheat! Laboratory testing was unable to pin-point EPO. A red-cell count from a blood test was only an indicator. It was a messy business. Prison cell interrogation produced better results. Squealers stepped forward. Richard Virenque, Festina team leader and French knicker-droppin' fave, looked his adoring public in the eye and denied all knowledge.

But plenty grassed up the weasely Virenque. Richard was confronted with the evidence. He sobbed in the back of a car, like a turned-over rent boy.

'I didn't mean to. I couldn't help it,' he mewled.

There were other suspects. Names were dropping like flies. But Virenque was the most pathetic. Like Christophe Moreau, another cheesy French apologiser, he got the boot and he got the ban. But he never held his head high. And he should've done. Six years after that incident, the Football League does not test players for EPO. Nor do many other sports of a less arduous nature. The knock-on effect of allegations across the millennium nearly did for Le Tour de France and cycling in general. The athletes on wheels have been pursued by purist accusations all down the line. Often accurately. So what? These men are heroes for racing great distances over massive mountains. And then they take drugs. Double heroes.

Michel Pollentier won a Tour stage at Alpe d'Huez in 1978. As the stage winner, he was automatically called for a drugs test. He went along and was caught with a length of tubing and a rubber bulb strapped to his body. It contained somebody else's urine. A simulated piss, a quick squeeze and he should've been off the hook. He deserved to be for invention. Full marks for tryin'. It's the same contraption that Withnail uses, with the same disastrous, hilarious consequences, when he's breathalysed in his beat-up old Jag. Even this was trumped by the tale of a rider who hid a condom up his arse, connected by tube to his willy for realism. The rubber johnny held a sample of his mechanic's urine. Sadly for the rider, the roadie had got bored during long slack moments of the race. He'd dipped into his master's gear on the sly.

If one team has the money to afford high-altitude training in Mexico, or oxygen tents and high-pressure wind tunnels, does that give them an 'unfair advantage' over some cheapo outfit stuck in a run-down velodrome on the outskirts of Marseille?

Choppy Warburton was a visionary. He was the British cycling coach and manager at the end of the nineteenth century. He cut a dash like a modern football manager on the touchline, with an ankle-length cashmere coat and a wide-brimmed fedora. His star was world champion Jimmy Michael. At Catford track in 1896, Choppy passed Jimmy a bottle. Jimmy got spaced out and rode all over the place. Choppy was banned for life. Not before he'd shared his secret wisdom with Welshman Arthur Linton. In the Bordeaux–Paris Race of the same year, Arthur was starin'n'wobblin' wildly at midnight in Tours. By five in the morning at Orléans, he looked a wreck, corpse-like.

He gained an eighteen minutes over the 45 miles after that. Arthur died two months later. No one ever figured out what Choppy put in his bottled elixir.

Drugs are of their time. In Choppy's days and up to the end of the First World War, a decent sort of chap could buy drugs in Fortnum'n'Mason. Sheets of gelatine were sold, impregnated with morphine and cocaine. Very popular in the trenches. Like amphetamines were with the Royal Air Force in the Second World War. Gritted teeth in Spitfires. Black bombers over Dresden. Hell, even Winston Churchill was at it. The old brigade were up-front about their need for pharmaceutical assistance. There were three Pelissier brothers, Henri, Francis and Charles. They were top dogs in French cycling. They had a chat in a café with a journo in 1924. They were pissed off with being treated so harshly on Le Tour. The only way they could keep on track was cocaine for the eyes, chloroform for the gums and boxful of pills. 'Dynamite', they said. The article caused a bit of a stir. Henri, the oldest, was in love with the rock'n'roll world, although it wasn't officially invented until Elvis came along. He was in permanent contretemps with Tour directeur Desgranges. His wife, Léonie, got fed up and shot herself in 1933. Henri's lover, Miette, was twenty years younger than him. In one of their many rows, Henry went for her with a blade. Miette pulled out the same gun that Léonie had used on herself and, moments later, Henri lay dead with five bullets in him. Miette got off on self-defence. Guns'n'drugs tale not so far away from Anita Pallenberg, Keith Richard's long-time belle. She was in bed with a young man. The boy toyed with her gun and left his bloody brains on the pillow. The Pelissier brothers were champions and heroes. Charlie stayed in the game. Francis did as well, talent-spotting a young rider from Normandy, Jacques Anquetil, who won Le Tour de France five times.

He was quite prepared to stand up and be counted.

He said, 'Why not? So what?' about taking big stimulants.

He led a strike in '66 at Bordeaux against testing. He reckoned that by not allowing drug use in the open, black market contamination was a serious health risk. He said doctors should be allowed to administer freely to riders. Many contemporary workers in the substance field say the same today. His stance was that everyone in all areas of life takes substances when necessary. His example was of an office worker with a headache. Jacques reckoned that it was asking too much of cyclists to be clean and different. Hypocritical too. He held his head up and looked his accusers in the eye. Just as the great Fausto Coppi had done a few years earlier. He was asked on television if he had taken drugs.

He replied, 'Only when necessary.' Asked how often that was, he replied, 'Almost always.'

Henri Desgranges always wanted his Tour de France to be a dangerous game. He got it in ways he didn't foresee. That's why we love it.

After Tommy Simpson died, another drug crackdown was announced. It coincided with the explosion of mind-expanding psychedelics from California. The skinny frothin'-at-the-mouth boys had had their day. Body consciousness came in. Muscles rippled to ludicrous dimensions. Steroids were passed around. They weren't a lotta good for people who fell off bikes regularly at velocity. Cuts and wounds are real slow to heal on the anabolics. Body bulk is fine in a tight sprint. It's a liability to drag up the mountains. And so to EPO in the '90s.

Now that it can be tested for, Le Tour agreed to run tests before many other sports.

A popular excuse of many a rider down the years has

been, 'Honest, I never knew what was in the trainer's needle.'

Vitamin shots have long been in use on rock'n'roll tours. B12 has always been a favourite. A jab in the buttocks from some local doc! Tired'n'run down? Try this. Long-haul two and three month tours across Europe, the States, the Far East could be guaranteed to run down both performers and crew. Crap food, plenty of booze, chain-smokin', long hours, and just plain hard work. Jagger reckoned to lose 10 lbs through sweat on a good night. The Beatles didn't fit their flappin' suits at the end of a tour because they'd worked off so much weight on-stage. Pep pills were mandatory. Preludin in Hamburg. Elvis shipped home three lab bottles of uppers from his German army base. The Who used hollowed-out speaker cabinets for transport and storage. Nowadays, bands are lazy. A few monster gigs a year. A coupla showcase bookings to pump up the new album. Those year-long epic travels around each country, playin' to every town, are largely gone. Television does the work now. So multi-vit pick-me-ups came in. I've had them. They worked. I forgot to ask for a legal certificate of contents in the works. I trusted the man. It's a justification given by many a cyclist on the wrong end of a doping test.

Another option is not to put in but to take out. Blood transfusions are back in vogue. Cleans the blood, literally. Fresh stamina. In his heyday, Keith Richards spawned persistent rumours that he regularly visited a clinic in Switzerland. Under sedation, his blood was filtered and transfused. He would awake free from addiction. There would be no trace of substance left to register on a test. This was the dodge used by a bunch of Winter Olympics cross-country skiers a few years back. When they left their rented house, they forgot the blood transfusion machine. The cleaner found it and turned it 'n' them in.

Why bother? We ask our athletes to entertain us. So long as they do, who are we to dictate their preparation? Hell, athletes are giving drug-taking a bad name. If the stuff is freely available, the same as a strong cuppa coffee in the morning, everyone has the same chance. If it's out-front, we all know about it.

We ain't trying to reproduce a shining perfect world in a pure sporting event. We're celebrating a fucked-up world, heroic because it is flawed.

The trouble with illegality, even for asthma-inhalers and codeine, is that it doesn't work. The prohibition of booze in the States was a laughable flop. So too the present-day drug wars. More people take stuff more than ever before. There's the dichotomy. Our culture runs on drugs for work and play. As it always did. I'm including alcohol, nicotine and the deregulated supermarket shelf. What's so different about Le Tour de France?

The respected French journalist, Pierre Chany, said of Anquetil, 'You can't be a champion like that just by taking a pill from a bottle.'

Drug testing on the Le Tour takes up too much attention, energy and time. I stood outside the little battered cream caravan high in the Pyrenees. It was the drug van. It was parked, discreetly unmarked, behind the winner's podium. All that distinguished its role was a sheet of paper with half a dozen handwritten names gaffa-taped to the door. I stood next to a tasty bird. We watched Richard Virenque go in. He was wearing his red'n'white polka dot shirt. She was holding a matching cap. She squealed and squirmed. I thought she maybe needed a wee. The Rent Boy certainly did. He had to give a urine sample. The girl asked to borrow my pen. She wanted the Weasel-Faced One to sign her peak. I wanted to see how he related to a fan, one on one. We both stood there for a good quarter of an hour. How long could it take to piss into a bottle? Did the staff run the taps? I gave up. It wasn't that interesting.

Testing is always gonna be behind the game. There will always be a time gap between the molecular creation of a substance and its subsequent detection. When there's that much dosh and prestige at stake, a lotta effort goes in to drug innovation. The old communist bloc was renowned for its chemical excellence. Russian gymnasts, Polish hurdlers, East German cyclists. Their laboratories were reputedly second to none. Since Glasnost, the system has fragmented and crumbled. The hot word is that the outfit has merely upped sticks and moved lock, stock and barrel. It's gone to where the serious money is: the United States of America. The privacy of the Rocky Mountains. The entrepreneurial freedom of California. Just the same as happened after the Second World War with rocket science. When Germany folded in '45, Von Braun and his outfit found a welcome home in the Land of the Free. Now it's maybe the same thing for a new generation of white-coated pharmaceutical pioneers.

Chapter 12

America gave the world Elvis. Earl was wearin' Elvis shades as he parked up. They were beauties. Big'n'fat. Gold-sprayed with holes punched down the sides. He'd got 'em for a quid in a joke shop in Derby. The shades went a treat with his greasy slicked-back hair. Brylcreem; 'Dixie Three Peaches' wax was hard to find in Europe.

Barry was directin' motors to the press car-park. He was called Barry because his moon-face, residual hair 'n' gormless jaw reminded us of Barry from *EastEnders*. Barry was prone to flyin' off the handle, like Barry. Barry's main gig was back-stage security right after the finish. He was volatile muscle. Barry leaned in the driver's open window. We were insiders, Regulars. Shared confidences.

'Hey, great shades. Did you see Elvis back at the line? An Elvis impersonator. Full threads.'

'Uh-huh,' said Earl.

But we hadn't. As sure as eggs is eggs, we'd go lookin'. Black Magic was stuck under the trees in the shade. It was a scorcher. Clear blue skies, sun high. Silver pointy granite peaks of the Aravis around'n'above us. Opposite the car-park was a brand new stone alpine chalet nearing completion. The builder's board outside announced him as Noel Bastard. It was gonna be a good day.

A piss-call had been made back down the long valley. A cheese sandwich in Thônes, past Alex'n'Bluffy. The Brief and I had stretched our legs. Four cyclists came up the road and stopped at the public toilets. Each of 'em had a fluffy brown Kiwi bird stuck on his helmet.

'We're from New Zealand,' one said.

'Really?' I replied.

'Yes. We're following Le Tour de France.'

'Really?' I said. I was wonderin' why people from the Antipodes had to raise their voices at the end of every sentence as if they were asking a question.

The main square of this pretty little alpine town was packed. It was on the day's route. A dip before the last of the five big climbs, the Col de la Croix Fry. Every chair at every café table was taken. Americans. They were in relaxed, affluent mode. In position to watch the procession. The victory procession of Lance'n'his Postal boys. The epic slog of Alpe d'Huez was behind 'em. Now it was sit back with a café au lait and a slice of gâteau. It was like being at Disneyland. The French alpine café experience. Or perhaps Las Vegas. 'Alpeville – a complete themed environment'. A facsimile, a perfect reproduction. I once took my mate, the Baker, to the Louvre to see the *Mona Lisa*. I thought a spot of serious culture would lift up this transpontine yob on a day off giggin'. We queued in the ante-room to the Great Work of Leonardo. A closed-circuit TV on the wall showed that famous enigmatic smile to us waitin' punters.

'Let's go. I've seen it now,' said the Baker.

'No. No. The real thing is in the next gallery,' I urged.

'Fuck that. It's all the same,' he said and marched off.

All Lance had to do was stay upright on the bike over this last day in the mountains and the crown was his. America loves winners. Lance was most certainly that. He was magnificently unstoppable. The newsagents were fresh outta *L'Équipe*. Every Yank was readin' a copy with a pic of their man on the front. There was a lotta cheese in the shop windows. Reblochon was the regional speciality. We rustled up dirty great baguette sandwiches, using my six-inch lock-blade 'picnic' knife in the lay-by.

The road-blocks were fascinatin'. We had zipped through a few, being privileged insiders. My tolerance towards stroppy interlopers was in steep decline. As the line of traffic on an about-to-be-closed main road inched up to the gendarmes, there were always one, two, a few, who stopped to argue the toss.

'My grandmother lives a kilometre up there. She is urgently awaitin' the cylinder of oxygen in my boot.'

'I am on a call-out for a gas-leak at a children's home.'

All I knew was that it held me up. The more Le Tour went on, the less inclined any of us were to be distracted. Interesting cultural side-shows, like the Thiepval Memorial, had been forgotten. Waxworks, Chambers of Horrors and Museums of Wigs listed in the Guide were blanked. A scenic mountain road was over-ruled for a fast dual carriageway.

At the head of the valley, Le Grand-Bornand awaited Le Tour. The locals, all 2,000 of 'em, had gone to town on the festivities. It was a ribbon development strip, up the riverbank. Another freshly tarmacked road would carry the race on the other bank. A charming bridge linked the two. Being pasture terrain, cows were the theme. Fuckin' hundreds of 'em, mostly on bikes. Life-size straw cows pedallin' bikes. In fields, in files, on roofs, in gardens. Bovine Worzel Gummidges. Must've kept the whole town busy all winter, in between caterin' for the skiing tourists. They looked wonderful, inspirin', original. Dotted around the town in the unlikeliest places. Roofs turned into beaches with deck-chairs'n'parasols. Roofs as astro-turf fields of brightly coloured paper butterflies. Bunting of course. The town's prize silver band were pumpin' out a selection of folk tunes'n'Lennon–McCartney in the Place Gambetta. Suddenly, Le Tour had become French again. An Event, a celebration of visions'n'dreams. Not a single-minded race with a single winner. The square was dominated by a merry-go-round. I had never seen the like and I've got five kids. Le Manège Magique was a fantasy

straight outta the early twentieth century. Movin'
Edwardian panels, eyes'n'tits on murals, very Monty
Python, with bunched red crushed-velvet drapes, a tall
flagpole with a little boy on top, a life-like model. I was
astonished. I sat'n'drank a citron pressé. It was art.
Surrealism? Dada? A sign said it was made in 1992.
Recherché? It was a kiddies' ride. Except each vehicle on
the Magic Roundabout was hand-made, unique. No
Swedish catalogue number. A T-Rex, a hangin' bi-plane, a
giant squid, a rocket with a glass cockpit that rose up
above the roof, a potted aspidistra, a balloon with basket.
The children thronged to it. The hurdy-gurdy music
played. 'Live out your fantasies,' it was sayin'.

Lance Armstrong was in a group of six on the giant TV
screen. I'd nibbled the fresh-water crayfish at the
sumptuous buffet, too full of fuckin' Reblochon cheese.
The Brief was making a beast of himself with Tartes
Myrtilles. It was mystic chef time. Havin' a hundred 'n'
fifty mad cyclists on the other side of the hill, bearin'
down on me, gave an urgency to every step. I could feel
their manic charge. Le peloton had knocked off four of the
bastards. The Cols Glandon'n'Madeleine'n'Forclaz were
big 'uns. I would most certainly need whatever drugs
you've got to reach the top. Richard Virenque grabbed the
early mountain points, gave what he thought was an
endearin' smile to his fans, and packed in his race.
Coastin'. Plenty were quittin'. Roberto Heras, a previous
mountain lead-out man for Armstrong, stopped. The
names flashed up on screen. Didier Rous, Giunti, Becke.
They were droppin' like flies. Their race was run. Tombak
caught his finger in his wheel spokes, nearly rippin' it
right off. Hospital job. Didn't his mummy ever warn him
about bein' careful? The six were all that was left at the
summit of the Croix Fry, just over the 4,000-foot mark.
Floyd was lookin' mighty fine. It's a great name, Floyd, to

roll a tongue around. It drawls. Floyd's a country boy from Pennsylvania. Amish roots, it's said. I dunno if his mamma wears a white bonnet. He was a BMX trix boy till he switched to drop handlebars. He sure likes to party-on-down hard, they say. Big George had been dropped back down the road apiece. That was rare. George Hincapie was the other sidekick for Armstrong. He's been alongside Lance on every one of the winning six Tours. The only one. My mate, E Factor, lives in New York City. One-time main-man roadie with the Patti Smith Group. Loves this big ol' bike race, like all road men. Tells me he useda see Big George (as a youth, maybe Middle George) burnin' it round Central Park time after time when the rest'd gone home. Floyd'n'Big George watch out for Lance's arse, front'n'back, side to side. For sure, the whole eight-man US Postal team are specialists to enhance Lance 'n' stick him on the podium. These Good Ol' Boys are special.

I dunno if Big George'n'Floyd laugh at Lance's jokes, especially if they ain't amusin'. I dunno if Lance buys 'em fancy convertibles from downtown automobile showroom windows. The pattern is American, down south, straight outta Memphis, Tennessee. This is Elvis Presley territory. Elvis always had his mates around him to closet him from a harsh world and provide him with company and stimulation. Until he was shipped to Germany as a GI, the King had never strayed far from home. His constant companion on the road was his cousin, Junior Smith. Junior had gone psycho with a semi-automatic while serving as a soldier in Korea. He stayed psycho whenever any boy or girl got close to his cousin, the first rock'n'roll star. He slept in the same bed as Elvis, on Mama Gladys' orders, to stop his cousin sleep-walkin'. Junior died young of an overdose. Rat poison was his choice. The King had some gang around him. The Memphis Mafia covered every need for Elvis, except sex'n'drugs. Dr George C.

Nichopoulos always travelled on tour with Elvis. There are those who shake their heads'n'mutter, 'Sycophants.' Hell, fame can be a lonely'n'desperate place.

Pals can ease the pain. Billy the Kid, William Bonney, valued his friends. He saw himself as part of a gang, not as a lone celebrity outlaw. Pat Garrett gunned him down at Fort Sumner, New Mexico. Billy's two chums were shot dead too. Some years ago, I visited the compañeros' grave on the edge of that dusty little town. I had to climb a high fence to get close. Burghers. I pissed on the grave. Just outta badness; as a mark of respect for Billy. It had the three names on the gravestone, under the word, 'Pals'.

Lance Armstrong was only ever on his own on a solo time-trial or the final shove of a mountain stage he wanted to win. On the giant portable screen in Le Grand-Bornand, Lance let Floyd go. A swift descent and he could have a precious stage win. A reward, a thank you.

Ullrich and Basso, the leading Italian contender, were kinda chasin'. These boys were 7 miles away. The crowd was startin' to shuffle their feet, raise their arms, talk loudly. One smallish knot of solid American support was accurately positioned by the line. Flag-wavin' time. I watched Kloden, the young German team-mate of Ullrich, but in third place to Jan's fourth, sail past the lot. White shirt of the National champion. The last mile. In the bag. Comfortable. Hands drummed the beat on wooden advertising boards track-side. Jean-Louis Pagès stood on the empty line making last-second checks. His job done immaculately, as always. Kloden was well clear. Armstrong urged Landis on. No response. Basso was hangin' on the back. Ullrich was labourin'. Le maillot jaune launched himself forward. My head swivelled down, looking along the road. They were real, straight at me. Armstrong charged and lifted his arms. Two seconds and he'd braked to a stop alongside me. Flushed. Kloden

207

right behind in disbelief. Then the three. A cloud of jabberin' journos like insects covered 'em. Cameras every which way. I was breathless. I hadn't moved. Armstrong had made a majestic moment. A sprint to win by an inch. It was like a 100-metre Olympic final, a winnin' goal at a play-off final, a marathon finish, a knock-out punch in a World Title fight. All in one go. I looked up'n'watched several replays on screen. It was very U2 in Chicago. Except that I could see every sweatin' pore on Bono/Lance's face for real. I could've actually reached out'n'wiped away his sweat.

That was a job for his minders. He had two of 'em. One was his bread'n'butter man. He steadied the wobblin' bike, a towel round his neck, rehydration bottle in hand. He was tough: shaved head, face carved outta granite, hooked nose. Shoulders like a bull. I could see him in the corner of a Bethnal Green boxing ring. I called him Magwitch, after the escaped convict on Cooling Marshes in *Great Expectations*, who terrorised young Pip. Magwitch's positioning was superb. At Lance's re-entry into the public domain, immediate post-race, Magwitch smothered him with his powerful presence. Lance would surrender, be led to his bus or the winner's enclosure behind the blow-up podium. Magwitch was alert'n'single-minded in the protection of his master. He took no shit.

The other minder was for Lance's brain. He was PR. He sorted journos'n'officials, hangin' off Armstrong's side. He whispered advice and gave the nod. I couldn't place his origin. My own travels are not extensive enough. Kinda Asian. Maybe South Seas. He looked exotic and relaxed enough to wear a garland of orchids round his neck. I wouldn't have been surprised if I learnt that he'd been brought up on Tetiaroa, Marlon Brando's atoll heaven. He was as smooth as Magwitch was brusque. They made a fine team. It was as much a delight for me to watch the pair in operation as the riders. Heart'n'mind. Journos, of course, have to be kept sweet. They've gotta fill their column inches. Lance wants 'em filled with tweet! tweet! tweet! A strong co-dependency. In rock'n'roll, it's just the same. Bottles of chilled white wine to the journos. Hotel room, a ride on the band's bus, first in the dressing-room when the band's slipped outta sweaty stage shirts, a line of cocaine if he's really influential. Might even, even, get his end away with a bit of spare. All for a jolly good write-up.

TV is the key to the heart of America. Newspapers carry fuck-all clout, except in the big cities of the coast. I useda read the *Lubbock Tornado* when I lived in West Texas. I'd be lucky to read stuff from outside the state, let alone beyond national borders. Still, Texas is big enough to be its own country. 'Secede' indeed. The ol' country song gets it: 'The sun has risen, The sun has set, And you ain't outta Texas yet.' OLN have the deal to screen Le Tour de France in the States. It stands for Outdoor Life Network which is known as a Huntin', Shootin', Fishin' channel. It's hardly a must-see major network. In '03, they had a big-top canvas marquee as their portable studio. That was now ditched for a great shiny chrome'n'glass two-tiered job. Lance's growing fame was boosting the station's profile. The ratings must be on the rise. Sheryl Crow used the studio as a handy hideaway. The preppy crew of last year, spots'n'whinges, had morphed into a slick team of 150 people in crisp pale blue shirts.

I have always taught my children, 'Never trust a man in a pale blue shirt.' Cops, customs men, bankers.

OLN had picked up on a bunch of young Americans travellin' with Le Tour. They called themselves 'The Cutters'. They wore cut-offs and carried a giant inflatable killer whale. They were all called Tommy. Like all people trying hard to be wacky, they weren't. The Cutters got a daily slot on OLN, doin' zany stunts. They reckoned it was 'Jackass meets Canal +'. It wasn't funny. They got the chop from the network after a week or so.

A world-weary cameraman said to me, 'No one wants to watch cheese tasting.'

The Cutters had filmed a sequence about smelly French cheese.

'The public wants the bike race.'

To a point. No one wants a bunch of rich embarrassing self-conscious twats.

Lance kept to the point in his interviews. Lance kept outta the way most of the time. A few soundbites through Mr Aloha and he was off. As the show in Le Grand-Bornand wound down, I watched a group of six-year-old nursery children with their teacher leanin' on a barrier. They were holding up coloured pictures they'd painted. Bicycles, flowers, mountains, cows. They were lovely. One kid dropped her drawing onto the roadway. A journalist was stompin' along, on his purposeful way to some post-race interview. One brown, English deck-shoe landed full-on the pretty picture. The paper was ripped'n'torn. The bloke never noticed. The race was all. The child's face showed her upset. Earl crossed the road, bent down, picked it up and handed it back.

Armstrong's image is honed. Anton Corbijn took a whole wedge of arty photos of him. Black'n'white, almost sepia, around the ol' homestead, soft focus, nice house, big brick-work fireplace. Lance gazin' into eternity. Corbijn had done U2. He was Mr U2. *Joshua Tree*. Bono'n'The Edge in the desolate Californian desert. Very rock'n'roll, all Gram Parsons'n'Keef Richards, cacti'n'UFOs'n'death. And with Lance, a deeper, softer side. Not a bike in sight.

'What goes on in this remarkable man?' it said.

The thing with Lance Armstrong is death. Most people

shy away from the whole subject. His very story hits the nail on the head. He just about died from cancer. He was startin' to get there as a cyclist when he was diagnosed with testicular cancer in '96. A rush job of treatment to his lungs, brain, and the loss of one of his balls. Did that give him an unfair advantage on a saddle? I've never heard anyone say, 'Bollock-cheat.' His photo post-chemo was chilling. No eyebrows, baseball cap hidin' hair loss. His vulnerability shinin' outta his desperate crossed eyes. Lance's great phrase is 'Le Tour de France made me wanna get outta bed in the mornin'.'

He has done that with a vengeance every mornin' since he first pulled le maillot jaune over his battered head in July '99. He started that morning in yellow for the very first time right here in Le Grand-Bornand, breathin' pure alpine air. He wore it all the way to Paris. His first Tour win. Years down the line, he was still head'n'shoulders better than anyone else in le peloton. He could ride out pain better. He'd stared death in the face.

The look of this Tour, the must-have accessory was a Lance band. A yellow plastic bracelet around the wrist. Riders from all teams wore 'em, crew, journos, right across the board. I didn't notice a Lance band on the Pork Butcher. It was the symbol of Live Strong, Armstrong's charity for cancer people. They were sold every day in a very American kinda way. Bright yellow logoed transit vans dumped a gaggle of bright-faced college kids from Iowa or some place to work the crowd. It was very in-yer-face aggressive marketing, eyeball contact. Janglin' the bucket of coins. One of the banders, a funny woman called Fanny, said liftin' the heavy money buckets was doin' wonders for her breasts. The merchandising-with-compassion did well. I had no idea how much a Lance band cost. A lotta dough must've helped a lotta kids with cancer in a country that refuses to provide free public health care for those sick people who can't afford it. Shades of Bono'n'world debts.

Armstrong has been through the full gamut of chemotherapy in beating his cancer. Armstrong, today, as winner, must be the most drug-tested athlete in the race. Not once has he tested positive. I don't give a flyin' fuck that the French nation is deeply suspicious of Lance Armstrong.

To me, Lance is magnificent. He is the most complete sportsman I have ever seen.

Lance Armstrong didn't help himself when tongues were waggin'. His fuck-you attitude was brilliant. An Italian rider, Simeoni, got himself into a couple of early breakaways. He threatened to reveal naughty drug-taking stories in court about the Italian trainer, Dr Ferrari. Lance has taken a lotta fitness advice from Ferrari. So what? He's as loyal as Elvis to those that help him. When Simeoni took off down the road, Lance was obviously well annoyed. He took the smear on his pal personally. Armstrong could've easily sent one of his Blue Boys after him. A lieutenant to do the job on his behalf. He went himself, on his tod, in the yellow. He was the Patron, the Senior Figure, the Champion. As such, he controlled le peloton. He called the shots and he showed he could pull the trigger himself. Like Ronnie Kray shootin' George Cornell perched on a bar-stool in the Blind Beggar pub in Whitechapel. Open'n'honest, for all the world to see. Lance pulled alongside the sneaky Italian telltale and mimed zippin' his mouth shut. Simeoni hung his head and dropped back to the bunch. A pariah. It was a clear message that took a lotta bottle to deliver. The mark of a true champion.

The style of a star. Lance Armstrong has moved on up. His scene with Sheryl Crow, his mates come round, Will Smith, Robin Williams. Hell, the President Dubbya rang him on a mobile while he was on the podium in the Champs Elysées. That's some tough jump when you've been brought up by a single mom on the outskirts of a dump like Dallas, Texas. Livin' in the rarefied world of celebrity and big dosh, it is all the more remarkable doin' what he does. Pushin' himself more than anyone around and far more than the rest of us can imagine. Chapeaux, Lance.

Glidin' outta the mountains, down the hairpins towards Lac Leman, slalomin' through the pine trees in Black Magic, on a soft, warm summer's evening, it was a shock to re-enter the real world. Motorways, filling stations, toll-booths, cheap shoddy motels that guarantee a feelin' of white trailer-park trash. I like that feeling. At one with my disengaged world.

On the way across the Jura, the Brief was extolling the beauties of the juxtaposition between modern autoroute and scenic rolling hills. He looked hard at the maps on his knee.

'Stop,' he ordered.

Earl pulled the motor over onto the hard shoulder. I sat up in the back and leaned forward between the two front seats. Our three heads were in a line. All lookin' outta the windscreen.

'Why've we stopped? What're we lookin' at?' I asked.

The Brief said nothing. He pointed a finger forwards. A few trucks. Cars. A bridge over the road. Nothing. We sat. A rush of cars across the bridge. My heart quickened. Cops on motorbike, blue lights flashin'. And there above us, was the multi-coloured peloton, flowin'n'fillin' the road. Serene'n'urgent. Self-contained, in a bubble. For that moment, time stood still. It was broken by car-horns, motorbikes, dozens of team-cars, roof-racks piled up with spare bikes. Chasin' their riders like a pack of dogs. And they were gone. Earl started the engine.

'Paris,' said the Brief.

There were a coupla calls en route. A few matters to put right. Before the room-pacin' could start. The unsettled confinement of a room after weeks on the road. Nowhere to go, nothin' special to do. No focus, no edge. Yet adrenaline being pumped around as before. Nervous energy that no chair can rest, no bed can relax. Stationary objects cannot hold the eye. The seventy-two-hour get-it-outta-the-system clean-up routine would be gone through. Pacin' the room. All of this awaited me in Paris.

First up was a visit to a side-street, windswept and wet. The Caravan was gettin' itself ready for the last of its journeys. The performers were primpin'n'preenin'. Damp J-cloths wiped down mud-spattered body work. Logos to the fore. Every sponsor wanted to look tip-top for its public, on screen 'n' on the main street. I wanted a bagful of freebies to take home. I bided my time and kept my cool. No jumpin' in the crowd for a key fob, no divin' under railings for a flimsy cap. I sauntered up to the row of waiting floats, stretchin' out my hand, raising an expectant eyebrow. The laminate around my neck answered the unspoken question. The Aquarel flat-beds were near the rear. I went to the fabricated church. Dom Leo, the Myopic Curate, was puttin' the final touches to his make-up. I posed with him for a photo. I told him he was way out front as most enjoyable act on the bill. I gave him a chocolate biscuit called a 'Leo'. I'd bought it three weeks before in Liège. The room, at the Hotel SiMaisNon, was missin' the Belgian equivalent of a Terry's Waiffa. It had melted and reset distortedly a few times. It was battered'n'grotesque, but it was still in one piece.

'You win this prize,' I said.

He seemed well pleased. Me too. He gave me a big smackin' kiss on my cheek. He had on bright red lipstick. Like the Everly Brothers' song, 'I ain't gonna wash for a week, oh no no.' Gifi were a kiddies' toy firm. My fave float was one of theirs. A yellow rubber duck on a yellow rubber ring. Kinda thing little 'uns wear in the swimming pool. A bloke had driven that duck every mile of the way, open to the elements. Blown to pieces, soaked to the skin, fried to a crisp. Through open countryside, bumped over cobbles, ground up the steepest mountain. He had one fuck of a tan. The inside drivin' seat was a motorbike set-up. I shook his hand.

'Want a go?' He indicated.

Did I? I climbed into the ring. The child within me fulfilled and gleeful. And he gave me a free T-shirt. I've seen record company executives in California lose it completely to get a free T-shirt. It's some very basic instinct. The cops were in four-wheeler off-roaders. Dark blue. I'd spotted a smart silver pen marked 'Gendarmes' they gave, not threw, out. I approached carefully. I asked politely in my best schoolboy grammar. He looked me up'n'down. He paused at my silver star earring.

'Non,' was all he said.

I climbed up onto a lump of artistic abstract sculpted metal to get a good view of the whole parade. Earl was already up.

'Fuck it. I forgot to get one of those pretty pink bags to take home for the missus.'

The marketing wagon train took off. I waved and shouted like a loony. I hoped the Brief wasn't watching. Leo and the Rubber Duck got it large. Boof! Something hit my leg, landed on my foot. I looked down. A small pink package sealed in plastic. I bent down carefully to grab it. It was a La Redoute bag. Such fine ju-ju.

Earl was collecting autographs. We were at the next town down the road. Besançon is a beautiful old city with great stone ramparts jutting high above the river. We were strung out on a rain-swept industrial estate, catching individual riders as they slumped to a halt at the completion of their 35-mile time-trial. Earl was elbowing his way through each little scrum of journos to wave his autograph book under each cyclist's nose. He was enjoying himself by annoying the press at work in their corral. They were getting soundbites but there ain't a lot to say about pointing a bike in the right direction and pedalling hard on your own. I felt kinda sorry for them but I sort of agreed with Clara Schumann's comment that 'Writing about music is like dancing to architecture.'

Earl was back to being a fan, with his freebie official kiddies' picture-book'n'pen. He was getting mixed results in his collection. Many riders were too knackered and keen to get outta there as quickly as they could. Floyd Landis was leading the field, ahead on the clock until the big boys came home. As he slowed to quaff his peach iced tea, I gave him a loud 'Floyd' Southern-drawled shout. He looked round, pleased with his turn, but I was already lookin' blank on purpose. Vladimir Karpets had timed his late run to devastating perfection, like scoring the winning goal in injury time. He had run Little Tommy Voeckler into the floor to snatch Best Youngster jersey. His eyes were narrowed into mean slits as he shot through. The sprinters were biding their time to slug it out on the Champs Elysées on the next and final day. Earl hopped from group to group.

'Best 'til last,' he said.

Meanwhile, back-stage security was falling apart. The huge crowd had spotted the gaps in the fence and were leaking into the reserved area. Armstrong came through last and first. As he whipped off his shades to reveal a pair of splendidly bossed eyes, he glanced up to see a mass of punters goin' doolally where they shouldn't be. Earl scuttled across to him just as Magwitch and Mr Aloha, his minders, got to him. They wheeled Lance around in a U-turn and off the track.

'Doh,' said Earl. 'I'll get him.'

Armstrong had the composure and bearing of a champion. He could do it all. Sprint, chase, climb and time-trial. He was magnificent. Even now, with his sixth win in the bag, he'd pushed himself one minute further clear of the rest. That's some impressive gap at this level.

The Brief joined us at the Micropolis, the Tour HQ for the day. He'd been out on the course, photographing the cyclists. He described the variety of riding styles; rolling shoulders, still spines, handlebar grips, high cadences of foot revolution.

'It made a change to watch each rider in fast action in detailed close-up,' he said.

The Micropolis was a vast modern exhibition centre. The multi-levels held every aspect of Le Tour's organisation. There were areas up'n'down tiled ramps that housed security, marketing, police, adjudicators, sponsors, time-keepers, transport. The set-up mirrored the start venue in Liège without the razzamatazz and elaborate foliage. The atmosphere, in comparison, was tense, weary functionalism. The remains of a sumptuous buffet was piled on tables on the lower level. The press room was a hall and busy. I palmed a stack of free Tour postcards with a postmodern arty design while I waited at the entrance for the Brief to return with the revised time-sheets of the day. A big hubbub began by the door. Journos were running, barging into each other. Photographers jostled to jump onto a small platform in front of a stage set up at the front with a couple of chairs. A table of microphones stood ready.

Lance Armstrong strode to the stage, wearing his yellow jersey. He was a man who had kept himself to himself these last three weeks. Apart from the odd quick quip, he'd let his legs do the talking. Now on the eve of his coronation, he was giving his undivided attention to the massed press corps. Like Le Tour de France, he had come to the people. Lance was accompanied by Pascale, the Françoise Hardy lookalike official translator. Lance was disliked for failing to be fluent in French after all this time. His US Postal team manager, Johan Bruyneel, was with him. The boss from Belgium was the sound tactical advice in Lance's earpiece when he was racing. Now he stood to the side, with a slight contented smile in a Brian Epstein manner. He looked smart and very clean. The two of 'em had been together since this remarkable run of success had started back in '99. Bruyneel, like many a football manager, had been a rider of moderate talent. He had ridden six Tours himself. He knew the score. The questions flew across the room.

'Which Tour was the hardest?'

'How do you feel?'

'Which Tour did you enjoy the most?'

'How did you feel?'

'Will you do another Tour?'

A thousand journalists all about to file the exact same copy. The pressure was on them and they were grabbing for the roving mike. Cameras were fizzing and popping for the same shot.

I hung out on the side. I turned to Earl and said, 'Do you know that quote of Frank Zappa? He said rock journalism is people who can't write, interviewing people who can't talk for people who can't read.'

I wasn't paying full attention when I heard Armstrong mention Richard Virenque. I snapped to alertness. Lance was sounding off about the criticism he gets at times here in France. He was questioning why he is not granted the full respect of being the greatest Tour de France champion of all time, yet Virenque is treated as the all-conquering hero, even though his winning tally is zero. Furthermore, said Lance, why do so many French people make sly digs and insinuations about his alleged doping, with absolutely no evidence, when they forgive and forget Richard who was caught bang to rights with self admissions and the testimonies of others of his profligate drug-taking. It ain't right and it don't square. I applauded. Lance seemed to embody that old Machiavellian adage, 'A man who would rather be feared than loved.'

I couldn't get near the man with the portable mike. I wanted to ask Lance one question.

'How would you feel if Willy Nelson wrote a song about you?'

And then the Texan was gone. Armstrong and his small entourage went out through a fire exit. He wasn't quick enough for Earl.

'I'll get him,' he said.

He looked determined and he'd done his homework while the press conference was on. He nipped down side stairs to the gravel outside where the US Postal car was waiting. As Armstrong got into the back seat, Earl opened the other door and sat down next to him in the motor. Before any minder could move, Earl gave his cheekiest smile and said, 'Sign this, please, Lance.'

As he met me back at the entrance, Earl waved his autograph book delightedly.

'I got him,' he said.

I beamed with pride at my boy.

I had also got what I came for. Far better than a press conference with Lance Armstrong was a chat with Jean-Louis Pagès. His official title is Directeur des Sites. I reckon he's the livin', pumpin' heart of Le Tour de France. I'd been asking Matthieu, the press officer, for a few days if I could meet Jean-Louis. I'd been so impressed by the cool way this elegant man ran his stage area, the rough and tumble of L'Arrivée, the finish line.

'Wouldn't you rather meet Jean-Marie Leblanc, the Directeur Générale?'

'No. Not at all. The Pork Butcher is a politician.'

Matthieu laughed.

'I will try to arrange it.'

And he did. In the middle of the time-trial, Jean-Louis had a tea break, popped into headquarters and told me how it was. He'd stumbled into this crazy, chaotic national institution of a race by chance twenty years ago. His brother-in-law needed a hand with the car-parking. Jean-Louis was teaching kids history at the time. Cometh the hour, cometh the man. He'd never gone back. It was a pure circus runaway story. Before that, he'd never seen Le Tour. Shaboom! It transformed his life. It hit him like a punch in the face. Like rock'n'roll at its best. In a parallel universe, I'd bumped into The Clash on a Belfast stage in '77 and never looked back.

As we talked, his eyes searched me out. His hand repeatedly lay on my arm to make a point. Jean-Louis smiled a lot, not politely but with great expression. The lines and wrinkles on his weathered face twisted and contorted as he spoke. He didn't care that much for cycling as a sport, he preferred football, but he loved Le Tour de France as an event. I concurred completely. He didn't knock about with the riders. Mostly he didn't know who they were, top faces excepted. Like a life-long football fan, you support a team. The individual players come'n'go. The team continues. Like the women in my life, some of whom I've loved, they pass on.

Teamwork and preparation count for a lot in Le Tour. On a day like this, when each cyclist rides alone, US Postal finished with six in the top sixteen. The team had spent the year riding the routes in advance, gaining knowledge and familiarity with every bend, straight and gradient.

Jean-Louis was a believer in foresight. He checked out each of the finishes well in advance. He walked the course beforehand. Hell, it's Jean-Louis who gives it the thumbs up or down when the mayor of some town out in the sticks comes to Paris with a fistful of euros to gain the prestige and honour of hosting the Great Race. So when there's a snarl-up that threatens the equilibrium, it's Jean-Louis' intimate knowledge of the terrain, as well as his spirit, that blows away the blockage.

Matthieu, sitting nearby, laughed in agreement.

'I'm new to this,' he said. 'When I get agitated about possible problems, Jean-Louis says, "Don't worry. It will happen. Don't panic."'

This reminded me of Meher Baba, Pete Townshend's Indian guru. Just before he took a vow of personal silence for the rest of his life, he issued the message to his followers, 'Don't worry. Be happy.'

I'd seen this ethos avert a couple of close shaves already on this Tour, like at Villard-de-Lans. Jean-Louis agreed that there were just too many vehicles following the Tour. The old tradition of roamin' from town to town by the back roads couldn't cope with the modern indulgence of one man and his car. All these motors were rippin' up the environment. Those pretty High Pyrenean mountain-top finishes were left devastated, like slash'n'burn clearings in the rain forest, when the motors moved on. The Brief had watched the process from his eagle's eyrie viewpoint and commented on it with a sad shake of his head.

Monsieur Pagès breathed intensity. His function, he said, was in the shadows so that the riders could shine. A perfect roadie's self-definition. He ran a team of 200 people and yet, time and again, I had watched him do it himself rather than delegate.

'Yeah. Show not tell,' he said.

I told him that his presentation was so cool, an almost

perfect blend of tough sensitivity.

'Have you ever had to hit someone to make the race happen?'

He cracked up laughing.

'Of course. If anyone invades my territory without good reason, gets in the way of the riders, they're asking for it.'

I have heard an almost identical answer some years ago from Keith Richards, after he'd decked a German marauder with his Telecaster.

As we stood up, Jean-Louis put his arm around my shoulder. I turned to him and asked, 'Jean-Louis, you are a hard man, yet you can act so softly. Is it difficult?'

'No. Not at all. It is natural. I act naturally with passion.'

As he strode off back to his position as King of the Line to welcome home Lance Armstrong, I could feel his heart pumping that passion all around Le Tour de France, regardless of who won. One sharp blast of his intimate intensity had inspired me.

Chapeaux, Jean-Louis.

Chapter 13

Paris. The capital city pulls me back. Paris has a huge power; it's a massive magnet. One-quarter of all French people live in or around the place, like iron filings. The layout is tight, confined, unlike London or Los Angeles, which sprawl. The Périphérique is a band of road, a modern city wall. Within are the treasured ju-ju centres.

Le Tour de France zeroes in on the Champs Elysées from a long way out. I felt the pull when the race reached Nîmes. With the Mediterranean at my back, I fancied I could see all the way to Paris. An ache in my weary bones, like a class A comedown, told me to head north. Cut'n'run up the Rhône corridor. Head for home, foot down on the autoroute. It was the temptation of resignation. But honour had to be achieved in the High Alps. Over every col, skimming every lakeside, the magnetism of Paris gets stronger. In Besançon, at the solo time-trial, I was thinking contradiction. I was luxuriating in the long drawn-out events of the day. Being able to focus on every loved one of le peloton. I was also whisperin', 'C'mon. Speed it up. Let's get outta here. Let's hit Paris.'

The official distance for this Tour de France was 2,120 miles pedalled in anger. Black Magic had clocked up a mileage of just over 5,000.

On that final Sunday, it was a short hop from fields to Périphérique. It was still early morning. The roadies were clunkin' barriers into position on the boulevards. I headed for my own personal spot in the capital. All the way round, the Brief, Earl and I had clocked the Gambettas. In every town of the nation there was a rue or avenue Gambetta. For us, it was a talisman. It was a handy in-joke. It was a guaranteed rendezvous. Whenever we got lost, or the situation was gettin' hairy, that blue sign on a strange wall would come to the rescue. So when it came to checkin' in to a Parisian hotel, there was no choice. Hotel Gambetta, on avenue Gambetta, beside Place Gambetta.

As Bilbo Baggins wisely put it, 'Third time pays for all.'

This extra triumphant entry to the city! So who was this angel who watched over me? Why was he my ju-ju guru? Léon Gambetta was a politician. I'm rarely drawn to politicians. Lyin', cheatin' scumbags on the make. As a kid activist, I once wrote, 'Harold Wilson is God' on my school ruler. My mates were putting 'Eric Clapton' in that phrase. Harold sold my youthful idealism down the Mekong River. Since then, very few politicos have caught my eye. Gambetta exploded like a rocket and was gone just about as quick. In 1870, Paris was besieged in the Franco-Prussian War. Emperor Napoleon III had thrown in the towel at Sedan, right next to Charleville, home of Rimbaud. Seventeen-year-old Arthur raced to Paris, looking for poems and kicks. He got nicked at the station. Léon Gambetta was a guy on the up. Young'n'gutsy for a politico. He learnt his hustling trade as a brief in Cahors, down to the south-west. Then it had to be Paris. His ambition towed him there. With his eye on the main chance, war proved that his time had come. The situation was desperate. Cafés were serving fried dog'n'roasted rat. Supplies weren't getting through. No food, no guns. Balloons were the answer to crossing the German siege around Paris. One ended up in the Atlantic, another in Norway. Minister Gambetta himself got in the basket. Up, up'n'away he went, to raise a relief army. Now there was a politician who actually did it, rather than getting others to do his dirty work. Maybe that's why the French have remembered him so famously'n'fondly. His time at the top was short-lived. Another reason I like him. While he was still milkin' it, he bought a house on the eastern edge of Paris at Ville d'Avray. He was cleaning his gun at home, as you do, when it went off. It shot him in the head. Not quite Kurt Cobain. Léon Gambetta was a revolutionary who died young. It's enough. His heart is buried in the Pantheon, between Jean-Jacques Rousseau and Voltaire. Over the way is Émile Zola and Victor Hugo. The bloke is one of the Greats.

This Hotel Gambetta is a two-star beauty on the wrong side of the tracks for the Eiffel Tower/Notre Dame brigade. It is functional rather than luxurious. Its comfort is in the name. It sits next to the dead centre of Paris. At the end of the avenue is Père Lachaise cemetery. Many of the good and famous, weird and wonderful are buried there. The florists, with elaborate colourful frontages, do a steady trade. Locals pay tribute to their relatives, who make up the bulk of the cemetery. The walls are militaristic in design, down to the barbed wire on top. Against these, the last of the Communards in May 1871 were lined up and shot. The man who ordered it, Adolphe Thiers, is six foot under here. Should've been an unmarked grave. The cemetery is a sculpture park. There are families in vaults shaped like castles, pyramids, small houses. Graves bear crosses, sacred bleedin'hearts and angels. Layer on layer are crammed between the avenues. Some are abandoned, derelict. Others are pristine and with loved photographs. The tombs are rough-hewn granite, marble of all hues. Grand avenues link up randomly. Graves are jammed higgledy-piggledy. It's a great place for hide'n'seek. The French use it as a park, a place to promenade and saunter. A flâneur's paradise. There are flowers everywhere. Trees too, chestnut and plane. It is an uplifting place, truly a celebration of life. Père Lachaise has sucked in many exotic beings. Edith Piaf started life as a dumped foundling but ended up here. Her songs of self and tragic heroism, fuelled by booze'n'morphine, touched regular people. In a burst of pre-Beatle mania, at her funeral 40,000 fans stormed the barricades at the cemetery gates to say goodbye to 'The Little Sparrow'. There are characters in here who, like Marco Pantani, deserve the doffin' of my cap. Their time might not have been long but the knowledge of it has sure enriched mine. There's a lion-tamer eaten by his beast. On top is a sculpture of him ridin' on the back of his lion. Two balloonists, hand in hand in stone, naked for all the world like gay lovers, asphyxiated 26,000 feet above India. The poet and decadent, Gérard de Nerval is here – a man who liked to take his pet lobster for a stroll in the park on a pink silk ribbon. At the age of 47, he was walking home from his auntie's. In an Ian Curtis kinda mood, he thought 'What's the fuckin' point?' He hanged himself from the next lamp-post. It was on the corner of Slaughter Street and Impasse.

As I drifted through this Death Heritage Park, I saw that it was a respectful Grand Day Out for the French. Elegant in suits and cashmere coats that brush the shoes, whole families promenaded with dignity. Women of a certain age, alone since their men tend to pop off first, had spent time in front of the mirror. This was no furtive backwater of gloom. Oscar Wilde would have approved of his remains being shunted here. Having broken the rules and paid the price, he slummed his final years in Paris, like Vince Taylor. He was born a hundred years too early, as Freddie Mercury should testify. Oscar's tombstone was well worth the detour. Epstein's sculpture of an Egyptian winged messenger was roped off. It struck me as way too late. His stone knob has already been chipped off. Legend has it that its huge size, especially on a ginger, offended two English women. They took revenge with a chisel. The cemetery superintendent supposedly has Oscar's cock on his desk as a paper-weight. Willies have some importance in this life after death. I walked on from Oscar Wilde to Victor Noir. Victor copped it young, aged 22, in the violent chaos of 1870. He was shot by Pierre Bonaparte, who was the cousin of Emperor Napoleon III. Victor was a journalist who had slagged off Pierre in print. I don't know what Vic said but it must've been quite terrible to get killed for it. And yet Victor's tomb is one of the most tender places in Paris. A full-size Victor lies flat out 'asleep' with his boots on. Victor's relaxed state makes this a place for lovers. In his hand he carries a top-hat. The inside of the topper is a clandestine letter-box for 'Hey Paul,' 'Hey, Hey Paula' sweet nothings. There are posies around his body, the dead flowers of romance. It is Victor's knob that is the big attraction. Word has it that if a woman is struggling to get herself pregnant, all she has to do is rub Victor's knob. The grave was ticker-taped off. It obviously stopped not a single desperate barren bird. Nothing would. Fertility ju-ju is strong stuff. I looked at it. The bulge in Victor Noir's trousers stood out a mile. Polished to a greeny-silvery shade. It was still popular. A serious rebuff to scientific reason. I hung around, hoping to catch someone in the act. I'd have given it a go myself but I'm a man with five kids already. I've done my bit for world over-population.

I passed one more warm-up on my way. Chopin's headstone said 'Fred Chopin.' I love slang'n'nicknames, but Fred, not Frédéric, stuck me as flippant and familiar. The bloke was a classical composer. For sure he'd lived a rock'n'roll life. He'd suffered TB, coughin' up blood over the piano keys, having to be carried off stage exhausted on a tour of Scotland. His great lover, the writer George Sand, was herself a Patti Smith lookalike. She was a no-show for the funeral here. She didn't show for his death-bed gig either. Twenty-five others did, though, crowded into his room, making sketches, writing poems, playing fugues. It was a fitting send-off for someone on his way to this high-profile requiem.

After all the support acts, it was time for the headliner, Jim Morrison. He has put Père Lachaise cemetery on the map for Americans. Just as Lance Armstrong has made Le Tour de France famous across the States. Morrison's grave pulls in the crowds like no single other. XXL black T-shirts and blue-jean babies are well in evidence. This is a Goth shrine to drape a barely living body over. Black lipstick, hair, clothes, black everything. Jim was a great advert for death. His lyrics were doom enriched. 'The End' was the perfect finale for the movie, *Apocalypse Now*. He was a poet. His pal in the band was Ray Manzarak, uncool as fuck in pale blue button-down shirt, tweedy sports jacket, dentist's glasses and a mummy's boy hair parting grown long at the sides. He played jazzy blues hunched over his keyboards. Jim knew better. He knew his Bo Diddley. He went down his local Transcendental Meditation Centre, an activity unknown outside Rishikesh and Los Angeles in '64, to recruit drums'n'bass Krieger'n'Densmore. These were not rockin' kids, as Eddie Cochrane would've understood. They were improvisational plodders. It was a solid base for Jim to stand up in his leather kecks and fix the scrambled hippies with his magisterial take on existence. Being a rock'n'roll star brings a feelin' of omnipotence. Alcohol, unusually for the late '60s, was Jim's drug of choice. The result was confrontation with the forces of repression. Cops onstage. Morrison out to outdo his poetic hero, Arthur Rimbaud, in shock tactics. He swore. He waved his willy around. The prison cell beckoned. The FBI, spotting a national rabble-rouser at an unstable time of Vietnam protests'n'race riots, opened a file on him. 'Mad, bad'n'dangerous to know?' Like another ancient role-model, Lord Byron, Jim skipped the country to lose the heat. He had a rock-star's interlude in March '71 at the swanky Hotel George V. Jim Morrison slipped away into the backstreets of Paris to prepare for sainthood. He holed up in a borrowed flat behind Bastille with Pamela Courson, his long-time bird. He walked for hours in anonymity, his chin freshly shaved. What is it about the ju-ju charge of Parisian pavements? He died in the bath. Three days later, he was buried in Père Lachaise. That's when the conspiracies started flyin' around. They keep on going. A smack o.d., with Marianne Faithfull shootin' off to Morocco next morning. Wiccan magical curses from New York City. Marathon wanking sessions. Government assassination. And of course, Jim ain't in the coffin. Only Pam saw the iced-up corpse in the cheapo coffin and she died of smack herself three years later in LA. The doctor's name on the death certificate was illegible and unremembered. Whether Jim faked it or not, it's no easy feat for a young American passin' thru' to grab a plot in prestigious Père Lachaise in a coupla days. Four people, including Pamela Courson and Doors manager Bill Siddows, were present at the eight-minute ceremony. A local woman, Mme Colinette, watched it happen while tending her husband's grave across the way.

She said it was 'Piteous and miserable. There was no priest, everything was done in a hurry.'

I found the remains of James Douglas Morrison a sedate affair. A jink of a dog-leg off the avenue de Lesseps, with its significant pyramid, brought me to the taped-off grave. An armed security man oversaw proceedings. The headstone was chiselled with graffiti. The surround was chipped too. Red roses lay on top. School girlie love notes mixed with the autumn leaves. We all stared down. Cameras were brandished. This was a stop on the modern Grand Tour. Aside from the rumours'n'speculation about his mysterious death, Jim still draws the crowds because he did it. He lived fast, died young. One extra rock'n'roll ju-ju touch was that he died on the same date as Brian Jones, four years earlier. Like Gambetta, he walked the walk as well as talking the talk. Mortality was Jim's thing. Like Rimbaud, he pushed it to the edge in complete disregard of death. All of 'em shiftin' in'n'out of the Parisian frame, leavin' a strong electric charge for others to pick up on. Not only were these contemporary mourners the young alienated outsiders, there was a whole bunch of ageing hipsters. Smart coats, new jeans, trendy hats to cover the bald patches, an optional pony-tail hangin' out the back. I wondered if, like me, they suffered the contradiction of finding life hugely fascinating, despite hoping to die before I got old and failing against the odds. Hell, I'd given it my best shot. Standing in front of headstones brings it all back home.

When you're American and you've done Jim Morrison, you walk excitedly down the hill to the main gates. You tell each other, loudly, that you've done Jim Morrison. I was pissed off that there wasn't any music playing. I have heard that in Turkey, Texas, the shrine to Bob Wills, King of Western Swing, is a full-sized statue that plays his tunes, like 'San Antone Rose', at the push of a button on his ten-gallon hat. Class.

Lance, Floyd, Big George and the US Postal boys rode into town with a swagger.

Chapter 14

There is something about capital cities. The residents consider themselves so fuckin' cool that raisin' an eyebrow would be hysteria. Provincial tossers and foreigners think metropolitans are rude, surly'n'offhand. Taking a capital city by storm is a big act. It's infectious. It's the heart of the nation. Léon Gambetta had taken to his balloon to stop the Prussians. Seventy years later, Germans goose-stepped down the Champs Elysées. Adolph Hitler flew in. A limousine was sent. He had the publicity photo taken in front of the Eiffel Tower. No one's saying how that was. Old newspapers of the time are kept at the back of the cupboard. But more than a few collaborators, like Maurice Chevalier, raised a glass to the swastika. The French still squirm at the memory. Four years on, de Gaulle insisted on a duplicate march down main street. An exile in return. Behind him was American muscle. It's got to affect the local thinking. Occupation. Military invasion must be a huge challenge, but it's obvious. Cultural invasion is insidious. It sneaks up and takes over before it's been noticed. It's often welcomed. It's usually necessary to kick the tired old culture up the arse.

An American dominating an event as French as Le Tour de France. Talk about coals to Newcastle. It's as unlikely and as essential as exporting rock'n'roll to the USA. By '64, rock'n'roll had gone soggy'n'floppy. Only eight years after 'Heartbreak Hotel' had lit up the world, Elvis was struggling to get a record in the charts. Crap movies came off his conveyor belt. His barnet was no longer cutting edge. Mummy's-boy crooners with quiffettes were all over the charts. Bobby Vee, Bobby Vinton. Buddy Holly was dead. So was Eddie Cochrane. Both killed in transit, on tour. Buddy's plane crashed in snow and ice at Clear Lake, Iowa. Maybe he'd have turned insipid. He had a penchant for orchestras. Eddie was terrified of flying. He was convinced that an aeroplane would be the death of him. On a tour of the UK, Eddie played steady guy to the wild man, Gene Vincent, he shared the bill with. Before his last gig, in Bristol, Eddie ran along the hotel corridor to his girl, Sharon Sheeley. He was sobbin'n'screamin, bare-chested. Drinkin' Gene's cheap wine, he foretold his imminent death in a plane crash to his fiancée. It took Sharon hours to calm Eddie down. After a great show, Eddie'n'Gene jumped into the motor, hot foot for London airport to fly Stateside. The roadie wrapped it round a lamp-post. Eddie Cochrane was dead. Gene Vincent was crippled, legs and psyche.

He limped on. The French in particular took a shine to his leather jacket'n'greasy quiff, but he was gone. Gene's look begat Johnny Halliday but great music needs attitude as well as style.

The Beatles brought the rockin' back to Paris in January '64. It was hard goin'. The place had gone flabby. Their tour of France was for three weeks with two days off. Plus ça change. Two shows, sometimes three a day. That band pushed it hard. They opened at the Olympia, near L'Opéra, to an audience of elite bourgeoisie. The burghers turned up in the full evening dress. Black ties, silk'n'taffeta. No dancing, no tappin' of the patent leather. No screamin' girlies. The back-line amps screwed up. George Harrison reckoned it was sabotage. Things were lookin' grim, man. The Beatles were used to ecstatic mania. This was not conquering hero stuff. The French burghers knew something happenin' was in the air. But they wanted to refine it, tame it. Make it fit into their orderly scheme of things. The French press were reserved and guarded. The Beatles' media man, Brian Somerville, started a ruck back-stage in an attempt to drum up stories.

It would've been a trudge back across the Champs Elysées to their hotel after the gig. The Beatles were staying at George V, round the corner from the Arc de Triomphe. In their suite occurred one of those defining moments in history. Brian Epstein opened a telegram. It told him that his boys had made number one in the *Cashbox* US charts. Their single, 'I Wanna Hold Your Hand', had shot to the 'Toppermost of the Poppermost', Lennon's long-time predicted goal. An amazing leap of forty-three places. McCartney jumped onto roadie Mal Evans' back. Round'n'around they roared, like the winner's enclosure on Derby Day.

Eppy was going, 'What could possibly be better than this?' as he always did at each new level of achievement.

Fuck Paris! Fuck the snooty French! Next stop the USA. And if you take New York City as the cultural capital of America, leaving Washington DC for diplomats, The Beatles stormed it. Turned the whole country into a state of frenzy. Rock'n'roll music and attitude were re-charged'n're-vitalised right around the planet.

The new take was respectful of the heritage without bowing down to tradition. No British rockers had ever cut it in the home of rock'n'roll. The Beatles did it their own way.

I was watching Armstrong and the other survivors on the big screen. He stood out a mile with his maillot jaune and wide grin. He was sippin' champagne with his gang as they wheeled through the suburbs of Paris. The Brief checked the route map.

'They're at Charenton? Your kinda place. Ain't that the famous asylum?' I asked him. 'That's where the Marquis de Sade was held.'

The Brief smiled. 'I think the madness and mania are over for another year. It's plain sailing to the finish line. A mere formality.'

I was still thinking about the Marquis. He was a lover of freedom in any form. The French authorities couldn't handle that, especially as he wrote down his thoughts. Dangerous dissemination. He was banged up for twenty-seven years. He avoided Joe Guillotine's cutting edge invention in the Revolution. Handily labelled a pervert with the term 'sadism'. Freedom through sexuality was only part of the game for him. His warden, Royer-Collard, made it his mission to stymie de Sade. No paper, no pens, no ink. The Marquis used his shirt and shit. His clothes were taken away. He wrote on the walls. He was unstoppable.

Le peloton cruised along above us.

'Not always,' I said to the Brief.

'Ah yes,' he said. 'The slip "twixt lip and cup".' Obviously, thoughts of his employment had jarred him awake. 'The tale of Bill Evans.'

Bill Evans is a great jazz pianist. This ain't him. Our Bill Evans is a Dutchman called Blijlevens, Jeroen Blijlevens had ridden in four Tours. He'd got himself a stage win in each of 'em. No slouch. He fancied himself as a bit of a sprinter. He was often thereabouts at the line. In the Millennium Tour, he'd dragged his arse over the hills and on up the Champs Elysées. He'd cracked it. A hero. There was one naggin' ache for Bill. It was Bobby Julich, an American. Bobby had been givin' Billy a bit of gyp for a coupla days before they'd got to Paris.

Stuff like, 'You're crap,' and 'Call yourself a sprinter?'

and 'My granny's got stronger legs than that.'

Fairly mild bit of stick. Sorta thing an annoyed vicar might shout at Arsenal. The impact on the road is different. Because of the close proximity of the mouth of the accuser and the ears of dozens in le peloton, the words are sharper. Because of exhaustion and isolation, the meaning is brooded on. Six hours in the saddle leaves plenty of time to mull it over. Victims are handy distractions on the road. Most road crews carry one. Just like most classrooms contain one. Wind-ups are excellent entertainment. I've known roadies gamble good money on the exact point of explosion of a victim's wind-up. It's a skill learnt young. Victims call it bullying. Aficionados who give as good as they get prefer to consider wind-ups as a game of psychological ping-pong. I don't think Bill Evans did. Bobby upped it as the pair lapped at speed in front of an adoring crowd. Insults flew. They crossed the line. Le Tour was over. Success'n'relief. Bill boiled over. He finally retaliated by slaggin' Julich off. Julich then pulled his master stroke. He just smiled back. This act of wind-up genius tipped Evans. He shoved Bobby, who now got annoyed. He threw his helmet at Bill, who threw punches back. A full-blown fight was on. TV cameras zoomed in on the action. Julich's face needed stitches. Blijlevens was disqualified from the whole race and banned for a month. Having flogged round France for almost a month, one moment's loss of cool meant his listing for the year 2000 reads, 'Did Not Finish'. Bill shrugged. He knew the score.

He said, 'You have to be intense to compete and sometimes that causes a problem.'

We had all felt that intensity. It was what I was there for. Rarely does it show its face on the last day. Le maillot jaune was tucked inside his gang, keepin' safe. Mountain man in dots coasted on the flat, soakin' up the love of his nation. Vladimir Karpets had timed his late run to perfection. He would be Best Young Rider in white. The coming man. I hope so. I was impressed that he looked completely unimpressed. Two talented nutters from Australia, Robbie'n'Stu, were scrappin' for green points. Erik Zabel always in the frame. The results were done and dusted. But the show must go on.

This was the slick, polished set piece. French bureaucracy may be difficult to deal with. It is meticulous on days like this. Black Magic was stacked away under the Place de la Concorde. The underground car park was commandeered by armed guards. So was the square, sealed off to rubbernecks. The obelisk pointed up to the clear blue sky. Egyptian ju-ju, old'n'new, with the glass pyramid of the Louvre at the far end of the Tuileries Garden. Across the River Seine was the Assemblée Nationale, all respectable gravitas, and the converted station of Musée d'Orsay, full of art. It felt overpowering to be standing in the centre of this big 'coffee-table book' city. I put my arm round my boy's shoulders. 'It's the end of the road.'

'Yeah, sad, ain't it?'

'Could you keep going?'

'Ask me tomorrow, when the adrenaline level's dropped. Some setting,' he added.

If Alpe d'Huez was the peak of alpine panoramas to stick a finish line on, this exact spot was its urban equivalent. Throw in a few medieval fortified hilltop towns along the way and you've got television heaven. Jacques Chirac had known that when, as mayor of Paris in '75, he had given Le Tour the honour of staging the finish here. The race had wound up in the capital right from the off. In 1903, 20,000 local cyclists had joined the remaining

Tour riders at Ville d'Avray alongside Léon Gambetta's shrine. The hoped-for formal procession to the stadium presentation had been a riot.

Nowadays, the up'n'down of the Champs Elysées is the nearest Le Tour gets to a Formula One/Olympic Games static spectacle. Great terraced stands are erected along the roadside. These 'Tribunes' are viewing platforms for the influential, privileged, rich'n'famous. I'd blagged a handful of tickets for them from Matthieu, the press attaché. In the end-of-Tour warmth, tight restrictions had eased a little. It seemed that if you'd stayed the trip, you qualified as an insider. It felt odd but I wasn't complainin'. My mate, Whisperin' Ian, was due in town on the Eurostar. He'd fancied taking a look at my passion.

'You've been rattlin' on about how good it is all year. I'm intrigued.'

I'd tried to explain that Paris was a gentrified version. Ah well. If you can't beat 'em …

Ian had been supposed to hook up with the Brief's son. They were both travelling from England on the same train. He arrived solo at the rendezvous, on the steps of Sainte Marie Madeleine.

'Where's my boy?' asked the Brief.

'Dunno,' whispered Ian. He's a quiet man. 'His mobile was switched off. I waited on the platform. I checked the concourse. I cruised the cab rank.'

A look of terror was in the Brief's eyes.

'I must away to the Gare du Nord,' he said in a strangled voice.

'The show must go on,' I replied. 'Shall we take our seats?'

The Tribune Gabriel was a novelty for us. Ian and Earl passed the security gate with tickets. The elderly guard had a face that looked like it had had a good kicking in the Algerian War and been dosed with pain-killing alcohol ever since.

He said 'Non' to me. I wasn't bothered. I limped down the side like the bloke in *Day of the Jackal*. I passed the gendarmes by flashing the press pass. Earl and Whisperin' Ian were being shown to their blue sculpted seats by some bird who was obviously moonlighting from her air stewardess job. I waved at them from the road. I climbed the barrier, walked up the aisle the wrong way and sat down next to them.

'Fuck 'em,' I said.

I was too long in the habit of goin' where I pleased.

It was hot. Chilled mineral water was distributed. The sun poured down. Across the road, in the public standing, groups of national identity were whoopin'n'wavin' flags. Even in this benign setting, I cared not a jot for jingoism.

'Common and vulgar,' I declared.

Shazam! It was show time. The publicity Caravan was upon us. Each vehicle zigzagged up the carriageway at a lick. Earl and I cheered our favourites. Father Leo manically ringing his Aquarel church bell. The Catalogue Boy in corduroy with a sickly grin and a fey wave. Phil Collins, still hidden inside his giant 'Le Vache Qui Rit' cheese box. The Rubber Duck. I had a feeling of unity. Through all the miles and trials'n'tribulations, we had made it. That in itself was a result.

The crowd was festive but restrained. Maybe it was big city cool. Maybe it was so fuckin' hot. Ian was getting worried. He could feel his pallid English forehead was starting to burn. Sadly for him, this was the one day that the Caravan wasn't giving out free hats. The companies usually made it a competition to see which brightly coloured sponsors' cap would show up best through massed numbers on the telly. Yellow Crédit Lyonnais were tops. Earl came to the rescue. He fished outta his bag that day's copy of *L'Équipe*. It had a large picture on the front of Lance Armstrong in his yellow jersey. Using origami skills that he must've acquired at art college, he fashioned a hat for Ian out of newspaper. It was a cracker. Pointed at the top and the front with a fold-up brim, it reminded me of little boys playing soldiers in the '30s. Earl had another image. 'Here you are, Ian. Robin Hood.'

Whisperin' Ian supports Nottingham Forest. He looked sheepish but he stuck it on his head with relief. He looked around nervously, as if he expected someone to shout, 'Look at the fuckin' state of that.'

This was a refined assembly, however. After a few minutes, several onlookers could be seen sporting similar paper hats. Ian looked delighted to find himself a mover'n'shaker. Fashionable in Paris! The knock-on continued. The hostesses appeared with armfuls of freebie caps. They were red'n'white polka dots, from Champion Supermarchés. A large 7 was on the front. A tribute to Richard Virenque's seventh win as King of the Mountains. As the caps were passed along the rows, a scary face appeared alongside the girl. It was the Brief. He was wearing one of the tasteless homages to the Weasely Rent Boy. He was flushed and taut.

'My boy's not there,' he yelled, 'What shall I do?'

'Oh, he'll turn up. He's nineteen. He'll be all right,' I said.

'No, no, no,' he cried and rushed back up the aisle.

I sympathised. I knew that road madness comes in many forms. I've had it in the unlikeliest places. Earl leaned across.

'His face. What does it remind me of?'

I knew.

'Captain Haddock. When Tin-Tin is being bundled head-first into a strange black car by two burly unshaven thugs with Kazakhstan accents,' I said. 'At least he's acting on his paranoia. He's seen it all in Broadmoor.'

I was curious how someone could get lost on a train.

We all returned to watchin' the Entry of the Gladiators. Such a sight. The helicopters foretold the coming. We looked up. The speakers shouted. We looked down. A blur of colour. So fast. We stood up. Le peloton shot off towards the Arc de Triomphe. We sat down. And so it went for eight laps. Each lap clocked in around the ten-minute mark. The prowess of the cyclists on their machines was gob-smackin'. So tight the formations. So close to each other. I feared a sneeze would cause a massed crash. All 147 were showing off their intricate skills. Better than an acrobat, because we knew all about handlebars, wheels'n'pedals. We've all done it. But not like this. Far better than the Red Devils at an air show. I've never been in an RAF jet, let alone flown one. It's a spectacle with a handle.

It was too detached for Earl.

'I'm off ringside,' he said, pulling his pass from his pocket.

I understood. We'd got used to wanderin' around checkin' different perspectives. It felt sterile and passive up here, applauding.

The final dash had all the fastest men. Plus a couple of mavericks. Jean-Patrick Nazon, last seen puking'n'prone, came in second. Jimmy Casper, the Lanterne Rouge, last man in the pack, was sixth. Just in case you had it all sussed.

Oh, yeah, Lance Armstrong won his sixth Tour de France.

Ronny Scholtz was a triumphant fifty-third. A big fancy podium was wheeled out for the perfect photo opportunity with the Arc de Triomphe as a backdrop. Everyone got their deserts.

As we drifted away from the protocol ceremony, Earl joined us. 'I nearly lost my head,' he said.

'Yeah, it's contagious, ain't it?' I replied.

'No, I nearly had my head knocked by a bloke on a bike. I leaned over the barrier to get a photo. Bloke missed me by a whisker.'

'You wouldn't be the first,' I said.

I looked around to clock the familiar faces. I wanted to go all gushy. Hugs'n'handshakes. Meaningful lingerin' looks with all the crew that had made the round trip. We few.

'Fuck it. Let's go.'

Whisperin' Ian had a train to catch. He was on a flyin' visit. We sat at a café over the most expensive cold Cocas it's not been my pleasure to drink.

'Funny old business, end of tour.'

Some end in explosive fall-outs, like The Clash in Canada. Some just melt away into a damp winter's night. I had a mate called Kenny who worked as a drum roadie for ABBA when they were massive. Before they became postmodern recherché darlings. The tour finished up in Dublin. The band threw a big sit-down dinner for all the crew after the gig. The tour manager, Thomas Johansson, announced that every roadie could choose between a tour bonus in cash or a snog from Anni-Frid and Agnetha. Kenny emphasised a snog, not a peck on the cheek. To a man, the entire road-crew chose the lips.

I passed on a trip across town to the official celebations. It was all over. The motor cruised slowly down a quiet small side road. In the warm, clear evening, all our passion was spent, at peace finally. Ahead of me were two riders in the red of Team Saeco, dawdling on their bikes. One of 'em was Salvatore Commesso with his dark goatee beard and devilish grin. As I pulled level, alongside, Earl climbed half outta the open passenger window, clapping his hands hard and shoutin', 'Chapeaux'. The cyclists bowed their heads in humble proud acknowledgement.

The Brief was back at the hotel. So was his lad. It turned out he'd got peckish after the train ride and gone for a crêpe. We had our own plans for celebration. Big eats. The Brief had booked a table for four at the Tour d'Argent. This restaurant was called the 'Bayreuth of Cookery' by Jean Cocteau. It goes back to Napoleon, Cardinal Richelieu, Madame Pompadour. Henri III ate heron pies here.

A doorman greeted us as we got out the cab. The view of Notre Dame across the river was stunning in the evening light. I overheard a group of Americans talking on the corner, still flushed with their success.

'I can't believe it. Here we are — the Île de France, Paris, France.'

I turned to the Brief.

'It's got to be the duck here.'

The 'canard au sang' is their signature dish. I knew. He had told me. How the chef, Frederic, had started a tradition in the 1890s of pressed duck, each served with its serial number. It now ran towards a million. A gourmet experience enjoyed by Charlie Chaplin and every Prince of Wales. The magnificent presses were operated on a small stage, 'le theatre du canard'. We entered. Earl wore an Italian cycling shirt. I had on my yellow Hawaiian with the nudes. The maître d' in the lobby froze. He looked down his considerable nose at us, 'Jackets and ties, messieurs.'

It was our turn to freeze. A frosty woman in the corner made a furtive sign with her fingers to the man in charge.

'Perhaps we could provide ...' he suggested.

She removed several coat-hangers bearing formal attire from the wardrobe.

'No. Sod that. I'm not dressing up in pantomime clothes,' I said. 'It would choke me.' We turned 'n' walked out onto the quai-side.

The doorman grinned. He pushed his peaked livery cap to the back of his head to reveal an ageing quiff.

I grinned back. 'Fuck 'em.'